Routledge Revivals

Patterns of Kingship and Authority in Traditional Asia

There has been a tendency to neglect the political life of Asia, in favour of religious and aesthetic considerations. The myth of the 'changeless East' dies hard. Few people are aware that the earliest legislation for the rights of the common man go back to the Sumerians and that outlines for a social contract were drawn up by Indian Buddhists two thousand years before Locke and Rousseau.

First published in 1985, *Patterns of Kingship and Authority in Traditional Asia* provides an excellent survey of traditional Asian ideas of government, from the earliest kingdoms of the Sumerians and the Egyptians to the time when Western influence first made itself felt. Each chapter is written by a specialist on a particular country or region of Asia, who seeks to identify some of the essential features of its traditional royal or imperial authority. Particularly fascinating is the way in which traditional institutions continue to have a vital influence upon Asian countries.

The serious reader will obtain a clear outline of traditional Asian ideas and systems of government and will indirectly acquire a deeper understanding of other aspects of Asian civilisations.

Patterns of Kingship and Authority in Traditional Asia

Edited by I. W. Mabbett

Routledge
Taylor & Francis Group
Routledge Revivals

First published in 1985
by Croom Helm Ltd

This edition first published in 2024 by Routledge
4 Park Square, Milton Park, Abingdon, Oxon, OX14 4RN

and by Routledge
605 Third Avenue, New York, NY 10017

Routledge is an imprint of the Taylor & Francis Group, an informa business

Publisher's Note
The publisher has gone to great lengths to ensure the quality of this reprint but points out that some imperfections in the original copies may be apparent.

Disclaimer
The publisher has made every effort to trace copyright holders and welcomes correspondence from those they have been unable to contact.

A Library of Congress record exists under ISBN LCCN: 84045701

ISBN: 978-1-032-90485-6 (hbk)
ISBN: 978-1-003-55825-5 (ebk)
ISBN: 978-1-032-90486-3 (pbk)

Book DOI 10.4324/9781003558255

Patterns of Kingship and Authority in Traditional Asia

Edited by: Ian Mabbett

CROOM HELM
London • Sydney
Dover, New Hampshire

Croom Helm Ltd, Provident House, Burrell Row,
Beckenham, Kent BR3 1AT

Croom Helm Australia Pty Ltd, First Floor,
139 King Street, Sydney, NSW 2001, Australia

British Library Cataloguing in Publication Data

Patterns of kingship and authority in
traditional Asia.
1. Monarchy – History 2. Asia – Kings
and rulers – History
I. Mabbett, Ian
321.1'4 JC375

ISBN 0-7099-3509-9

Croom Helm, 51 Washington Street, Dover,
New Hampshire 03820, USA

Cataloging in Publication Data applied for.
Library of Congress Catalog Card Number:
84-45701

Printed and bound in Great Britain
by Billing & Sons Limited, Worcester.

CONTENTS

PREFACE

A.L. Basham

This important and interesting collection of papers is the outcome of a symposium held under my chairmanship at the first biennial conference of the Asian Studies Association of Australia, which took place in Melbourne in August, 1975. It was inspired by a seminar which was planned for the International Congress of the Human Sciences in Asia and North Africa, which was held in Mexico in the following year, and at which I had been invited to organize a seminar on Kingship in Asia and Pre-Columbian America.

I was a member of the organizing committee of the Melbourne conference, and when I mentioned at one of its meetings that I had been invited to chair the seminar in Mexico, it was suggested that I might also conduct a symposium on a similar theme at Melbourne. I must admit that I had some misgivings about the proposal, but the committee was quite convinced that such a symposium would be useful, and I allowed myself to be persuaded. I had planned the Mexico seminar to be based on papers written as far as possible by natives of the regions concerned, while in the case of Melbourne I invited papers only from scholars working at universities in Australia and New Zealand. Thus both the contributors and their approach to the subject were different in the two cases. In fact the papers submitted to the Melbourne Conference were, on the whole, equally scholarly and interesting, in comparison with those at Mexico, and some were definitely better. The approach, moreover, was noticeably different. The discussions at Melbourne were keen and fruitful, and it was agreed on all hands that the symposium was a success.

It was envisaged that I should edit a volume of papers arising from the Mexico seminar, and it seemed hardly appropriate that I should also edit the papers of the Melbourne symposium. I was not a little embarrassed by the situation, until my good friend Dr Ian Mabbett, who had presented a fine paper at the Melbourne symposium, agreed to edit its proceedings. This he has now done, and he has added one or two further papers, which were not presented at the symposium, and which add to the value and comprehensiveness of the collection.

The result forms an excellent survey of traditional Asian ideas of government, from the earliest kingdoms of the Sumerians and the Egyptians down to the period, varying from region to region, when Western influence began to make itself felt. The serious reader who works through the whole of this comprehensive and perceptive book will have obtained a clear overview of traditional Asian ideas and systems of government, and indirectly he will also have obtained a deeper understanding of other aspects of Asian civilizations.

There has, perhaps, been a tendency to neglect the political life of Asia, in favour of the religious and the aesthetic. This book may help the reader to realize that in politics also the life of Asia was marked by freshness, variety, and originality. The myth of the 'changeless East' dies hard, and few people other than specialists are aware that the earliest legislation to protect the rights of the common man goes back to the Sumerians, that ideas of social contract were adumbrated by Indian Buddhists nearly two thousand years before Locke and Rousseau, and that for nearly two thousand years the Chinese Empire chose its public servants by open competitive examination. Students of political science have too often been inclined to dismiss all Asian government as mere 'oriental despotism'. Such views are still sometimes heard, and this book should do much to counteract them.

This book will, it is hoped, be of more than academic value. With the growing importance of Asia in the affairs of the world some knowledge of the political principles of Asian civilizations is necessary for an adequate understanding of contemporary Asian politics. The attempts of the Muslim nations of Asia to adapt the precepts of the Quran and Hadith to the needs of the modern state require no emphasis in this context. Politicians in present day India search their ancient literature assiduously in order to find precepts which are valid for a democratic welfare state. For many years a debate has been taking place in communist China as to the significance of the doctrines of the great classical theorists, beginning with Confucius, for the present day, and the scales seem to be now tipping in favour of tradition. Quasi-feudal Japanese traditions of government helped to promote an unprecedented phase of expansionist imperialism, and have more recently helped to bring about the economic miracle whereby Japan has become one of the world's major industrial powers. Though adapted to twentieth century needs and given veneers of rationalism, many of the ideas discussed in this book are still valid and influential in the lands where they originated. For this reason, among many others, I hope that this book will be a success, and I thank Dr Mabbett for editing it and seeing it through the press.

ACKNOWLEDGEMENTS

It is not often that an editor finds all the organizational work done before he comes on the scene. Most of the papers in this volume were presented at a symposium presided over by Professor Basham, who thus inspired and assembled the collection, and placed the papers in my hands; I am grateful to him for bringing the project into being and for entrusting it to me. I would also like to thank the contributors for their patience and co-operation, Mrs J. Prince for her most meticulous typing of the volume on a word-processor for publication, and the Monash University Publications Committee for a generous grant towards the cost of publication of this work.

I.W. Mabbett

PATTERNS OF KINGSHIP AND AUTHORITY IN TRADITIONAL ASIA

1 INTRODUCTION: THE COMPARATIVE STUDY OF TRADITIONAL ASIAN POLITICAL INSTITUTIONS

I.W. Mabbett

> Now rises aloft the sky's golden jewel. He gazes far and wide as he speeds on, radiant, to his far destination. O let the sun-god inspire men to reach their goals and perform their tasks.
>
> Hymn to the sun god, Ṛg Veda 7.63.4

The study of Asian kingship is an arduous task, and its goals are distant. Indeed it might be said that its object is a mere figment.

For, some say, Asia does not exist: it is an artifact of Europocentric generalization. There is no Asia; there are many Asias. Vigorous and independent civilizations throng the avenues of oriental history; they do not belong to each other, and each of them has at least as much in common with others outside Asia as with its neighbours.

Indeed, within this volume, the route taken through Asia approximately follows the sun-god, beginning with his rising in the east. Like him, it encounters no natural limit at the western extremity of Asia. Brian Colless's paper on ancient Mesopotamia, Egypt and Israel, though spilling into Africa, deals with ideas and values that quite obviously belong together with the subject matter of the earlier papers; quite possibly almost any of the papers could be just as profitably put together with studies of quite different parts of the world.[1]

The view that orientalists have in an important sense invented the orient they study has come to be associated especially with the name of Edward Said, a specialist in comparative literature whose book, Orientalism,[2] has been much discussed.[3] Now, the orient is that part of the heavens where the sun rises. Its location therefore, like beauty, is contingent upon the eye that perceives it. An old definition of the orient, long current in France, sets it squarely in the Middle East and nowhere else. Said's book is almost wholly concerned with this orient. Where other parts of the wider orient, the Far East, are mentioned, it is usually to say that what applies to the study of the Arab Middle East does not apply to them.[4] Said's orient is a special case. Therefore, generalization from Orientalism to Asia as a whole is implicitly prohibited, a fact which, curiously, has been almost unanimously ignored by those orientalists who have applied his critique to various parts of Asia. It would be profitless to enter here upon the issues of debate elicited by Orientalism; but let us acknowledge at least that the prior assumption of 'Asia' as a meaningful category is an assumption that can be questioned.

Further, it could be argued that kingship does not exist: it is a word for an infinite variety of political relationships, and they cannot be studied as a unity. Each Asian civilization has its own language, its own cosmology, its own problems to solve, and its own unique styles of government.

All this is true. A fortiori, Asian kingship does not exist. This goes far to explain why historians rarely essay comparative studies of traditional political institutions in different parts of Asia. Each usually prefers to ask questions about one country or one civilization; and the choice of pertinent questions is governed by the available source-material. The possible pertinent questions are different in each case.

This self-denial is an index of wisdom. The student who seeks the truth about traditional Asia finds it in fragments which are generally as tantalizing as they are ancient. Some of them are very ancient indeed. Confucius allegedly wrote: "Every truth has four corners. As a teacher I give you one corner, and it is for you to find the other three." The fragments of truth about Asia are like these dismembered corners; we must work out for ourselves where the missing corners belong. To use a different metaphor, they are like jigsaw pieces which do not make one complete picture, but form parts of several. The danger with comparative study, if it strays far into theory, is that we may invent a picture and force the pieces into it.

But in the long run, of course, the attempt to relate different cultures to each other, to identify and account for the differences, must be made. Of course the political institutions of different countries differ from each other in kind as well as degree; but by patient enquiry we may yet discover why they differ in the ways they do. Of course Asia is a cartographical artifact, but the very circumstance that countries and civilizations can have such separate personalities when their geographical relationships are (often) so close is a good starting-point for study.

Indeed, the vivisection of Orientalism into area and culture specializations masks a quite genuine unity that is founded on geography. Asia is not the sum of certain agricultural civilizations defined by particular sacred languages, cosmologies and dynastic traditions. It is, most of it, a huge, bleak, land-locked waste sparsely peopled through its history by mobile tribes; the agricultural societies which dominate the record belong to the coastal fringes of this great land mass, and in various ways their histories have had imposed upon them a rhythm beaten out by the little-charted migrations of warriors and traders, Buddhists and Muslims, to and fro across the arduous passages of the interior. South Asia too needs an Owen Lattimore.

Historians are boxed into regional compartments by their source-material, and their source-material by definition speaks only for the outer zones of Asia where agrarian civilization and literacy developed. Therefore the relatively empty interior is too often and too easily forgotten. But throughout history there has been a constant traffic, military, commercial and cultural, linking the agrarian societies by the land routes as well as by sea and mediating common experiences.

Quite apart from this, the shared underlying pattern of monsoon and harvest has made for similarities of social and hence political organization. It is therefore not surprising that the studies in this volume exhibit a number of common themes that inform the workings of political authority in many different places. Let us identify some of these themes.

1. In ideology, almost no Asian society distinguishes between sacred and profane. Almost every Asian culture possesses a language of ideas pervaded through and through by 'religion'; one of the most basic mistakes is to suppose that we can treat Asian ideas of the sacred without making a subtle and difficult translation from the language of modern international culture, organized as it is around a fundamental dualism. One form of the

mistake is to suppose that 'divinity' meant in a traditional Asian society the same thing that it means to us. It is not surprising if we find sacredness even in China, the most apparently 'secular' of the Great Tradition cultures, but the sacredness needs to be carefully defined. As Paul Rule says below, the Chinese ruler is "sacred in a specifically Chinese way".

2. This illustrates the question of 'god-kingship', a specific case of the infusion of the profane with the sacred. It is difficult to avoid it in any extended discussion of the ideology of kingship in Asia, and several of the papers in this volume touch on this theme. Whether kings really were seen as gods in any given culture has been much debated; one mistake easily made is to suppose that the answer must be the same in all centuries, that there is no historical development, and S.D. Singh in his detailed diachronic study of India brings out the danger of this assumption. The most valid general answer for the whole of Asia must be ambivalent: the proponents of rational secular states cannot ignore the evidence that in many times and places the idea of god-kingship was certainly there; but on the other hand we must recognize that it did not have the implications in practice that it would have in modern society; it was a term in a symbolic language that everybody knew rather than a tool of despotism. Further, as several of the papers here demonstrate, the relationship between ruler and divinity could assume any of many subtly variant forms.

3. Rulers were preoccupied with legitimacy, for reasons that the foregoing discussion may suggest. Often they stressed their (frequently spurious) links with royal ancestors. Often they commemorated their rule with impressive rituals, which sometimes contained echoes of prehistoric fertility cults. Often they invoked special relationships with gods, as just noticed, for the same end. Very often they identified the ritual source of their power with the paraphernalia of their regalia, with magic palladia. Notably also, a ruler needed to be able to commemorate his authority throughout his kingdom by cunningly working a mutual assimilation between his own cult rituals and those of the constituent communities in his realm.

4. In many societies a sort of sympathetic magic was supposed to link the virtue, legitimacy and mystic power of the king with the course of nature. Time and time again, in different cultures, we meet with the idea that national prosperity attended the

king's virtue, calamities followed his misdeeds.

5. Whatever the realities of power, the language in which it was expressed frequently appealed to moral ideas. Even where institutional limits on royal power were lacking, traditional notions of harmony, convention and wise conduct inevitably engendered psychological constraints, though these are difficult to measure.

6. It is a truism that traditional societies were conservative and looked back to ancient models, at least for rational justification of present polity. Chinese idealization of the legendary past rulers Yao and Shun is paralleled by the Indian theory of cyclic time in which a golden age is followed by descent into anarchy, making necessary the institution of kingship.

7. The quest for the actual origins of kingship commonly brings out one pair of functions: those of the priest and of the warrior. There can be no single mechanism that applied throughout the continent, but different forms of interaction between military and ritual necessities appear to have been at work in most societies.

8. The ebb and flow of power entailed the sort of rhythm of centralization and fragmentation that is documented in several of the studies here. Whether it be the decline of the caliphs, the fragmentation of Chou society, or the 'Balkanization' of India, the pattern is the same.

9. Similarly, the preoccupation of the ruler with control of resources is readily documented. We see him claiming rights over all the land by virtue of his office (though it is not necessarily a modern, absolute style of ownership), building up a following by developing his patronage network (Brian Colless discusses the role of the New Eastern monarch as 'rewarder') or buying friends with the perpetual alienation of rights and immunities.

All these themes are abundantly illustrated in the articles that follow. The very fact that so many common elements should appear in studies that were planned independently of each other is impressive: there is a rich store of material waiting for comparative study - but it must be sensitively handled.

The attempt at comparative Asian studies is therefore certainly worthwhile, and the present symposium, though each contribution stays within the geographical purlieu of its author's own studies, is an assemblage of material useful for the attempt; certainly, the concurrence of many common themes in separately undertaken studies is impressive. But many dangers beset the road that must be travelled before conclusions can be drawn.

Many of these dangers arise from the nature of the sources, which are both fragmentary and, in a particular way, partial.

They are partial because they consist very largely of written records which filter history through contemporary perceptions, and, in doing so, they impose upon us the assumptions embodied, even unconsciously and implicitly, in the thought of the sorts of people who wrote or inscribed the records. Now, a great deal has been written, especially recently, about the ways in which viridical perception of the societies we study may be vitiated by our own cultural bias; much more practical a problem, and much more germane to the actual concerns of orientalists, is the way in which our perception may be vitiated by the cultural bias of those societies themselves.

The point to be emphasized here is not the hackneyed, if apt, caution against the 'élitist bias' of the sources for largely illiterate societies. It is that these sources are the products of cultures dominated by cosmologies of stasis or equilibrium (the kalpas and mahākalpas of Indian thought, for example, or the yin-yang and Five Correspondences theories of China), which insidiously tempt us to analyse the politics and society of these cultures in conformity to stable and self-perpetuating 'systems' which we hypostatize before our enquiry begins.

Sources almost invariably presuppose equilibrium systems, and it is very difficult for the student to resist adopting the same cultural vocabulary, if not also the same system, as do his sources. This predisposes him to analyse the political institutions of a society as if they belonged to an equilibrium system. It also discourages him from seeking to account for the actual origins of the institutions in the system: the temptation is to assume that they were consciously created, as it were from above, as parts of the system - usually by the founder of a ruling dynasty, sometimes by the co-operation of an élite class such as brahmanas. This approach entails that, when institutions change or come into conflict with each other, this must be seen either as 'decline' or as 'transition'. History is seen as the passage from one fixed point to another, lingering for a longer or shorter time at each point.

What is wrong with this is that, in real life, equilibria are being upset all the time by myriad forces - not simply organic 'decline' - and 'systems' are always changing much faster than cultural perceptions of them. Thus, for example, the Tokugawa shogunate in Japan was in a cultural sense a system that lasted from the sixteenth century to the nineteenth, during which most of its outward forms remained unchanged; but that does not mean that in 1869 it was still essentially the same thing, only rotten with decay. That is an old view, but it is time, if some scholars are right, to recognize the importance of social changes that took place under the surface, changes that are not adequately described as 'decline'.[5]

Comparative study may benefit from the attempt to discard cultural lenses, if only partially and as a salutary exercise, and account for the origins of variant traditions in different parts of Asia by working from the bottom up - by looking at the influence of environmental, economic and military factors upon the development of political cultures. Two of the concepts which belong to this approach, 'oriental despotism' and 'feudalism', are so familiar and so often used that they must be examined here.

Oriental Despotism

The idea of oriental despotism has a venerable pedigree. Western writers since Locke have often been influenced by the idea, and its early currency can be partly attributed to Bernier[6] (who was retained at the court of Aurangzeb) and Montesquieu.[7] Bernier was no fool, though, and he does not deserve to be naïvely or hastily interpreted. His pages show that the power of the Mughals was often exercised capriciously and arbitrarily; they show no less clearly that, in a *sauve qui peut* ethos, that power was never secure, permanent or reliable behind the back of the man who wielded it.

Among modern scholars J.H. Steward[8] and K. Wittfogel[9] have been prominent in associating totalitarian power of Asian rulers with the hydraulic systems over which they presided. Of these two, the first blunted his early emphasis on the importance of irrigation systems in later writings; the second sharpened his, and *Oriental Despotism: a comparative study of total power* stands as the most forthright and authoritative statement of the thesis with which his name has become identified.

Its central argument is easily stated, though summary cannot do justice to it. Oriental despotism is a type of political system which developed in

Asia, did not embrace the whole of Asia, and was diffused to some places outside Asia. Its origin was in the needs of the 'hydraulic society' which appeared in various parts of Asia. As agriculture became more sophisticated, it became able to thrive in arid and semi-arid zones by developing techniques of water storage and distribution. These systems became increasingly extensive until they could no longer be designed and created by individuals or simple communities. Hence the state was born: the "agromanagerial bureaucracy" necessary to oversee the hydraulic system upon which the livelihood of the people intimately depended. This monopoly bred power. It gave the master of the system political control over society, a control which was maintained by the levying of arbitrary taxes and corvée labour for big projects which often served the ends of royal self-indulgence as well as communal economic well-being. The king sustained his power with a standing army and a monopoly of arms; he prevented rival economic centres of power from arising by keeping merchants in subservience and reserving control of all land to himself. The system was underpinned psychologically by a theocratic, conservative, universal ideology, and individual freedom scarcely existed. This cultural whole, although historically dependent upon hydraulic systems for its origin, could to some extent be diffused to despotic agrarian regimes that were not.

This is the heart of the theory; in Oriental Despotism it is extended into a view of the difference between European and Asian traditions. According to this view, Europe hatched the industrial revolution and democracy because of its pluralism and freedom; in Asia, oriental despotism ensured power for rulers but also entailed stagnation. It is this theory which has incurred much of the animus inspiring criticisms of the thesis as a whole.

Of the criticisms, some are effective, some are not so effective.

First there is the theoretical argument that K. Wittfogel's account of the state in 'hydraulic society' involves a vicious circle.[10] The centralized state is necessary to extensive irrigation; extensive irrigation is Wittfogel's way of accounting for the rise of the centralized state. Neither can come into being without the prior existence of the other. But this is not a fatal objection. Irrigation and the state grow together. This possibility has been pointed out by a number of writers; W. Mitchell refers to the process as a 'synergistic' one.[11]

Another theoretical criticism is not so easy to assess. It is that the sort of state organization envisaged is impossible in a simple agrarian society. It may be represented by B. Hindess and P.Q. Hirst, who wrote:

> Max Weber's conception of a rational bureaucracy, of an administrative machine which works through stored written documents according to a system of rational rules which employs salaried career officials appointed on the basis of technical competence, is the pre-condition of a *managerial* form of administration. Such a rational bureaucracy cannot exist without a rational legal system and a developed money economy - this presupposes modern capitalism and the modern state.[12]

As it stands, this argument is easily refuted. One may riffle through the pages of the authoritative *Arthaśāstra* (traditionally attributed to the third century B.C. but more probably compiled during the following three or four centuries) and one will find, *passim*, abundant evidence that ancient Indians were thoroughly at home with the theories of archive organization, pedantic regulations, appointment of officials by carefully weighed criteria, complex commercial codes, and all the paraphernalia of bureaucracy. And since ancient India did not have modern capitalism and the modern state, the conclusion offered cannot be true.

But nothing is as simple as this. Neither the proto-kingdoms of the Gangetic basin where Indian kingdoms developed, nor the Mauryan empire, witnessed the rise of anything like the modern state. The reason, however, is not that Indians lacked the theories or even the institutions. They had plenty of both, but the theories and the institutions did not work out in practice in a 'modern' way for socio-cultural reasons. The modern notion of a state was not developed; loyalty was personal, not abstract; politics were dominated by factions and patronage networks; officials regarded their appointments as ways of gaining money and influence ('The two worst places to stand in are behind a horse and in front of an official,' as the old Indian saying has it; Chinese parallels are legion), and corruption often made nonsense of tidy theories.

Thus it is true that ancient Asian kingdoms were not like modern states, and in this respect the argument against 'oriental despotism' is correct. But the difference lies not so much in the possession of different institutions as in the fact that institutions worked differently for social reasons.

The theoretical argument against the 'hydraulic society' thesis is therefore weak after all: it does not succeed in showing that the managerial resources were necessarily lacking. Even if corrupt and inefficient by modern standards, bureaucratic institutions may have been adequate even from early times to the task of creating and maintaining an irrigation network.

The damaging criticisms of 'oriental despotism' are the empirical ones. Irrigation can be many things, and these need to be identified in the many places where they are found. Systems vary in complexity. Farmers may take small or great steps away from simple dependence on rain. They may use the water that floods depressions or former loops of rivers after annual inundations, when this coincides with the season for their crops (as in Sind); they may dig simple ditches to direct surface drainage to their crops, even to encourage crops of wild grains (as may have happened in prehistoric times); they may make small ponds or tanks or erect dams across slopes; they may make reservoirs of any size, up to the enormous barays which rulers of Angkor in Cambodia raised above the surrounding plain with walls built by colossal manpower levies; they may lead complex many-tiered patterns of canals along valley sides until they are high above the parent river (as in Java). Many permutations of reservoirs, rivers, canals, length and scale of system, and sophistication of technology are possible.

Scholars have not neglected to look more closely at the types of irrigation appropriate to the zones where in fact centralized polities first appeared in Asia - notably Sind, Bihar and the loess lands of China. They are probably right in arguing that in these places we do not find evidence of the elaborate systems linking many communities desired by the theory, or of the need for such systems. (What has been written about India needs to be treated with caution, however. The present state of knowledge about ancient Indian irrigation is still a little raw.)

In China, Wittfogel's leading case, kingdoms first arose in environments where extensive irrigation was not actually necessary, and in their later history it was not usually governments that were responsible for large irrigation systems. In the hills of the loess region in the North-West where the earliest states appeared, rainfall regimes are likely to have been adequate, and in the Yellow River plain to the North-East water management involved drainage rather than storage. So far as the historical record shows, later hydraulic works were the initiatives rather of private individuals or Buddhist monasteries than of governments.[13]

Thus, in the first place, states may arise without irrigation: in the second, quite complex irrigation systems may arise independently of the state. The complexity of a canal system feeding the crops of a densely populated valley or plain may, in its accomplished form, so impress the visitor that it appears to be impossible of construction through ad hoc co-operation alone; but historically the system may have grown up bit by bit, communities and canals developing together and adapting to each other. Villages may resent the invidious and unequal benefits of government initiatives and prefer to deal with each other. Several writers refer to systems developed in the past apparently without state management: one example is that of the Hohokam; this system was originally seen by J.H. Steward as a case of oriental despotism, but no evidence of state management was found by later investigators.[14] Often cited is the work of E. Leach who found hydraulic systems without state management in Ceylon.[15]

It remains true that certain kingdoms (not the ones actually examined in detail by Wittfogel) did use systems fed from large state hydraulic constructions. The reservoirs and associated canal systems on which Angkor throve involved organization on a staggering scale;[16] inscriptions frequently refer to officials in the management of corvée, who must have been numerous; kings recognized the importance to their office of undertaking public works - one said on his accession: "In five days I shall begin to dig."[17] One modern engineer, seeing the scale of the (now ruined) hydraulic works undertaken by Angkorian rulers, informally estimated that a fleet of modern bulldozers would have taken ten years to achieve the same results.

It is interesting, incidentally, to compare Angkor with Egypt. The Nile's flood conditions make it a special case, and in ancient Egypt evidently the demands of irrigation and drainage absorbed a great part of agricultural labour.[18] That manpower could indeed be organized on a large scale by the state is sufficiently attested by the extravagant mausolea favoured by rulers and dignitaries, mausolea which find their Cambodian analogue in the massive royal tomb-temples which dot the landscape even now.

Such material could indeed be used to argue for the 'oriental despotism' hypothesis, but the argument would be subject to severe qualifications. In the Egyptian Old Kingdom, there was a pronounced centrifugal tendency; regional nomarchs or governors gradually became more like hereditary local rulers, and mortuary endowments and temples became increasingly autonomous.[19] In Angkor, rulers had to bargain with local aristocrats whose ancestors had been petty kings, and there could be quite loose vassalage links in a superficially unitary kingdom.[20]

Perhaps, then, Asian states did not develop bureaucracies as necessary conditions to economic systems. But the student of political institutions is likely to be more interested in the second part of the thesis: regardless of how agrarian kingdoms in Asia originated, did their control of bureaucracies, armies and ideologies in fact make them despotic? Even though it is impossible to review the evidence here, it is safe to say that, even though they may have been despotic in theory all the time and despotic in practice occasionally when the interests of various groups happened to coincide, they were not permanent totalitarian despotisms. W. Eberhard stresses the role in China of cliques of gentry which necessarily hamstrung any central control; the idea of law imposed effective limits on the emperor's autocracy; officials were not, as required by the theory, a distinct class of imperial servants, but were drawn from the landlord class whose interests they were disposed to serve; central ministries were (at least in the formative Han dynasty) concerned not with the centralized control of the whole country but with supplying the palace and capital only.[21] Scholars differ over the precise measure of the real power wielded by Sons of Heaven, who perhaps deserve to have a little of it restored to them by a sceptical posterity; but few authorities would deny that limits on power existed.

The final criticism of 'oriental despotism' concerns its ideological dressing - the argument derived from it that Asiatic totalitarianism entailed stagnation, while Europe forged ahead.

This argument is not very convincing; here it will be sufficient to refer to the spirited attack on it by Irfan Habib.[22]

What general assessment of the thesis can be made?

It seems clear that it fails in its chief aims. It does not prove that complex hydraulic works attended, or were essential to, the rise of states, and it does not prove that Asian regimes were totalitarian and despotic in practice.

It would be a pity, though, if between them Marx and Wittfogel should permanently inoculate ideologically neutral scholars against comparative studies which start with facts of environment and economics. It is worth recalling that, although it is the 1957 Oriental Despotism that has attracted most attention, Wittfogel's work in earlier decades had considerable influence upon the studies of other scholars. It is only necessary to cite Chi Ch'ao-ting,[23] whose Key Economic Areas in Chinese History is valuable in relating the geographical power centres of successive dynasties to the parts of China where agricultural advances yielded the biggest surpluses, and Owen Lattimore, whose important work Inner Asian Frontiers of China[24] opened new windows on frontier history and made it possible to relate the development of Chinese institutions and attitudes to the interaction taking place on the perimeter between Chinese and barbarian societies. Both these studies acknowledged the influence of Wittfogel; neither is seriously disabled by the criticisms that may validly be made of Oriental Despotism.

Two possibly useful ideas can be extracted from the thesis. One is that it may be profitable to direct attention to the economic surroundings in which Asian political institutions developed. The other is that it may be possible to relate a ruler's power systematically to the degree of control over resources put into his hands by the system over which he presides. He may never be a total despot, but he may approximate to the status of a despot for reasons influenced by the way in which the agricultural surplus is yielded and distributed.

If it is a mistake to regard the ruler as the undisputed master of this surplus, this is quite largely because he has to reckon with the interests of other men in a good position to press their own claims upon it. And it is at this point that it is useful to turn our attention to the idea of feudalism.

Feudalism

Oriental despotism falls at one imaginary extreme of a spectrum. At this extreme, a given territory has a single political master, and the élite elements between him and his low-born subjects consist entirely of his salaried officials and dependent priestly, military and other experts; there are no independent power centres.

At the other extreme, a given territory contains a number of competing units each regarding itself as sovereign, and there is no political criterion for identifying the territory as a political unit, though there may be a cultural one.

Between these extremes falls a large range of situations in which it is possible to give a political definition to a territory because the territory has a single acknowledged overlord, but the overlord has to reckon with a number of power centres which may have greater or less autonomy. These power centres may be vassal states that are effectively independent and acknowledge their theoretical subjection only by occasional tribute; or they may be courtiers who enjoy, at their sovereign's pleasure, the revenues of certain designated lands in the home territory; or they may be anything between.

Students of Asian history very frequently meet with such intermediate situations - even in China, both during the Chou dynasty and later, around the frontiers.[25] In common usage, the term 'feudalism' is applied loosely to most, or even to all, of this intermediate range, denoting a relationship between an acknowledged overlord and a subordinate who enjoys a certain measure of autonomy.

But we need a more specific definition. It seems appropriate, firstly, to exclude the extremes of the whole spectrum. The courtier enjoying his master's largesse in the form of revenue assignments is too like a salaried servant; the remote South-East Asian state sending trading missions under the protocol of tribute to the Son of Heaven every few years, or every few decades, is too like an independent country. The difficulty, of course, is that of finding effective criteria to demarcate the inner core of genuine 'feudalism'. Courtiers and vassals can slide into it or out of it with the ebb and flow of royal power. The descendants of Aśoka's servants, it is reasonable to assume, became governors, and governors became kings. Tibet, in the course of her history, has been lord, vassal and sub-vassal of China, as well as (most recently) assimilated territory. The changes come with changes in the reality of power rather than with the adoption of different overall 'systems'. This is a hint that the useful categories we seek are likely to apply to types of transient political situations rather than to imposed constitutional systems.

A related difficulty besets a second step we might wish to take: that of confining 'feudalism' to relations within a kingdom, excluding relations between a ruler and feudatory kings elsewhere. J.W. Spellman, for example, finding 'feudal' too loose a term to apply to the feudatory relations of ancient India, distinguishes between these subordinate rulers and contracting feudal vassals within a kingdom.[26] On the analogy of European history, where the idea of 'feudalism' was born, this may seem only proper; but the difficulty is that the boundaries of kingdoms in Asia were not fixed for all time; they were carried backwards and forwards by armies. In one generation, a province of a kingdom may be securely controlled under the governorship of the ruler's appointed servant, often a reliable relative; in a later generation, the province may become a vassal kingdom. Early Mauryan rulers in India appointed sons as governors - Aśoka, as a prince, served as a governor, and so did his son after him - and Mughals appointed salaried district officials, but the provinces were eventually lost to the Mauryas, and the Mughal home territory shrank to almost nothing. The reverse process occurred in China, where the Ch'in absorbed a number of kingdoms into their own home territory.

All the more, then, if we wish to adopt an even more specific definition of feudalism, which makes of it a particular type of contractual relationship, there is a correspondingly greater danger of losing touch with political realities. There is no Platonic 'feudalism' in heaven to which actual situations approximate, and whose definition we can distil from them; there is only a confusion of actual situations.

It will be helpful to enumerate briefly some of the characteristics of actual situations. Each of the categories listed below is a range of characteristics which might be possessed by the relationship between overlord and vassal, and a definition of feudalism should specify what part of the range qualifies the relationship as feudal.

1. The relationship between overlord and vassal may be dictated by the former from a position of power, or it may represent little more than the

inheritance by an independent 'vassal' of ritual symbols useful as legitimizing devices, or it may come somewhere in between. Founders of dynasties like Babur or William the Conqueror might be thought to fall near one end, museums of past glory like Mughal Delhi when the British arrived, or the Chou in the Warring States period, near the other.

2. Invasion and 'stratification' may be present or absent in feudalism. W. Eberhard, writing about Chou 'feudalism', lists 'ethnic superstratification' as one of its defining characteristics.[27] The 'ethnicity' of this stratification has not convinced some other scholars, who are unimpressed by the evidence that the Chou were from a distinct and alien race. We may wish to incorporate this social layering by invaders into our definition; if so, we will be interested in such regimes as those of the Kassites, Hittites and Hurrians in Mesopotamia. The Hittites had a tribal peerage and the institution of partition among sons of rulers.[28]

3. A related criterion is kinship. In many cases, ruling classes have characteristics that may be called 'tribal', the claims of vassals to their fiefs stemming wholly from their kinship and little if at all from contracts with rulers. We may feel tempted to exclude this from true feudalism. With this criterion, Daniel Thorner has sought to draw a line between the Rajputs, among whose vassals kinship claims were strong, and at least the early Mughals, whose muqtidars could be unrelated adventurers from anywhere in the Islamic oecumene.[29] The role of kinship among Rajputs is however not straightforward, and the relationships among them oscillated according to the varying impingement of outside political forces, as Richard Fox's important (thbugh not uncontested) study argues.[30]

4. There has been much discussion of the importance of landholding to the feudal relation; for Marxists of course, and for many others, it is the core of the relationship.[31] Even with a purely political relationship, we would ordinarily expect that the vassal would enjoy at least some rights over the revenue from specified tracts of land; otherwise it is difficult to see him as other than a salaried servant of the king.

5. The beneficiary's land may be in a single bloc, like the medieval European manor; or it may be in fragments, and the fragments may even be exchanged from time to time. We have to decide whether to admit such fragmented holdings to the

definition. In eighth century Japan manors or shoēn became important, accounting, by the tenth century, for the greater part of the agricultural land; these however came to be broken into separate parcels and rights over them were negotiable.[32] The question of primogeniture is also important here. In India, holdings were usually inherited whole; in China, where primogeniture was outlawed in 127 B.C., the lands of aristocrats were fragmented over the generations, a process integral to the supersession of 'feudal' relations by the bureaucratic state.

6. Beneficiaries may or may not have jurisdiction in the territories assigned to them. European lords of the manor had considerable jurisdiction; Japanese daimyo did too, though in some ways it was circumscribed. The development of the Japanese shoēn in earlier centuries is a complex one, and highly instructive in various ways. The shoēn were not a preconceived system of economic integration but an institution which grew up more or less haphazardly outside the centralizd revenue organization and eventually overshadowed it. Private lands could be given exemptions from government claims and regulations, and local dignitaries often commended their lands to members of great families in the capital as a protection against provincial government, relinquishing a share of their entitlement to the surplus. Often initiatives came from temples or great families at the centre, who installed agents as managers on their lands. A hierarchy of interested parties developed, each entitled to specified shares of the agricultural surplus. The high status of the landholders, and the legal exclusion of government agencies, meant that private individuals acquired considerable powers over the people who cultivated the shoēn lands.[33]

This sort of jurisdiction over patches of land, which grew up gradually within an originally more centralized state, may be contrasted with the responsibility for government in tracts originally given as part of a parcelling out among supporters. The authority of Chou feudatories varied with Chou power, but was considerable even initially. The feudatories of Indian rulers were usually autonomous within their petty kingdoms.

7. The exclusion of central government agencies from the Japanese shoēn is an example of immunities. A beneficiary might have ceded to him few or no legal powers over the inhabitants of his fief, but he might at the same time have a parcel of carefully defined fiscal rights contractually equipped

with detailed immunities, for himself and often for his descendants. Such immunities, with or without political jurisdiction, stud the historical record right across Asia. The shoēn gained tax-free status; so did monastic holdings in China and elsewhere in the Buddhist world. Gupta India is a complex case, for its 'feudalism' consisted partly of relations between overlord kings and subordinate rulers outside the home territory, partly of relations between kings and beneficiaries who received from them rights to revenue from specified tracts; the inscriptions recording these grants have sometimes been interpreted as bestowing jurisdiction, though this is not obvious; what is undeniable is that they include long lists of types of revenue made over in perpetuity to the beneficiaries, including apparently types of fines levied for violations of law, and frequently under the terms of these grants even future royal officials are expressly forbidden to enter on business. Similar immunities crop up in far distant parts of the world. Immunities contributed to hopeless fragmentation in Assyria before the reunification by Tiglath Pileser III,[34] and Egyptian grants to mortuary endowments and temples were similarly equipped with prohibitions addressed to the agents of future kings.[35] In the east, the inscriptions of Angkor, whose immunities are often sanctified with impressive oaths, make a close parallel.

8. The general question of land ownership is of course much involved with the questions of jurisdiction and immunity, which were special rights in specified territories, but they need to be distinguished. Most Asian societies did not have the simple notion of undivided 'ownership' current in western law, and this is a complication that has bedevilled the discussion of royal power: in one sense, kings may indeed have been owners of all the land, but it was a limited sense. A particular piece of land could be subject to the claims of tenant, landlord, temple or mortuary endowment, tax farmer, courtier, subvassal, vassal or suzerain, in almost any combination. Thus under the Kamakura shogunate the centrally appointed jito shared revenues with a series of co-beneficiaries - partly as a level in a vertical hierarchy, partly as one of a number of equal parties.[36] And this sort of complex combination of property rights, with its checks and balances, is apparent in India too; it is even more highly developed in Angkor.

9. So far we have been considering relations

between an unspecified overlord (who would ordinarily be called a king or an emperor) and his vassal; but we may wish to extend the definition we seek to further relations between vassals and their own dependents. Asia offers examples of several degrees of sub-infeudation. India before the Muslims came may be the most striking example: here there was a progressive devaluation of the language of politics, until even sub-feudatories of several degrees with a few score villages to govern could call themselves maharajas.[37] This progressive sub-infeudation can be seen as having eventually undermined the autonomy of the Indian village.

10. In Asia, religious institutions often play the part that feudal manors play in Europe - they lay claims on tracts of land, having rights to specified shares of produce and labour guaranteed by lords and kings. Buddhist monasteries were prominent in the formation of the Japanese shoēn; Egyptian mortuary endowments and temples enjoyed the same sorts of revenues and immunities as secular lords; temples throughout the Hindu-Buddhist world enjoyed the fruits of land alienated by pious kings. The example of the lamaseries of Tibet and Mongolia is of course familiar; and in the colonization of the Cambodian ricelands by the expanding Khmers we find recorded a process of infeudation which it is very tempting to call ecclesiastical feudalism: rights over tracts of land were reserved to priestly favourites who established shrines, with royal largesse, as the embryos of new villages. A rather similar process occurred in Japan.

11. A formal contractual relationship is usually thought essential to the definition. Sometimes the descendants of a vassal have to be ceremonially installed at every generation by the ruler, as was originally the case with the Tokugawa shogunate; sometimes the original dependence on royal patronage may pass forgotten and uncommemorated. The legal and contractual nature of the feudal relationship is indeed on some views fundamental. For J.R. Levenson and F. Schurmann it is something that contains the embryo of capitalism, and distinguishes both feudalism and capitalism from Confucianism.[38]

12. A vassal or beneficiary may or may not live on the lands assigned to him. Whether he does or not may depend on the commercial development of the society in which he lived; it has been argued that medieval Europe was too under-urbanized to draw the barons from their castles into cities. If the

landholdings are fragmented into plots here and there, the beneficiaries may live in towns and employ stewards on the property. Under the Tokugawa shogunate the 'feudal' lords were required under the sankin kotai system to spend half their time in the capital.

13. Much depends upon whether the grant made by overlord to vassal may be resumed at will; but this above all is a feature that varied according to the reality of power rather than according to a quasi-constitution. Founders of dynasties had to choose between buying the permanent attachment of supporters by rewarding them with fiefs that they could keep in their families, on the one hand, and preventing rival power centres from forming by keeping control over succession to local office in their own hands, on the other. Chinese magistrates were moved from place to place every few years, and nobody would wish to call their régime 'feudal'; in India the Mughals began with the same theory (and suffered for it because the jagirdars had no interest in nurturing the long-term prosperity of their districts, as Irfan Habib has shown[39]), but in the course of time office tended to become hereditary. Similarly in Egypt under the fifth and sixth dynasties the governors or nomarchs were shifted around less and less often, and began to turn into local lords with their own shrines. This trend has been extremely common in most parts of Asia; beyond a certain point it may appear to turn bureaucrats into feudal lords.

These then are some of the characteristics which may be possessed by the relationship between lords and vassals. They have important lessons for the study of 'feudalism', indeed of political institutions in general.

One lesson concerns the diachronics of political history. Strong rulers concentrate power at the centre, and according to their own ability and the traditions they inherit they may or may not be able to create a state that is not feudal at all, even in the loose sense, but bureaucratic. But if, as was normal outside China, they seek to rule by buying service with revenues and lands, their régimes are inherently unstable, and power slips away generation by generation as the descendants of favourites owe less and less to their monarch, more and more to the cultivation of local interests. If power is to be concentrated again, it is likely to be returned suddenly and violently by a new strong man. This of course is a cycle; it may be a dynastic cycle, though it need not, because the new strong man may have a good claim to the throne. Such cycles occurred all over Asia. In Indochina, for example, Jayavarman II, the founder of Angkor, initiated a cycle, and several among his successors (notably Sūryavarman I and Jayavarman VII) initiated their own. In India, Candragupta Maurya and his son and grandson began one; Babur and his son and grandson began one. In every cycle, the gradual dispersion of power passed through a series of stages several of which would be called 'feudal' according to most definitions. Asian feudalism, on this view, represents a stage in a movement, not upwards towards a more advanced type of society, but sideways between centralization and dismemberment.

Another lesson is methodological: that societies' perceptions of their own political cultures are likely to be more static than the constantly and subtly shifting relationships of real power. Societies could readily visualize themselves as unitary states, or as collections of unitary states; but many spent most of their time shifting uneasily in one direction or the other somewhere in between, and therefore needed a third type of intermediate theory. Most such societies produced such theories. The danger for the historian is that of treating these theories as pictures of enduring 'systems', when the situations they depicted were inherently unstable. The myth of the unchanging East is not dead yet, but it is high time it was scotched.

NOTES

1. The symposium from the Thirtieth Congress of the Human Sciences in Asia and North Africa, Kingship in Asia and Early America, edited by A.L. Basham, demonstrates the value of such comparisons.
2. E. Said, Orientalism, New York, 1978.
3. See for example the symposium in the Journal of Asian Studies, vol. 39 No. 3 (1979-80), pp. 481-517, and the series of articles in the A.S.A.A. Review beginning in vol. 6 No. 3 (April, 1983).
4. See particularly E. Said, op.cit., pp. 261f.
5. H. Bolitho, Treasures among Men: the Fudai Daimyo in Tokugawa Japan, New Haven, 1974.
6. F. Bernier, Travels in the Mughal Empire, London, 1891. See pp. 211-212.
7. Montesquieu, Charles Louis de Secundat (baron) de la Brède et de, The Spirit of the Laws, tr. T. Nugent, London, 1923.
8. See inter alia 'Cultural Causality and Law', American Anthropologist vol. 51 (1949), pp. 1-27.
9. See inter alia K. Wittfogel, Oriental Despotism: a Comparative Study of Total Power, New Haven, 1957.
10. See B. Hindess and P.Q. Hirst, Pre-Capitalist Modes of Production, London, 1975, p. 216.
11. W.P. Mitchell, "The Hydraulic Hypothesis: a reappraisal", Current Anthropology vol. 14 (1973), pp. 532-534, with a useful bibliography for the subject.
12. B. Hindess and P.Q. Hirst, op.cit., p. 217.
13. See W. Eberhard, Conquerors and Rulers: Social Forces in Medieval China, Leiden, 1970.
14. Cited by W. Mitchell, op.cit., p. 533.
15. E.R. Leach, "Hydraulic Society in Ceylon", Past and Present, vol. 15, No. 2 (1959), pp. 2-26.
16. B.P. Groslier, Angkor et le Cambodge au XVIe Siècle d'après les Sources Portugaises et Espagnoles, Paris, 1958, pp. 107-121.
17. G. Coedès, ed., Inscriptions du Cambodge, vol. II, pp. 17-31, 'Stèle de Preah Koh,' at stanza VII.
18. W.F. Edgerton, "The Question of Feudal Institutions in Ancient Egypt", in R. Coulborn, ed., Feudalism in History, Hamden, Connecticut, 1965.
19. W.F. Edgerton, op.cit., p. 124.
20. See C. Jacques, "Etudes d'Epigraphie Cambodgienne:7: La Carrière de Jayavarman II," Bulletin de l'Ecole Française d'Extrême-Orient vol.

LIX (1972) pp. 205-220; See also Ibid, vol. LVIII, pp. 168 ff.

21. W. Eberhard, op.cit., p. 83.

22. I. Habib, "An Examination of Wittfogel's Theory of 'Oriental Despotism'" in K.S. Lal, ed., Studies in Asian History, London, 1969.

23. Chi Ch'ao-ting, Key Economic Areas in Chinese History, London/New York, 1936.

24. O. Lattimore, Inner Asian Frontiers of China, Boston, 1940/51.

25. See J.R. Levenson and F. Schurmann, China: An Interpretive (sic) History, Berkeley & Los Angeles, 1969, especially pp. 34-40; H.G. Creel, The Origins of Statecraft in China, Chicago, 1970; O. Lattimore, Studies in Frontier History, London, 1962.

26. J.W. Spellman, Political Theory of Ancient India, Oxford, 1964, pp. 163-165.

27. W. Eberhard, op.cit., p. 27.

28. B.C. Brundage, "Feudalism in Ancient Mesopotamia and Iran", in R. Coulborn, op.cit., pp. 93-119. This volume contains a long essay on the comparative study of feudalism by the editor, as well as a series of valuable articles by other writers on their several areas. On Asia and the Near and Middle East, see the articles by E.O. Reischauer, Derk Bodde, B.C. Brundage, W.F. Edgerton, and D. Thorner.

29. D. Thorner, ibid., pp. 133-150.

30. R. Fox, Kin, Clan, Raja and Rule, Berkeley, Calif., 1971.

31. B. Hindess and P.Q. Hirst, op.cit., pp. 221-259.

32. E.O. Reischauer, in R. Coulborn, op.cit., pp. 29-30; see also E. Sato, "The Early Development of the Shoēn," in J.W. Hall and J.P. Mass, eds, Medieval Japan, New Haven & London, 1974, pp. 91-108.

33. See E. Sato, ibid.

34. B.C. Brundage, loc.cit., p. 106.

35. W.F. Edgerton, loc.cit., pp. 124-125.

36. J.P. Mass, "Jito Land Possession in the Thirteenth Century: the Case of Shitaji Chūbun," in J.W. Hall and J.P. Mass, eds, op.cit.

37. The most useful general account of this sort of 'feudalism' in India is R.S. Sharma, Indian Feudalism A.D. 300-1200, Calcutta, 1965.

38. J.R. Levenson and F. Schurmann, op.cit., pp. 71-78.

39. Irfan Habib, "The Agrarian Causes of the Fall of the Mughal Empire", Enquiry, vol. I, No. 2 (1964), pp. 81-98; No. 3, pp. 68-78.

2 JAPANESE KINGSHIP

Harold Bolitho

One of the clearest impressions I retain from my early education is of the way I learned my multiplication tables. I dare say most people in Australia have had the same experience - that is, of repeating the tables over and over again, to a sort of half-chant, until they were committed to memory. This has always been for me the quintessence of primary education - the murmuring, obedient acquisition of a set of facts which you don't yet know how to apply.

At around much the same time as children of my own generation were learning their tables, schoolchildren in Japan were using the same technique to acquire a totally different kind of information. They were learning the names of the successive emperors of Japan, all one hundred and twenty-four of them, beginning with the legendary Emperor Jimmu. The subject matter was different, but the learning method was the same - a chanted repetition of the emperors' names - Jimmu, Suizei, Annei, Itoku, Kōshō, Kōan, Kōrei, Kōgen, Kaika, and so on.

There was one difference, though. The Japanese children may have been as mystified as we were about the uses to which this memorized information could be put, but they were at least more inventive about finding uses of their own. They would compete with each other in the playground to see who could recite the list of imperial names the fastest. The habit has died hard. A friend of mine, who had this sort of education - incidentally, one of the very last generation to have done so - once recited the list for me, and a most impressive performance it was. Against a stop-watch, he could go through all one hundred and twenty-four imperial names in a little over a minute; the world record, he claimed, was held by a man who could do it in forty seconds from a standing start.

Looked at objectively, or, more particularly, listened to in all its sonorous majesty, this list of monarchs is impressive. It is also, at least in two respects, significantly different from most of the world's other royal lines. In the first place, it is unusually long. The Japanese constitution of 1889, which referred in its preamble to "a lineal succession unbroken for ages eternal", was guilty of only a slight hyperbole. Not too many people would now claim that the Japanese imperial dynasty can trace its descent back as far as the Sun Goddess, nor would they assert that her great-great-grandson, Emperor Jimmu, began to rule Japan in 660 B.C. For that matter, the existence of the first twenty-seven of his successors on the traditional list of emperors is not supported by incontrovertible historical evidence either. On the contrary one must view with suspicion any royal line of which ten of the first sixteen occupants were allegedly centenarians, and of which the twelfth lived to celebrate his hundred and forty-third birthday. Yet, despite such quibbles, the Japanese imperial line can certainly be traced back to the sixth century, at least as far as the Emperor Kimmei, twenty-ninth on the traditional list, who is now generally believed to have come to the throne in the year 531.[1]

A royal line stretching from 531 to the present is no mean achievement, even if direct heavenly descent now appears difficult to substantiate. While the Carolingians, Capetians, Plantagenets, Tudors, Bourbons, Hapsburgs, Hohenzollerns and Romanovs have come and gone, together with countless Middle Eastern caliphates and Chinese dynasties, the Japanese imperial family has remained, its lineage unbroken. Even during the fourteenth century, when there were two rival courts and two rival sets of emperors, each contender could trace his descent back to the same thirteenth century monarch.[2]

It should be remembered, however, that conventions governing succession to the throne were rather more liberal in Japan than elsewhere. Whether it be Emperor Saga in the ninth century with his nine consorts, or Emperor Goyōzei with a similar number seven hundred years later, no Japanese emperor ever fretted over a barren wife. Polygamy was permitted and expected, and if numerous wives, too, by some unlikely chance, failed to produce an heir, then there was always a retinue of court ladies in reserve to spare the monarch further concern. At the same time, no issue of the imperial loins was barred from the succession. Not one of Emperor Saga's forty-seven offspring, nor of Emperor Goyōzei's twenty-five, whether male or female, was totally ineligible. For that matter, succession from father to son (or, to a lesser extent, daughter), while it seems to have been preferred where possible, was not mandatory. Brother could succeed brother, or cousin succeed cousin, or nephew succeed uncle (or vice-versa), or even, in one case, great-uncle could succeed great-nephew. As long as the imperial blood-line - and therefore the particular relationship with the Sun Goddess - was preserved, little else mattered.[3]

The other respect in which the imperial roll call is impressive is this. Listening to the names of these remote figures, one is intrigued to realize just how little known they are. Of the one hundred and twenty-four, there would perhaps be only half a dozen to a dozen known with any degree of certainty to the average Japanese. He would of course know the three most recent emperors, but his familiarity with any earlier sovereigns would be limited to one or two of the glamorous history-book emperors. Perhaps he would have heard of Emperor Kammu, who founded the city of Kyoto in 794. Perhaps he would remember Antoku, the seven year-old drowned during the naval battle of Dannoura in 1185. Perhaps, too, he might be able to identify one or two of the four emperors involved in famous civil wars - Sutoku, Goshirakawa, Gotoba, or Godaigo. This would probably be the extent of the average man's knowledge - even the average educated man's knowledge. Only scholars or zealots would know of a significantly larger number.

We are, then, confronted by a royal line which has two distinctive features - first, that it has grasped the Japanese imperial institution for a very long time, nearly one and a half millennia; second, that its members, apart from the merest handful of exceptions, appear to have had little historical impact. In my opinion, each of these aspects can be explained by the other. The Japanese imperial line has survived for so long simply because its members have had no practical influence.

To those of us familiar with kingship along traditional European lines, the notion of a monarch who may reign without ruling is startling. In Christendom, at least, the king has always been required to do both, ruling as chief executive, lawgiver, and champion in battle, and reigning by his consequent right to be regarded as the Lord's anointed. St. Paul, who announced that "the powers that be are ordained of God",[4] had made the connexion between temporal and spiritual power clear enough. Whether representing his people before God in his own right, as an Erastian prince, or as the Pope's own chosen delegate, the European monarch has blended both the administrative and sacerdotal aspects which combine to make a king.

The position of the Japanese emperor was very different. Where the European ruler - or the Chinese ruler, for that matter - was both administrator and high priest, in Japan the two elements of kingship were kept quite distinct. The responsibilities of politics and administration, which involved objective criteria of performance, and which called for heavy penalties if these standards were not met, were held by a variety of figures, in greater or lesser proximity to the throne.

Unlike monarchs elsewhere, the Japanese emperor was no lawgiver. All major legal codes were announced by others: the seventeen-clause constitution of 604 was produced by a prince of the imperial house, and the Taihō and Yōrō codes of 701 and 718 were the work of the same member of an aristocratic family; the Jōei code of 1232 and the Osadamegaki of 1742 were both produced by military governments in which the emperor played no part. The Ōmi code of 668, the year in which the Emperor Tenji ascended the throne, may be an exception, but we will never know, since the circumstances under which it was announced - if, indeed, it ever was announced - are as little known as its contents, which have not survived.[5] Nor was the Japanese emperor a leader in battle; on the contrary, Godaigo was the only reigning emperor ever to venture near a battlefield, and he was deposed for his pains.

What both preoccupied the Japanese emperor and assured the survival of the imperial line was something quite different from these more energetic attributes of kingship. It was not what he did, but rather who he was which was of prime importance. In all religions blood descent is believed to confer special privileges. Christians approaching their God once relied on a rather roundabout system by which requests were passed from St. Anne to her daughter Mary, from Mary to her

Son, Jesus, and from Jesus, finally, to his Father, God. The Japanese, no less convinced of the efficacy of lineage, chose a more direct path; for them, requests were most likely to be granted when recommended personally to the Sun Goddess, chief of all the gods, by whichever of her lineal descendants was head of the imperial family. Therefore it was the emperor who assumed responsibility for those rituals and ceremonies by which the nation was assured of those things most vital to it - good harvests, and freedom from natural disasters. Who better to intercede with the gods than the descendants of Emperor Jimmu, great-great-grandson of the Sun Goddess, and related, on his grandmother's side, to the God of the Sea?[6] To whom did the imperial regalia of mirror, sword and jewel - so endowed with supernatural power that, unlike England's Crown Jewels, they are even now hidden from mortal sight - belong if not to the descendants of the man on whom the Sun Goddess bestowed them?[7] The imperial family, with its special relationship with the gods, stood apart from other Japanese, consciously and deliberately. Elsewhere, adoption was not considered unusual, but for the imperial family it was unthinkable. Adoption would have destroyed that claim to divine attention upon which each successive emperor relied.[8] It is the supernatural power of the imperial line which is, and always has been, of prime importance. The very first Japanese ruler to appear to us, in the pages of the Chinese dynastic histories, the Queen Pimiko, was held to have had just such powers. "She occupied herself with magic and sorcery", note the compilers of the Wei chih, "bewitching the people." From the description it is likely that she was a shamaness, making known to her attendants, while in a trance, the wishes of the nether world.[9] Despite the later appearance of emperors who, like Emperor Kōtoku (r. 645-654), "respected Buddhism more than the gods",[10] and despite an endless flirtation - never consummated - with the principles of Confucian monarchy, the historical emperors have continued in this thaumaturgic mould. Ever since the casting of the first calendar under the Empress Jitō in the seventh century, for example, this magically important function has been a monopoly of the imperial house. Obviously, something as vital as the calendar, on which the determination of lucky and unlucky days depended, could not be left in the hands of ordinary mortals. The same was so with the selection of era names. This, too, from the announcement of the first Japanese era name in 701, has been regarded as another imperial prerogative. Since all sorts of misfortune were believed to come from the choice of inauspicious characters, what more natural than that it should be entrusted to a descendant of the Sun Goddess.[11]

More than anything else, however, it is the central position of the emperor in court ritual which stamps him clearly as chief priest of the Japanese nation. The complex religious ceremonies of the early emperors, gathered together in 927, in the Engi shiki, were in constant use thereafter, and many of the one hundred and eighty-one annual imperial ceremonies are still performed.[12] One can hardly wonder at the English trader who, in 1615, referring to the emperor as the "Pope of Japan", described a figure who was "the greatest magician among the Priests, having devils in constant attendance upon his person".[13] Nor can one marvel that in 1687 so sensitive a position should have been denied an otherwise legitimate heir who had had the misfortune to be born during an eclipse of the sun.[14] Whether praying to his ancestors, worshipping the four points of the compass, or eating and drinking rice and sake in anticipation of, or thanks for, a bountiful harvest, the reigning emperor was undoubtedly the central figure in the nation's ritual life.

It is true that, with the growing sophistication of early Japanese society, particularly through its contacts with China, and its exposure to Buddhism and to government in the Chinese manner, the magical role of the emperor sometimes came to be overlooked. Clearly its significance had escaped the lady diarist of the eleventh century, who, ignorant of, and totally indifferent to, the idea of the Sun Goddess, could write in her diary that "I wondered where this deity might be and whether she was in fact a Goddess or a Buddha. It was some time before I was interested enough to ask who she actually was."[15] The indifference, naturally, could occasionally encompass the emperors themselves. The reluctance of the government to provide money to bury the Emperor Gotsuchimikado in 1500, resulting in his remaining unburied for more than forty days, is well known.[16] So too is the inability of his successor, Gokashiwabara, to get from the same government the money he needed for his coronation, as a result of which his ceremonial enthronement was postponed for twenty years.[17] Even more famous is the case of

Gonara, Gokashiwabara's successor, who allegedly had specimens of his calligraphy hawked around the streets of the capital in an effort to recoup his financial situation.[18]

By contrast, if his sacerdotal role is paramount, historically the emperor's part in national administration has been minimal. The evidence for this is largely of a negative sort; few are to be seen either making administrative decisions, or trying to make them. According to one historian of the imperial institution, there were just four emperors between 673 and 806 who ruled as well as reigned, "perhaps", he writes, "the only ones in the whole long history of the imperial institution".[19] Even this may be too sanguine, given that the only sources we have for the political history of the period in question, compiled by court officials, are deferential in the extreme. It is true that, in 743, announcing his plan to build a great image of the Buddha, Emperor Shōmu appeared willing to claim much more than priestly authority. "It is I who hold the wealth of the empire, and it is I who hold the power of the empire", he declared. "I have decided to use this wealth and power to build a sacred image".[20] Yet this was a most uncharacteristic claim for a Japanese emperor, even at a time when conscious imitation of T'ang China was at its height. In theory the reforms enunciated in the seventh century - that the land of Japan and its taxes, and the people of Japan and their allegiance, belonged to the emperor alone - augmented the emperor's authority. In practice, however, as several historians have pointed out, the reforms also produced a bureaucratic system which became "the highest, and only, public agency", and left the emperor with little more than ceremonial functions.[21] This was not all. A further barrier to direct imperial rule lay in the restrictions which denied access to high office to all but the hereditary aristocracy. It is odd that the Japanese should so willingly have turned their backs on one of the major strengths of T'ang government; stranger still that they should have restored to the aristocracy, in a different form, that very influence of which they were to have been deprived.

Perhaps the most noteworthy feature of all, however, is that this principle should have been enunciated by the Emperor Temmu, believed by some to have been, like his brother Tenji before him, one of the most powerful of Japanese rulers. Certainly, on the evidence available, such a judgement is difficult to sustain. There is, for a start, very little information about their reigns. What does exist is to be found in the Nihon shoki, the first, and least credible, of the six dynastic histories compiled by publicists of the imperial line. Even on the evidence provided here, there seems reason to doubt that either of these men was an absolute ruler. Emperor Tenji, for example, if he was a powerful emperor, was not so for very long, since he reigned for only three years, from 668-671, and during that period seems to have done little but go herb gathering, move his court, and introduce the water-clock. He may - and equally may not - have announced a code of laws in 668; if he did, then from this, as from his ambitious prohibition of "heedless slanders and foul falsehoods", there has been little lasting impact.[22] Emperor Temmu, at first glance, seems a rather more promising candidate. Not only did he reign for thirteen years until his death in 686, but he also seems to have wanted the throne enough to start a civil war to get it, deposing his nephew, the Emperor Kōbun, in the process. Yet his civil war was fought by others on his behalf, by aristocrats, "meritorious vassals", to whom he then had to offer a monopoly of high office.[23] As he appears in the Nihon shoki, he is at least as much involved in court social life, quizzes, banquets and concerts (he is said to have "made trial of the sound of drums and flutes and caused them to be practised in harmony") as he is in government. Indeed the most vivid impression is of his supernatural powers, not his administrative ones. Not only could he make himself invisible at will, but he could also command the tempest to cease. He was a skilled astronomer, and - in an age when astronomy and divination were closely tied - could foretell the future. His prediction, for example, that there would be a civil war in which he would win the throne, was indeed correct, although cynics might observe that Temmu himself did everything possible to see his prophecy come true. On the other hand, the gods spared no effort to hasten his victory, giving information, through oracles, on the disposition of enemy troops. There is no room for doubt that the Japanese chroniclers, in trying to establish the legitimacy of his succession, lingered unerringly on those thaumaturgic powers which alone could distinguish a true emperor from a usurper.[24]

Apart from Tenji and Temmu, those emperors most frequently indicated as participants in direct imperial rule are those of the early ninth century, and in particular the Emperor Kammu (r. 781-806), founder of the city of Kyoto, and his son Emperor Saga (r. 809-823). Yet here there is even less evidence than is the case with the two seventh century figures. Once again the only source is an official one - the Nihon kōki, which covers the years 792-833 - and this time, since work on it was begun in 819 under the patronage of Saga himself, one can hardly look to it for an impartial judgement of either its patron or his father. That is not all, however. Of the forty volumes of this work, only ten have survived, offering historians little chance to read between the fulsome lines.[25] For this reason the early Heian period is, of all periods of Japanese history, the least known. What we do know, however, is that Kammu, while he remained on the throne for a considerable time, had been forced to move his capital, not once, but twice, just as earlier emperors had done, in obedience to the ebb and flow of power between aristocratic factions at court.[26] Saga, his son, may have been an autocratic ruler, attentive to, and personally involved in, administration, but this is not his profile in the history books. Rather he seems to preside over the early growth of Fujiwara power, since he began his career in a Fujiwara household, and ended it by appointing the redoubtable Fujiwara no Fuyutsugu minister of the left. Saga retired at the age of thirty-seven, and spent the remaining nineteen years of his life engaged in his real passions - poetry, calligraphy, scholarship and esoteric Buddhism - and in both these respects his career set a pattern followed by so many of his successors.[27]

Early retirement, coupled with devotion to anything but government, have in fact been the hallmarks of the imperial house throughout its history. The abdication figures are highly suggestive in this context. If one calculates from the reign of the twenty-ninth emperor, Kimmei, abdication is very much the rule. Of the ninety-three emperors to have completed their reigns after Kimmei's death in 571, fifty-eight, or nearly two-thirds, abdicated. Of those fifty-eight abdicated emperors, more than half lived on for upwards of ten years, suggesting that whatever caused them to resign their office, it was not ill health. One can also judge that proven administrative talent and experience were not usually demanded of an emperor. Of the ninety-four who came to the throne after Kimmei, the majority were less than twenty years old at their accession, and indeed more than twenty-five per cent of the ninety-four were less than ten years old.[28] The youth of so many of the emperors must surely be an indication that the position was not particularly taxing throughout most of the historical period. The readiness of so many of them to abandon it may well suggest that the position was no more interesting than it was demanding.

It is significant, in fact, that, with just one exception, the notable emperors in the pre-modern period became noteworthy only after retirement. Of the half-dozen emperors most Japanese would be likely to have heard of, those mentioned on page 26, four were in fact ex-emperors when they became famous. This applies of course to Antoku, the boy emperor, who, while only seven when he was drowned, had already been retired for two years. It applies equally well, however, to Emperor Sutoku, who became emperor at the tender age of four, retired at the marginally less tender age of twenty-two, and then, in 1156, having been an ex-emperor for fifteen years, won himself a place in history by helping launch the Hōgen Rebellion against the incumbent emperor. The latter was Goshirakawa, who thereby earned some fame for himself during his brief reign of three years, simply as the object of an uprising. But it was in his subsequent career as ex-emperor, which spanned thirty-four years (some ten times the length of his reign), that he really bloomed as a political force. The Gempei Wars of 1180-1185 are his abiding monument. Emperor Gotoba, last of the four, certainly did little while he was emperor. Perhaps this is not surprising, since he succeeded to the position at the age of three, and left it at the age of eighteen. During this lengthy retirement of forty-one years, however, he had ample opportunity to make his political presence felt, which he did most notably by helping launch the Jōkyū Rebellion of 1221.

It is just possible, therefore, that of all the pre-modern Japanese emperors, the only one to distinguish himself in the position was Emperor Godaigo, who, in 1321, began to raise forces in an attempt to restore the prestige of the imperial house. It did not get him very far. He was speedily deposed by his government, and ended his life as emperor of a tiny fugitive court, sheltering in the mountains around Yoshino. It is a rather melancholy reflection that, had he succeeded in winning back his old court, he would then, in all likelihood, have had to struggle for power against his former supporters. Kitabatake Chikafusa, the courtier and publicist of the Yoshino court, really believed that government by courtiers was much more satisfactory than personal rule by emperors. The loyal warrior Nitta Yoshisada, too, was clearly itching for an opportunity to establish himself, not his emperor, as leader in place of those he hoped to overthrow.[29] The impression is overwhelming that, wherever political power may have resided in traditional Japan, it was most certainly not with an incumbent emperor, who was expected by everybody around him to be a ritual figure, not a political one. Where, then, was political power held? If kingship is composed of both administrative and sacerdotal elements, and the Japanese emperor accounts for only one of them, who carried the other half of the kingly burden? The answer is, of course, a variety of different people at different times. Like political figures everywhere, the political rulers of Japan have found it difficult to win power, and still more difficult to keep it. In consequence, the history of the ruling families of Japan - as distinct from the fairly placid history of the reigning family - resembles that of ruling houses anywhere, being characterized by ups and downs, riots and rebellions, murders and assassinations.

Broadly speaking, the rulers of Japan have come from three groups. The first is the imperial family itself. The pattern here can be observed as early as Queen Pimiko, the priestess-ruler described in the Chinese chronicles, for while she transmitted oracular messages, it was her brother, the only man with access to her, who interpreted and implemented them.[30] Prince Shōtoku, who governed on behalf of his aunt, the Empress Suiko, in the years 593-622, represented a more sophisticated variation, as did several other crown princes during the seventh and eighth centuries. Perhaps the most notable of them was Prince Naka, who, invited "to take charge of all important military and national affairs", is believed to have been the ruler of Japan during the reigns of Emperor Kōtoku and Empress Saimei,[31] and is recognized as the presiding genius of the Chinese-style Taika reforms.

Prince Naka's activity and influence as Crown Prince contrast dramatically with his three lack-lustre years as Emperor Tenji, indicating again the distance between emperors and administrative power.

Early retirement provided another avenue to administrative involvement and political influence. When Empress Jitō abdicated in 697, it was in favour of a fifteen year-old successor, and with the explicit intention of becoming his prime minister.[32] Later, in 758, Empress Kōken was quite open about her hopes for retirement, announcing that she would now take charge of major court affairs, while Junnin, the new emperor, could assume responsibility for minor matters and court ceremonies.[33] The complex structure of rule by retired emperors reached its peak in the period 1086-1185, when in succession three former emperors maintained their own political machinery for by-passing the state, and ran the affairs of the imperial household - including the control of the vast imperial estates scattered over fifty-nine provinces. The reigning emperors, by whom they were addressed as "your majesty", offered no interference.[34]

The second, and rather more important, of the three groups to provide Japan with civil rule, was that comprising the aristocratic families associated with the court. This, too, would seem to have had a long tradition. There are frequent references in the early parts of the Nihon shoki to figures who direct affairs of state on the emperor's behalf, and by the time Japan moves into the historical period there are several powerful families - among them the Soga, the Ōtomo, the Mononobe and the Nakatomi - jostling - and jostling rather vigorously - for political control.[35] The Soga family, which won supremacy for a time by destroying the Mononobe in 585, managed to arrange the assassination of Emperor Sushun in 592 and install its own nominees Emperor Jomei, and then Empress Kōgyoku, on the throne, before being destroyed in its turn. So great was the Soga reputation that the influence of some members of the family was held to extend beyond the grave. Several untimely deaths at court after 655 were popularly attributed to the malevolent spirit of Soga no Emishi, the former chief minister who had been forced to commit suicide in 645, and it was widely reported that a dragon had been seen emerging from his tomb and ascending into the clouds.[36]

Powerful as they were, the Soga, even at their height, were no match for the family which was to help destroy them, the Nakatomi. Under the family name Fujiwara, granted to them in gratitude by Emperor Tenji in 669, they controlled Japan almost exclusively from the ninth to the eleventh century. One sign of their dominance was the success of their daughters in the marriage market. Of the twenty-seven emperors to ascend the throne between 806 and 1155, all but three were born to women of the Fujiwara house.[37] Another was their monopoly of important advisory positions close to the throne. If the emperor was young, the Fujiwara would cheerfully rule as regents, in an office which, from its foundation in 858 to 1165, they filled exclusively.[38] If the emperor was mature, the Fujiwara would be equally happy to select just what state documents he should see, doing this in their capacity as kampaku, a post which they also filled exclusively between 880 and 1158.[39] In all respects the famous Fujiwara no Michinaga, four of whose daughters became imperial consorts, was the ruler of Japan. Certainly his admiring descendant Jien, author of the Gukanshō, thought so, for he compared him unabashedly with the great T'ang Dynasty emperor T'ai Tsung, and even with Yao and Shun, the model princes of antiquity. Michinaga himself seems to have thought so too; in 1017, at the wedding of one of his daughters, he composed a poem beginning "This world I do believe is mine".[40]

The third and final group from which traditional Japan drew its rulers was the warrior aristocracy, the samurai. In a pattern established by the Minamoto family in 1185, and repeated thereafter with some variations, first by the Hōjō, then by the Ashikaga, and finally by the Tokugawa, until 1868, political power in Japan was formally held by the shōgun - that is, commander in chief of all Japanese warriors - and his representatives. The business of national government - taxes, justice, defence and diplomacy - was now in the hands of the samurai, remote both genealogically and geographically from the courtiers and members of the imperial family who had previously held power. The transfer could hardly have been more complete. Indeed, as time went on, the various shōgun seemed less and less interested in preserving even the polite fiction - so scrupulously adhered to by generations of regents, prime ministers, crown princes, and the like - that they were simply ruling on the emperor's behalf. Both

Ashikaga Yoshimitsu, who, in a diplomatic letter to China in 1401, referred to himself as "King of Japan", and Tokugawa Iemitsu, in a similar context more than two hundred years later, appropriating to himself the title "Japanese Sovereign", seemed ready to state the brutal truth.[41] During the two hundred and sixty-eight years of Tokugawa rule, in fact, the emperor, although closely guarded and watched, became almost a non-person. Between 1626 and 1868, only one reigning Japanese emperor so much as set foot outside the imperial palace.[42]

This picture of the relationship between the emperor and his government is a familiar one. In essence, I am saying that the emperor did not, could not, govern. It is an old-fashioned view, since it reserves for the emperor only those functions which, to foreign observers in the seventeenth and eighteenth centuries, made him seem a kind of Japanese Pope, or, in Kaempfer's words, "an Ecclesiastical Hereditary Emperor".[43] Now entitled the 'myth of the two emperors', this view has received a fair amount of scholarly abuse over the last hundred years.[44] Yet I would uphold it, with reservations; those reservations, incidentally, would be on the grounds that to see the emperor as a Japanese Pope is to give him too much temporal power. Historically the emperor has seldom had as much influence as, say, an Archbishop of Canterbury, who at least has been responsible for the management of an ecclesiastical bureaucracy on a national scale. Even this much has been denied the emperor of Japan.

If I am correct, if the emperor has always been personally powerless, confined to ritual observances which, although performed in private, have nevertheless been of vital concern to the agricultural life of his nation, and if his unique link with the gods has been regarded as the crucial element in his success in this duty, then at least one of the common questions directed to historians of Japan loses its meaning. Those who expect an emperor to rule, but yet observe that in Japanese history he does not, usually ask why nobody ever bothered to usurp his title. The answer is very straight-forward. His title, although now translated 'emperor',[45] has never had quite the same connotations in Japanese; the common western associations - whether with Tiberius, Charlemagne, or Charles V - simply do not apply. In Japan it has meant, above all, that person who, as head of a particular family, is best fitted to represent the nation in its dealings with the gods.[46] To overthrow such a figure would be not only pointless, but also wickedly irresponsible.[47]

Yet, if I am correct, while that question disappears, another one takes its place. If the emperor is as I have described him, how is it that I should be constrained, in a paper on Japanese kingship, to spend so much time discussing a figure who was at best only half a king?

The reason is that the emperors since 1868 have become confused with their predecessors; the eminence given to the modern emperor has been read back into the past. But the modern Japanese emperor is in many respects totally different from those of traditional Japan. He is the result of a deliberate publicity campaign which began in the 1860s, when, in the national crisis of those years, malcontents of all sorts - imperial relatives and court nobles, of course, but also great provincial barons, samurai, ruffians, and even some foreign diplomats - saw in him the most appropriate justification for political change. Without pausing to consult him, they combined in his name to destroy a government they disliked, and proceeded to install him as a figurehead for something more to their taste. In the process, the emperor became more visible than ever before. His government dangled him before the country - significantly enough, they referred to him among themselves as "the jewel" - whether on royal tours around the country, or military parades, or numerous state occasions, as no previous emperor was ever dangled.[48] To make him, and his country, acceptable to the outside world, he was given all the attributes of European monarchy - neat moustache and beard, resplendent uniform, inspiring national anthem, and finally Britain's Order of the Garter. To quiet any public criticism of government policy, he was made to say in 1868 that "we decide all things ourself",[49] and, twenty years later, was put at the very centre of a European-style constitution.

At the same time, a whole new imperial myth was created, to give retrospective eminence to all those emperors who had lived out their lives in obscurity. They were rescued from oblivion, some of them being assigned great pre-historic tombs, whether they were actually buried in them or not, some being worshipped in newly-built shrines, or commemorated on newly-established public holidays, and <u>all</u> having their names memorized by every Japanese schoolchild.[50]

It was all a myth, but a most successful one. If anything, it was rather too successful. Not only did the Japanese convince themselves of the importance of emperors throughout their history, but they managed to convince the world outside as well, with some rather unexpected results. A book entitled Japan's Imperial Conspiracy,[51] in which the Emperor is given sole responsibility for Japan's decision to enter World War Two, is merely the most recent of a series of perverse tributes to the success of the imperial publicity campaign.

NOTES

1. The Kadogawa Nihonshi jiten, Tokyo, Kadogawa shoten, 1968, edited by Takayanagi Mitsuhisa and Takeuchi Rizō, is prepared to commit itself to Emperor Kimmei. Where earlier emperors are dismissed with a perfunctory "according to the Nihon shoki", Kimmei receives rather fuller treatment. "It is almost certain", the dictionary notes, "that he came to the throne in 531". (See entry under Kimmei Tennō).

2. See, for example, the genealogical chart in Kuwabara Takeo, ed. Arai Hakuseki (Volume 15 of the Chūō Kōron Nihon no meichō), Tokyo, Chūō Kōron-sha, 1969, p. 397.

3. For a summary of the major patterns of imperial succession, see Richard Ponsonby-Fane, The Imperial House of Japan, Kyoto, Ponsonby Memorial Society, 1959, p. 5; the information on Emperor Saga is from Nagahara Keiji, ed., Jien, Kitabatake Chikafusa (Volume 9 of Chūō Kōron Koron no meicho), Tokyo, Chūō Kōron-sha, 1971, p. 93; that on Emperor Goyozei is in Funabāshi Seiichi, "Gomizunoo Tenno", in Edo no kaifu (Volume 11 of Jimbutsu Nihon no rekishi) Tokyo, Shōgakkan, 1975, p. 118.

4. Romans, 13, i.

5. See Seki Akira, Inoue Mitsusada and Kodama Kōta, eds. Shiryō ni yoru Nihon no ayumi, Volume 1, pp. 49, 117-118. The 604 Constitution was produced by Prince Shōtoku, rather than by Empress Suikō, who was then the reigning monarch. Both the Taiho and Yoro codes were produced on behalf of the reigning sovereign - in the case of the former, the eighteen year old Emperor Mommu, and, in the latter, the Empress Gensho - by the same noble lawgiver, Fujiwara no Fubitō. For the Ōmi code, see Naoki Kōjiro, Kodai kokka no seiritsu (Volume 2 of Chūō Kōron Nihon no rekishi) Tokyo, Chūō Kōron-sha, 1965, p. 300.

6. For the divine ancestry of the Japanese imperial line, see W.G. Aston, tr. Nihongi, London, Allen and Unwin, 1956, I, pp. 76-108.

7. Ibid., I, p. 373, no.2; H. Paul Varley, Imperial Restoration in Medieval Japan, New York, Columbia University Press, 1971, p. 195.

8. Herschel Webb, The Japanese Imperial Institution in the Tokugawa Period, New York, Columbia University Press, 1968, p. 11.

9. Quoted in Ryūsaku Tsunoda, Wm. Theodore de Bary, and Donald Keene, eds, Sources of Japanese Tradition, New York, Columbia University Press,

1958, p. 8; see also Ishii Ryosuke, Tennō, Tokyo, Kōbun-dō, 1951, pp. 3, 13-16.

10. Nagahara, p. 83.

11. Ishii, pp. 143, 162.

12. Webb, p. 116.

13. Peter Pratt, History of Japan Compiled from the Records of the English East India Company, New York, Barnes and Noble, 1972, II, p. 86.

14. Ikeda Kōen, Tokugawa shi, Tokyo, 1909, pp. 556, 560.

15. Ivan Morris, tr. As I Crossed a Bridge of Dreams, Middlesex, Penguin Books, 1975, p. 72.

16. Nihon rekishi dai jiten, Tokyo, Kawade shobō, 1968.

17. Ibid.; Ishii, p. 141.

18. See A.L. Sadler A Short History of Japan, Sydney, Angus and Robertson, 1962, p. 130; common enough in English-language works, the allegation does not appear in recent Japanese studies on the period.

19. Webb, p. 27.

20. Quoted in Ishii, p. 71.

21. The quotation is from Ishimoda Shō, Nihon no kodai kokka, Tokyo, Iwanami shoten, 1972, p. 185; see also G. Cameron Hurst III, "The Development of the Insei", in John W. Hall and Jeffrey P. Mass, eds, Medieval Japan, New Haven, Yale University Press, 1974, p. 58.

22. Aston, II, pp. 287 ff.

23. Ishimoda, p. 220.

24. Aston, II, pp. 301-381, passim.

25. The remnants of the Nihon kōki cover only one fifth of the twenty-five year reign of Emperor Kammu; Emperor Saga, with perhaps as much as one-third of his reign represented, does rather better - although perhaps hardly well enough to warrant any too confident appraisals of his reign. Saeki Ariyoshi, ed. Zōhō Rikkokushi, Tokyo, Asahi shimbun-sha, 1940, Volume 5, passim.

26. See Roy Andrew Miller's review of some Japanese archaeological works, Journal of Japanese Studies, I, 2, p. 495; see also Sakamoto Tarō, Takeuchi Rizō, and Horie Tomohiko, eds, Sho no Nihon shi, Tokyo, Heibonsha, 1975, vol. 12, p. 9, where an estimate of the achievements of Kammu's reign mentions only the building of palaces, in which no doubt Kammu was directly involved, and the pacification of the Emishi, in which he most certainly was not.

27. This impression of the early Heian court, also shared by Varley (p. 9), is strengthened by

Kitayama's assertion that Saga left affairs of state to the court nobles around him. See Kitayama Shigeo, Heiankyō (Vol. 7 of Chūō Kōron Nihon no rekishi), Tokyo, Chūō Kōron-sha, 1965, p. 132.

28. Calculated from information provided in Webb, pp. 269-273. In each case I have taken the double reigns of Kōgyoku-Saimei and Kōken-Shōtoku as one reign each.

29. Varley, especially pp. 14, 74, 107, 111.

30. Tsunoda et.al., p. 8; Ishii, pp. 13-18.

31. Ishimoda, p. 162; the quotation is from Nagahara, p. 83.

32. Ishii, pp. 64-65.

33. Hurst, p. 64.

34. Ibid., p. 65.

35. Ishii, pp. 20, 40; Naoki, p. 19.

36. Nagahara, p. 84.

37. Calculated from Kadogawa Nihonshi jiten, pp.922-923.

38. Ibid., pp. 924-925.

39. Ibid.

40. Nagahara, p. 176; Joseph K. Yamagiwa, tr. The Ōkagami, London, Allen and Unwin, 1967, pp. 381, 389.

41. For Ashikaga Yoshimitsu, see Ishii, p. 138; for Tokugawa Iemitsu, see Tsuji Tatsuya, Edo kaifu (Volume 13 of Chūō Kōron Nihon no rekishi), Tokyo, Chūō Kōron-sha, 1966, p. iii.

42. Ishii, p. 166; the exception was Emperor Kōmei, who visited the Kamo shrine in 1863 to pray that the foreigners might go away.

43. Englebert Kaempfer, A History of Japan, Glasgow, 1906, Vol. 1, p. 260.

44. See, for example, Cyril H. Powles, "The Myth of Two Emperors: A Study in Misunderstanding", in Pacific Historical Review, XXXVII, I, 1968, pp. 35-50.

45. It seems clear that the English word "emperor" came into regular use as a translation for current Japanese terms - dairi, mikado, tennō - only after British diplomats had begun to lose patience with the Tokugawa Bakufu. In this context, see Sir Ernest Satow, A Diplomat in Japan, London, Oxford University Press, 1968, pp. 197, 244; see also Lord Redesdale, Memories, London, Hutchinson, 1916, Volume I, pp. 377-379, 393.

46. That the word tennō itself was more strongly linked to religion than to administration we may guess from Arai Hakuseki's analysis of it in his autobiography. See Miyagi Michio, ed., Teihon

'Oritaku shiba no ki' shakugi, Tokyo, Shibundō, 1964, pp. 299-300.

47. "It would be unwise", wrote the seventeenth century philosopher Kumazawa Banzan, "for a warrior to become emperor, or for an emperor to govern." Quoted in Ishii, p. 168.

48. Irokawa Daikichi, Kindai kokka no shuppatsu (Volume 21 of Chūō Kōron Nihon no rekishi), Tokyo, Chūō Kōron-sha, 1966, pp. 27ff.; David Anson Titus, Palace and Politics in Prewar Japan, New York, Columbia University Press, 1974, pp. 48-49; for the use of the word "jewel" in relation to the emperor, see Tōyama Shigeki, Meiji ishin, Tokyo, Iwanami shoten, 1967, pp. 210, 221-222.

49. Quoted in Ishii, p. 189.

50. On the subject of imperial tombs, see Miller, p.490; for public holidays, see Titus, pp. 32-33.

51. David Bergamini, Japan's Imperial Conspiracy, London, Heinemann, 1971.

3 TRADITIONAL KINGSHIP* IN CHINA

Paul Rule

Discussions of traditional kingship in Asia, as elsewhere, are haunted by a ghost: the ghost of the King of the Wood, prowling his grove at Nemi, red-eyed from lack of sleep, sword in hand, waiting for his successor to appear and slay him; in short, Sir James Frazer's magic or divine king.[1] Studies of ancient Chinese kingship are no exception, as can be seen in the contribution on China to the seminar on Sacral Kingship at the VIIIth International Congress for the History of Religions in Rome in 1955.[2] The reasons for the persistence of this Magic King image, despite its obvious inadequacies,[3] even in its original Mediterranean context, are not hard to find. Traditional kingship is characteristically 'sacred', religious in origin and sanction. The problem lies in the morphology of the sacred in each cultural and historical context. The Chinese monarch is not a Frazerian 'Magic King', but neither does he fit any of the other standard patterns of sacred kingship. He is sacred in a specifically Chinese way. It is one of the purposes of this paper to attempt to delineate the modalities of the sacred in traditional Chinese kingship.

If Frazer's general pattern of magician-king,

---

*For purposes of comparison I have mostly used the term 'king' and 'kingship' in this paper rather than the more strictly correct 'Emperor'. In pre-Ch'in China wang, 'king', was theoretically reserved for the high king or feudal overlord. After 220 B.C. the supreme ruler was called Huang ti, usually translated as 'Emperor', while wang became a title of honour usually reserved for close relations of the reigning Emperor, and almost always devoid of political significance.

developing into divine-king, and rationalized into king by divine right, will not do for China, or perhaps any other specific case, what other models are open to us? Recent writings have tended to concentrate on the ancient Near East in the search for models[4] and rightly so. In the Near East, as in China, we are not dealing with 'primitive' or tribal monarchies, restricted in geographic range and material culture; but with extended empires, firmly rooted in an agricultural society and a neolithic or bronze age culture. Both foci for the development of civilization share a common socio-economic base in control of the water resources of an essentially arid environment, whether by flood control measures or irrigation works. However, early Chinese civilization is not nearly so strictly water-based as Karl Wittfogel suggests in his thesis on 'Hydraulic Society'.[5] And his 'oriental despotism' thesis breaks down under the weight of the evidence for near total disparity. It, like its Marxist ancestor, 'the Asiatic mode of production', proves to be a chimera. What we find in both the Near East and China is an intimate relationship between the king and the god or gods of his society, with a wide and fine variety of differentiation, from the king as god incarnate, to the king as favourite of the gods.

Gilgamesh of Uruk is definitely mortal, marked off from other men only by his nobility of spirit and the special interest the gods take in him.[6] Naram-Sin who proclaimed himself late in the third millenium B.C. 'Naram-Sin, the God, King of the four corners of the world' was, Henri Frankfort tells us, unique in Mesopotamia in the explicitness of his claims to divinity.[7] The Sumerian, and later Babylonian and Assyrian, kings were typically mediators between their people and the city-god, and if they had claim to divinity it was by adoption rather than birthright.

In Egypt, on the other hand, the king or pharaoh was a god, born of congress between his aunt mother and the great god, Re, Horus, Amon or Osiris. 'What is the king of Upper and Lower Egypt?' runs an inscription in the tomb of the vizier Rekhmire. 'He is a god by whose dealings one lives, the father and mother of all men, alone by himself without an equal.'[8] Yet even the pharaoh was not unambiguously divine. He was not worshipped till after his death, and was carefully referred to as the 'good god' in distinction from his father the 'great god' with whom he was united on the dissolution of his body.

It would seem, then, that even in its archetypal form, divine kingship does not imply an unqualified identification of the king with the god. Frazer's simple-minded conclusion that a Chinese 'Son of Heaven' must be a 'human god'[9] does not necessarily follow. In the first place, even if Heaven is unequivocally a deity, and the sonship taken literally, the Emperor as t'ien-tzu or Son of Heaven is only a demi-god; he is mortal; strictly divine honours are posthumous, and his powers latent and limited. Moreover, both these assumptions are questionable. T'ien, 'Heaven', especially in later times, tended to be depersonalised and rationalised into something more akin to the forces of Nature than a personal god. On the other hand, the earliest form of the character for t'ien is clearly anthropomorphic, and the rhetoric and ritual surrounding the imperial cult of Heaven always retained the personalist overtones of earlier beliefs.

The question of Sonship is more complicated. The term t'ien-tzu is used several times in apparent reference to the king in the Shih ching, and would appear to have been a common title from the beginning of the dynasty.[10] However, its implications are nowhere, to my knowledge, spelt out in the early literature. The comparatively late Li chi glosses it as 'ruling over all under Heaven' and lists it with other royal titles such as 'I, the one man', which are clearly not claims to divinity.[11] In short, there is no evidence that it ever implied more than the 'Dei gratia' in the British royal title, and perhaps its symbolic claims were even less.

Other possible models for Chinese kingship suggested by the work of ethnologists and proto-historians are the priest-king and the hero-king. Both patterns are quite widespread, and both have obvious relevance to Chinese kingship. The Chinese Emperor as high-priest performed a series of annual sacrifices reserved to him alone. His behaviour models were taken from the culture-heroes of a legendary past enshrined in such works as the Shu ching or 'Book of History', who established their fitness to rule by heroic deeds, and confirmed it by victories in battle and untiring exercise of virtue in office. Yet, again, the analogy breaks down. The Chinese Emperor was a priest to no greater extent than any head of family in his realm. The dominant Confucian value-system had no place for priests as specialised functionaries, and certainly not for a religious hierarchy. The Emperor's main concern was the cult of his ancestors and the great state cults were largely modelled on the forms of the ancestor cult, may even have arisen out of it. Chinese Emperors liked to appear as heroes of the battlefield, or, in the case of the Manchus at least, of the hunt. But in no way was this seen as their raison d'être or even as a legitimation of their rule.

Theorists about kingship commonly take coronation or enthronement ceremonies as the key symbolic acts which reveal the essence of kingship.[12] Perhaps the most curious aspect of Chinese kingship is that these or their equivalents did not exist in China. I do not mean just the obvious point that without crown or throne as symbols of royalty - the Chinese had others - they do not figure in the ceremonies marking the accession of a new king. Simply, there was no crucial ceremony of accession, at least so far as I am aware. There were, of course, rituals acknowledging the position of the newly chosen king, but these were not of any special significance, and certainly not regarded as, in some way, constituting or intrinsic to his legitimacy.

This is all the more remarkable in a polity where succession was not by strict primogeniture and dependent on contingencies and political manoeuvring. In practice, the member of the ruling house who managed to secure acknowledgement, either by designation as heir apparent by his predecessor, or by acclamation of the dominant court clique at the moment of death of the old Emperor, was henceforth, and from that moment, Emperor. The Chinese had no concept of interregnum, even though there were occasions when the unexpected death of a monarch caused, as it were, the cosmic order to suffer a hiatus. Normally, as an early Han dynasty theorist indicated, there was a strict continuity of rule: 'That, after the Greater Dressing of the (deceased) Son of Heaven, (his Heir) is called King, indicates that his people and subjects cannot be without a ruler (even) for one day'.[13]

The ideology of Chinese kingship was not symbolised by a special rite of consecration but by the act of accession itself. This, per se, was evidence that Heaven had bestowed its mandate on the new Emperor. He was not a special kind of man, of a different order of being, but an ordinary human who had been given a very special charge. As Mencius said of the model Sage Kings of antiquity, 'Even Yao and Shun were the same as anyone else'.[14]

The case of Yao and Shun, which looms very large in Confucian theorising, is worth attention as the model for the handing on of kingship. As told in the Yao tien of the Shu ching, Yao, who had successfully fulfilled his functions as regulator of human society after the heavenly signs as interpreted by the royal astrologers, was faced with the problem of choosing a successor. He rejected his son as one who was unvirtuous and insolent, and eventually found his man, one Shun of Yu, a humble commoner who had displayed outstanding virtue in living peaceably with a blind and stupid father, a deceitful mother and an arrogant brother. Yao tests him by marrying him off to his two daughters (pleasing not one but two royal ladies at once must have been quite a task) and giving him various responsibilities. He passes all the tests and is then named by Yao as his successor. Shun modestly declines the honour but eventually accepts the abdication of Yao in the Temple of the Royal Ancestors, and proceeds to justify his selection by his deeds which are listed as performing all the current sacrifices at the right time and place (the priest-king theme?); ordering the calendar, weights and measures, and the feudal hierarchy (cosmic order or the king as magus?); punishing the wicked and suppressing the barbarian (the hero-king?).[15]

Thus far the ideology of the tests of fitness to rule. But is it no more than choosing the best man for the job? Why, in the end, are Yao and Shun not just the same as anyone else? Again Mencius provides the answer in the Fifth Book where he explains the role of Heaven in the affair. I hope you will forgive me for quoting at length because I believe that it speaks more loudly and more succinctly than volumes of commentary.

> Wan Chung said, 'Is it true that Yao gave the Empire to Shun?'
>
> 'No', said Mencius. 'The Emperor cannot give the Empire to another.'
>
> 'In that case who gave the Empire to Shun?'
>
> 'Heaven gave it to him.'
>
> 'You say Heaven gave it to him. Does this mean that Heaven gave him detailed and minute instructions?'
>
> 'No. Heaven does not speak but reveals itself through its acts and deeds.'
>
> 'How does Heaven do this?'
>
> 'The Emperor can recommend a man to Heaven but he cannot make Heaven give this man the

> Empire; just as a feudal lord can recommend a man to the Emperor but he cannot make the Emperor bestow a fief on him, or as a Counsellor can recommend a man to a feudal lord but cannot make the feudal lord appoint him a Counsellor. In antiquity, Yao recommended Shun to Heaven and Heaven accepted him; he presented him to the people and the people accepted him. Hence I said, "Heaven does not speak but reveals itself by its acts and deeds."'
>
> 'May I ask how he was accepted by Heaven when recommended to it and how he was accepted by the people when presented to them?'
>
> 'When he was put in charge of sacrifices, the hundred gods enjoyed them. This showed that Heaven accepted him. When he was put in charge of affairs, they were kept in order and the people were content. This showed that the people accepted him. Heaven gave it to him, and the people gave it to him. Hence I said, "The Emperor cannot give the Empire to another."'[16]

You will notice that, although couched in religious terms, the emphasis in this account is on legitimation by kingly deeds rather than by magical rites or divine intervention. The mystique of Chinese kingship, such as it is, is firmly grounded in expediency and popular acceptance. And Mencius, at least, did not hesitate to draw the logical conclusion that a king who did not act as a king should, was, in fact, no king.[17] This does not quite add up to 'the right of rebellion' as it is often depicted, but it is certainly a curiously attenuated form of sacred kingship which does not protect its exponent from his own subjects. But neither does it amount to a social contract or a constitutional monarchy. There are no legal or institutional limits to temper the exercise of power once bestowed by Heaven.

Nor, I must hasten to add, does this Confucian political theology square easily with the actual institution of monarchy in traditional China. It was not popular acclaim or divine intervention that brought the Chinese monarchy into being and kept it in power, but naked force. Leaving aside the arguments about the nature of the earliest forms of kingship in China, that of the Shang and Chou dynasties (i.e. whether they were feudal monarchies, or in what sense), how the latter succeeded to the former, and so on; there is no argument that the Ch'in, who united China in 220 B.C. and created the first Chinese Empire, were Realpolitikers, with no use for theory except such as would serve the interests of a centralising autocratic power. It is significant, I think, that recently the Chinese government attempted to rehabilitate the Ch'in as model rulers. The rebellion which replaced the Ch'in after a few years was partially at least inspired by a desire to return to the old theories as well as older practices - or, at least, so its apologists alleged.[18] So, the new Han rulers cultivated Confucian scholars who repaid them by depicting them for posterity as Confucian sage-kings. Not only did they come to power, as all earlier and later Chinese dynasties, by force; but once in power, they followed the principles of the much maligned Legalists, the ideologists of power politics, rather than those of the Confucians who dominated their governments.

The Confucians, in return, developed (or perverted?) the Confucian theories of government by virtuous men and the mandate of Heaven, in order to accommodate the new realities. And so we get Tung Chung-shu in his 'Luxuriant Dew from the Spring and Autumn Annals' (Ch'un-ch'iu fan-lu) elevating the king to a position of cosmic significance never dreamed of by Confucius:

> Those who in ancient times invented writing drew three lines and connected them through the middle, calling the character "king". The three lines are Heaven, earth, and man, and that which passes through the middle joins the principles of all three. Occupying the centre of Heaven, earth, and man, passing through and joining all three - if he is not king, who can do this?
>
> Thus the king is but the executor of Heaven. He regulates its seasons and brings them to completion. He patterns his actions on its commands and causes the people to follow them. When he would begin some enterprise, he observes its numerical laws. He follows its ways in creating his laws, observes its will, and brings all to rest in humanity.[19]

A sublime conception perhaps, but I think a more pertinent interpretation of this piece of cosmological nonsense is that the principles of Confucius have been made to correspond to the ways of the despotic monarch. The level headed humanitarianism of the early Confucians, aimed at tempering the wilfulness of the powerful by sage advice, has become the servile flattery of a courtier. It was this perspective which enabled later Confucians to call the Emperor and his works sheng, 'holy' or 'divinely wise'. Thus he is described as exemplifying 'sacred virtue' (sheng-te) and his rule is a 'sacred rule' (sheng-chih). And, in the Ch'ing dynasty, a carefully selected collection of moral maxims, focused on loyalty to the throne, is received as a 'Sacred Edict' (sheng-yu).[20] The moral sensitivity of Confucius has been reduced to one precept - loyalty. 'To be perfectly loyal to the Emperor, and to fulfil your filial duties to the utmost, is the whole duty of man.'[21]

I do not want to paint Confucian servility in too dark colours. The Emperors, as well as their scholar-bureaucrat servants, had to pay a price for their marriage of convenience. They accepted the limitations on their power imposed by a permanent bureaucracy with its own ethos. Furthermore, a sacred emperor must be seen to be one, must not tarnish his image.[22] As the mediator between Heaven and man, he must accept responsibility if that mediation fails. Natural disasters as well as policy blunders were sheeted home to him. And it was the Emperor who had publicly to acknowledge that his lack of virtue had precipitated the crisis. Heaven was displeased so, ipso facto, the Son of Heaven had failed in his task of maintaining cosmic order.

There still remains the question of how, in practice, the royal sacredness was regarded by the Emperor himself, his bureaucrats and his subjects. Even if the symbiosis of monarchy and bureaucracy can be fully explained in terms of expediency, the persistence of the rhetoric of sacredness, and popular attitudes towards the monarchy expressed in proverbs, stories and legends, suggests that the Chinese Emperor was, in some real sense, sacred. One popular conceptualization of this is Max Weber's 'charisma', but I feel it is one that gives us little explanatory mileage. It is, in Weber's usage, at once religious and political, suprarational and yet rooted in political expediency. When, in his The Religion of China, he attempts to elucidate it, he becomes so vague as to be almost irresponsible. All distinctions are dissolved in the all embracing notion of 'charismatic authority'.

> Thus (he says) the Chinese monarch remained primarily a pontifex; he was the old rainmaker of magical religion translated into ethics ... like all genuinely charismatic rulers he was a monarch by divine right ... (and so on).[23]

The evidence for this rehash of Frazerian ideas and Europocentric political theology as evidenced in his footnotes is drawn from a time range of three thousand years; and many of his <u>a priori</u> deductions, e.g. that the Emperor would be forced to abdicate, or even be killed, in case of natural disasters, or that he was subject to reprimand by the censors,[24] are simply untrue, at least in the Ch'ing period I know best.

The problem and the solution lie in the peculiar Chinese conception of the sacred. This would require another paper to develop fully (something I hope to do in the near future)[25] but let me dogmatically lay before you a few tentative propositions: that to the Chinese the sacred and secular are not separate spheres of reality as commonly conceived by the Western analytical mind,[26] but rather dimensions of meaning within one reality; that there was no logical or ontological contradiction in the Emperor being regarded both as subject to human frailty and yet the fount and focus of transcendent values; that his sacredness derived not from any personal charisma, nor even from his office as such, but from his social function as a pivot-point in the cosmic harmony. Chinese utopias, even those inspired by religious ideas such as K'ang Yu-wei's <u>Ta T'ung</u>,[27] are this-worldly because of, not in spite of, their religious ideals.

To turn from ideology of monarchy to its institutional and political reality, the terms most commonly used of Chinese monarchy in the Ming and Ch'ing periods are 'autocracy' and 'despotism'. I prefer the former term as less pejorative, and also less misleading. If they were despots, they were often 'enlightened despots'. It is interesting that the French Jesuit missionaries of the late 17th and 18th centuries so often saw the Ch'ing Emperors as counterparts of their own monarchs[28] and Jacques Gernet in his masterly new history of China, <u>Le monde Chinois</u>, entitles his study of the high Ch'ing period, 'les despotes éclairés'.[29] The central point seems to be that their power did not rest on a legal fiction[30] or a theological dogma[31] but on a lack of legal or institutional controls.[32] The consequence of possession of a vast centralized empire was power unlimited by any but traditional, ethical and practical restraints.[33]

These latter restraints were however very effective in practice. Joseph Levenson in the second volume of his Confucian China and Its Modern Fate[34] has arrayed the factors limiting despotic control in China very persuasively. Some we have already seen - the imperial 'image' of benevolence and paternalism, the pervasive Chinese moralism, the tensions between bureaucracy and royal household, the mutual dependence and inescapable tensions between the will of the autocrat and its implementation. It was, according to Levenson, these very tensions that kept the system alive for so long, or to translate it into our terms, prevented autocracy from sinking into pure despotism.

> The tension between emperor and bureaucracy was not the old order's weakness but its strength. When it ended, when Confucianism ceased to imply conflict as well as confederacy with monarchy, this was the decline of Confucianism as the specific intelligence of the Chinese world. With that decline, the bureaucracy slid all the way (or seemed so, to a fatally large mass of the people), for the first time, to utter parasitism. And a ruling class of parasites incites to revolution.[35]

It might well be argued that the main result of the revolution which followed on the collapse of the monarchical/bureaucratic tension was precisely to restore that creative tension. The struggle between 'red and expert', bureaucratic continuity and 'continuing revolution', that has become familiar in China more recently is, in many ways, a continuation of the old struggle, and Mao Tse-tung's theory of non-antagonistic contradictions in Chinese society might be seen as a new version of the old Confucian/Legalist confrontation. I would not like to extend the parallel too far. Mao Tse-tung was not just the founder of a new dynasty, and the elements of sacredness and transcendence in the new China are quite differently expressed, if at all.[36] But it is true, as Etienne Balazs insisted, that the most dominant feature of Chinese civilization, and its most permanent institution, has been the bureaucracy.[37]

In conclusion, one characteristic of autocracy often forgotten is its variability. So much depends on the personality and capability of the autocrat himself. Recent studies of the great rulers of the mid-Ch'ing period - K'ang-hsi, Yung-cheng, Ch'ien-lung[38] - and my own research into the records of the Jesuit mission of the period, show the depth of the imprint made on government and society by the personal interests and sensibilities of the Emperor. In the light of this, the dynastic cycle appears not as an inexorable historical process, but as the result of the throw of the genetic dice. Each of us will have his favourites - I confess to a partiality for K'ang-hsi. But the point I want to make is that monarchy has been perhaps the greatest of vehicles for individual self expression in history, for better or for worse; and nowhere more so than in China.

NOTES

1. See J.G. Frazer, The Golden Bough: A Study in Magic and Religion, esp. the opening chapter, on the King of Nemi. For a succinct account of the evolution of the magician-king into god-king, see Lecture V of Frazer's The Magical Origin of Kings, London, 1920.

2. Benedetto Fedele, O.F.M., 'Il Sacrificio de Vecchio Re-Mago nella Cina Leggendaria' in The Sacral Kingship, Leiden, 1959, pp. 151-163. Another 'ghost' haunts Fedele's contribution beside that of Frazer's Magic-King, namely the Rev. Prof. Wilhelm Schmidt's Urmonotheismus. Like Frazer, Schmidt erred not so much in his insight, as in his insistence on its universal validity.

3. v. E. E. Evans-Pritchard, Theories of Primitive Religion, Oxford, 1965, esp. pp. 27-29; and J. Bowker, The Sense of God, Oxford, 1973, esp. p. 12.

4. See especially, Henri Frankfort, Kingship and the Gods, Chicago, 1948, and J.W. Perry, Lord of the Four Quarters: Myth of the Royal Father, New York, 1966. The most important comparative study, focusing on the ancient city rather than its ruler, is Paul Wheatley, The Pivot of the Four Quarters, Chicago, 1971.

5. v. Karl Wittfogel, Oriental Despotism, New Haven, 1957. Cf. the criticisms in Wheatley, Pivot, pp. 289-292, and 297-298; and by S. Eisenstadt in the Journal of Asian Studies, XVII, 1957-8, pp. 435 ff.

6. The Epic of Gilgamesh (various editions and translations).

7. H. Frankfort, Kingship and the Gods, pp. 224-5.

8. H. Frankfort, Ancient Egyptian Religion, New York, 1961, p. 43.

9. Frazer, The Magical Origin of Kings, p.146.

10. H.G. Creel, The Origins of Statecraft in China, I, Chicago, 1970, p. 494.

11. Li Chi, I.2.i.16 (James Legge's translation, The Sacred Books of the East, XXVII, p.107).

12. e.g. A.M. Hocart, Kingship, Oxford, 1927; and D.C. Holtom, The Japanese Enthronement Ceremonies, Tokyo, 1928.

13. The Po Hu T'ung, ed. Tjan Tjoe-som, Leiden, 1949-52, I, p. 227.

14. Mencius, IVB.32 (D.C. Lau's translation, Penguin, p. 136).

15. v. B. Karlgren, The Book of Documents, Stockholm, 1950, pp. 1-8.

16. Mencius, VA.5 (Lau trans., pp. 143-144).

17. e.g. in II A.4 (Lau trans., p. 81).

18. See Chia I, 'The Faults of Ch'in', in W.T. de Bary, Sources of Chinese Tradition, New York, 1964, I. pp. 150-152.

19. de Bary, Sources, I, pp. 163-164.

20. v. H.L. Kahn, 'Some Mid-Ch'ing Views of the Monarchy' in Journal of Asian Studies, XXIV.2, Feb. 1965, esp. p. 232.

21. The Sacred Edict, VII.15, cited and analysed in L.E. Stover, The Cultural Ecology of Chinese Civilization, New York, 1974, p. 89.

22. v. H.L. Kahn, Monarchy in the Emperor's Eyes, Harvard, 1971.

23. M. Weber, The Religion of China, trans. H.H. Gerth, Free Press of Glencoe, 1951, p. 31.

24. Ibid., pp. 31 and 32.

25. See my paper, 'Sacred and Secular in China', delivered at the inaugural conference of the Australian Association for the Study of Religion, August 1976, and published by it in Australian Essays in World Religions, Adelaide, 1977.

26. As, for example, in Mircea Eliade's The Sacred and the Profane, New York, 1959.

27. Ta T'ung Shu: the One-World Philosophy of K'ang yu-wei, trans. L.G. Thompson, London, 1958.

28. See, for example, Joachim Bouvet's Histoire de l'Empereur de la Chine presente au Roy, Paris, 1697, which explicitly draws a parallel between K'ang-hsi and Louis XIV.

29. Livre VIII, Ch. 2 of Le Monde Chinois, Paris, 1972.

30. Such as 'The King's Two Bodies' theory analysed in the study of that title by Ernst Kantorowicz.

31. As in the 'divine right of kings' theory, on which see the standard exposition in J.N. Figgis, The Divine Right of Kings, New York, 1963.

32. See C.J. Friedrich and Z.K. Brzezinski, Totalitarian Dictatorship and Autocracy, Cambridge, Mass., 1965, esp. p. 5; and Ch. 1 of Pei Huang, Autocracy at Work, Bloomington, 1974.

33. v. Ch. 4 of R.G. Wesson, The Imperial Order, Berkeley, 1967.

34. London, 1964.

35. Ibid., p. 77.

36. See my contribution, 'Is Maoism Open to the Transcendent?' in M. Chu (ed.), The New China: A Catholic Response, New York, 1977 (Italian version,

Esperienza Cinese e Fede Cristiana, Bologna, 1976).

37. E. Balazs, Chinese Civilization and Bureaucracy, New Haven, 1964, esp. Ch. 2.

38. e.g. J. Spence, Emperor of China: Self-Portrait of K'ang-hsi, London, 1974; Pei Huang, Autocracy at Work (on Yung-cheng); and H.L. Kahn, Monarchy in the Emperor's Eyes: Image and Reality in the Ch'ien-lung reign, Cambridge, Mass., 1971.

4 FROM VILLAGE ELDER TO KING: THE EVOLUTION OF KINGSHIP IN ANCIENT AND EARLY MEDIAEVAL KOREA

K.H.J. Gardiner

'They ain't born like us, y'know, them royals'

Alf Garnett

In the Samguk-sagi, a history of Korea presented to the throne in 1145 by the Confucian statesman Kim Pu-sik, we read the following account of the genesis of the kingdom of Silla:

> The Founder Ancestor was surnamed Pak and had the personal name Hyŏkkŏse. He ascended the throne in the first year of the Wu-feng reign of Emperor Hsüan of the Former Han, which was the first year of a sixty-year cycle, in the fourth month on a pyŏngjin day (6th June, 57 B.C.). At that time he was thirteen years old, and the kingdom was called Surabŭl. Before this, the people of the old Korean kingdom lived (scattered) amongst the mountain valleys; there were six villages.

(a list of their names follows.)

> These were the six divisions of Chin-Han. Lord Sobŏl, the elder of the village of Tolsan'goho, looked over to the forest on the slopes of Yang-san and saw that amongst the trees a horse was kneeling and neighing beside a well overhung with creepers. When he went to look, there was no horse to be seen; there was only a huge egg. He split this and a baby boy came out. He took the boy, and brought him up. When the child was little more than ten years old, he already had a remarkable air of maturity. So, taking his supernatural birth into account, the men of the six divisions made him their prince.[1]

Ignoring the artificial and totally misleading chronology which has been imposed upon this story, we can see two predominant elements. One is the supernatural origin claimed for the royal founder which is regarded, not merely as an interesting and unusual characteristic, but as the principal justification for his investment with the kingship. The other is that, before the institution of the Silla kingship, the account envisages a very different type of authority. There are six villages, each with its elder, none of whom appears in any way superior to his fellows. Even the title here translated 'Lord', attached to the name of Sobŏl, the elder who finds the egg, is simply a courtesy and in no way implies his superiority over the other five. In another version of the story, all six elders are said to have come down from heaven, and their rule is characterised as a time when 'the people were scattered and lived wherever they wished'.[2] Thus the change from village elder to king is associated with the change from small units to larger ones. The six villages come together into a proto-state.

Needless to say, these texts of the twelfth and thirteenth centuries A.D., although doubtless based upon some sort of earlier material, cannot be taken as any guide to what was actually happening in the Korean peninsula during the first century B.C. Writers of the Koryŏ period (918-1392) had their own ideas about what constituted a true king and how his authority ought to be exercised, ideas which were heavily influenced by cultural borrowings from China; when they wrote about remote antiquity, they could hardly avoid imposing various of these later concepts upon the traditions they recorded. To perceive the real as opposed to the fictional factors associated with the emergence of kingship in early Korea, it will be necessary to turn to a more contemporary witness, and this inevitably means Chinese records, principally the dynastic histories, since there is no extant Sino-Korean text which is earlier than the Samguk-sagi of 1145.

Other than the merest scraps of information, the first Chinese account of Korea is to be found in the Shih-chi of the historian Ssu-ma Ch'ien, written c.100 B.C. Ssu-ma Ch'ien tells us that, in about 195 B.C., someone called Wei Man, who had been implicated in an unsuccessful rising against the first Han emperor, fled from China into the northern part of the Korean peninsula with a band of over a thousand followers. Once there

> Little by little he brought under his control the barbarians and Chinese refugees from Yen and Ch'i who were living in the regions of Chen-p'an and Chao-hsien, and made himself their king, establishing his capital at Wang-hsien (P'yŏngyang).[3]

We are not told anything here about the social organization of the inhabitants of Korea before Wei Man's arrival. In another part of the Shih-chi, Ssu-ma Ch'ien states that Chi-tzu, the uncle of the last wicked ruler of the Shang dynasty (twelfth or eleventh century B.C.), was given a lordship in Chao-hsien (evidently part of northern Korea), but he says nothing about any descendants of Chi-tzu. A third century A.D. Chinese history, the San-kuo-chih, alleges that the descendants of Chi-tzu ruled in Korea for forty generations with the rank of Marquis, until the last of them usurped the title of 'king' (wang). It was this ruler, according to the San-kuo-chih, who was overthrown by Wei Man and who then took to the sea with the members of his court and eventually settled amongst the Han tribes in southern Korea, calling himself 'the King of Han'. The text adds 'The line of his descendants subsequently came to an end, but even today there are still men of Han who offer sacrifices to him'.[4] Nothing of this detail occurs in any earlier source, and one can only speculate whether, given the propensity for later writers to elaborate upon the statements of their predecessors, the entire story of the descendants of Chi-tzu is not a product of the Chinese desire to provide legendary heroes of the surrounding peoples with a respectable Chinese ancestry. Certainly at the time the San-kuo-chih was written there was no-one that we would commonly recognise as a 'king' amongst the Han peoples of southern Korea.[5] According to that text, in the mid third century A.D. the Han peoples fell into three broad tribal groupings, which in modern Korean pronunciation would be Ma-Han, Chin-Han and Pyŏn-Han. Even these were not units, since they were subdivided into kuo, a word which in the context of China Proper is usually translated as 'kingdom', but here clearly means something a good deal less imposing. In Ma-Han, where there were 54 of these subdivisions, we are told that 'a large kuo would consist of over ten thousand families, while a small one would consist of a few thousand families'.[6] Presumably the kuo of Chin-Han and Pyŏn-Han (which had 12 kuo each) were comparable in size. Unfortunately we are not told whether the various families in each individual kuo regarded themselves as having a common ancestor, and it would probably be begging too many questions to refer to the kuo as 'clans'. On the other hand, since they do not appear to have been much larger than a sizeable country town in modern Australia, 'kingdom' is out of the question; perhaps 'settlement' is the best we can do. We are further told that, although there are headmen in these settlements, 'the communities in which the people live are so disorganised that they (the headmen) can exercise no real control, nor is there any custom of kneeling (to such men) and saluting them'.[7]

Allowing for some Chinese bias here, since the writers were describing institutions of a people over whom the Chinese empire did not rule directly and for which they could find no obvious Chinese parallel, the impression given by these passages is strikingly reminiscent of the picture which the Samguk-sagi paints of Korean society in the days before the kingdoms. Both types of source describe a people for whom the highest form of native authority was that of the village elder or the headman of a settlement. This authority may have been somewhat more than the San-kuo-chih is prepared to allow; the countryside of southern Korea is dotted with numerous prehistoric stone monuments, many of which appear to be burial markers, and all of which would have required the united efforts of a sizeable labour force for their construction. Nevertheless, it is noteworthy that the writers of the San-kuo-chih and the Wei-lüeh go out of their way to assert that the heads of the kuo were not kings (wang) in any sense in which that word was commonly understood in China, whereas they were prepared to allow the title wang to the rulers of petty city-states in Central Asia, or even to some of the chieftains in what is now Japan. On this evidence we are obliged to believe that there were no kings in third-century Korea, and if this is so, it is likely to have been equally true of the earlier period. It is doubtless significant that the first fully historical king in Korea, Wei Man, came from China. Kingship was evidently not a native Korean institution.

The dynasty of Chinese origin founded by Wei Man was overthrown in 108 B.C. in the reign of his grandson. It was destroyed by armies sent out from Han China (although it is worth noticing in passing that the apparently purely Korean ministers of Wei Man's grandson made common cause with the Chinese invaders and killed the last king). From 108 B.C. until the middle of the fourth century A.D., Korea was dominated by the expanding Chinese empire through the Chinese commandery of Lo-lang which, like the kingdom of Wei Man which it replaced, was centred in the area corresponding to the modern city of P'yŏngyang. The Han tribes of southern Korea, as well as much of eastern Korea, were not ruled directly by the Chinese authorities in P'yŏngyang. Here again the San-kuo-chih gives us some idea of what happened:

> The various barbarian chieftains living in the prefectures were (recognised) as 'prefectural marquises'. Pulnae, Hwaryo and Okchŏ all became marquisates. But since the barbarians fought increasingly amongst themselves, it is only the Marquis of Pulnae who continues today to make appointments to the offices of kung-ts'ao and chu-pu... in all cases using men of Ye stock to fill them. The fact that the elders of all the Okchŏ towns and villages call themselves 'Thrice Venerable' is also due to the system which obtained in the (Han) prefectures and marquisates.[8]

Kung-ts'ao ('Promotions Official') and chu-pu (Recorder) were very junior officials in the Chinese local administration; even lower in the official scale was the Thrice Venerable (san-lao). Clearly the implications of this passage are that in these border areas some local headmen were given special status by the Chinese governors of Lo-lang, and that these men in turn appointed subordinates to whom they gave the titles of Chinese junior officials, perhaps the only kind of official with whom these petty chieftains came into contact. As to the motive of the Chinese in appointing such chieftains as 'prefectural marquises', this becomes clearer if we look at what the San-kuo-chih has to say elsewhere about 'the Marquis of the Pulnae Ye'. We are told that in 247, when he

> visited the imperial court to pay tribute, it was ordered that he be promoted to the rank of 'King of Pulnae Ye'. (The King) lives amongst his people, but comes to pay a ceremonial visit to (Lo-lang) commandery at each of the four

> seasons. Whenever the two commanderies (Lo-lang and its southern neighbour, Tai-fang) are at war, they levy taxes and require supplies or military corvée (from his subjects) in just the same way as they do from those under their direct rule.[9]

This passage makes it clear that the principal reason why the Chinese border administration conferred royal titles upon tractable neighbouring chieftains was to facilitate the empire's exploitation of groups outside its direct control; it was in fact a classic colonial technique for which more modern times can furnish abundant examples in other parts of the world. And just as was the case with Pulnae Ye in eastern Korea, so perhaps also in the south with Chin-Han, where there was someone called 'the Chin King' who, however, did not reside amongst the people of Chin-Han in south-eastern Korea, where the kingdom of Silla later developed, but was always a man of Ma-Han, in the south-west, closer to the Chinese colonial administration in Tai-fang.[10] Another parallel and, interestingly enough, a much earlier one, was the so-called 'Marquis of Koguryŏ', evidently the chieftain responsible, in Chinese eyes, for communications between the Chinese frontier authorities in the north beyond the Yalü, and the five tribes which made up the confederacy of Koguryŏ. We catch a glimpse of this relationship only in A.D. 12 at the crucial moment when it was breaking down. At this time, the Chinese usurper Wang Mang

> had ordered troops from Koguryŏ to go out to attack the northern barbarians. They were unwilling to march, and when the commandery tried to compel them, they all fled out across the border, violating the law and becoming brigands. T'ien T'an, the governor of Liao-hsi, pursued and attacked them but was killed. The authorities of the circuit and the (relevant) commandery put the blame for all this upon Ch'u, Marquis of Koguryŏ... (the commander on the frontier) Chuang Yu enticed Ch'u, Marquis of Koguryŏ, into his presence, and executed him as soon as he arrived, sending his head to Ch'ang-an.[11]

This incident as described in the first century

A.D. Han-shu led to a breakdown in relations between the Koguryŏ tribes and the Chinese empire. Henceforth the tribes were usually hostile to China; they repeatedly raided Chinese outposts in the centuries that followed, and in 32/33, when they resumed relations with the Han court for the first time since the killing of Marquis Ch'u, we are told that their paramount chieftain 'styled himself king for the first time'.[12] As the San-kuo-chih tells us elsewhere, whereas once the Koguryŏ nobles used to come to Hsüan-t'u commandery to receive issues of court robes and caps, now 'they grew prouder and would not come to the commandery'.[13]

If we are correct in arguing that the 'kingship' or 'marquisate' of Koguryŏ was not an office which grew directly out of the structure of the Koguryo tribal aristocracy, but one which was largely superimposed by China, the suzerain power, to fulfil its own administrative needs, then the revolt against China placed the Koguryŏ king in an anomalous position. His role as intermediary between the tribes and the governor of Hsüan-t'u was no longer so important, and he needed to make himself essential in other ways, perhaps as a war leader. By the third century A.D., as the San-kuo-chih informs us, the Sonno-bu, the tribe which had once provided the Koguryŏ king, had been replaced as royal tribe by another of the five, the Kyeru-bu. Moreover, the kingship of the Kyeru-bu was clearly still hedged about with restrictions derived from the power of the tribal nobility in general:

> All those great nobles who belong to the same ancestral tribe as the king have the title koch'uga. Furthermore, even amongst the Sonno-bu, the original masters of the kingdom, although they no longer provide the king, yet their successive chieftains in direct descent have the title koch'uga; they also have the right to set up shrines to their ancestors, and to worship the spirits of stars, earth and harvest (on their own account). The Chollo-bu provide the king's wife in each successive generation, and likewise have the title koch'uga.[14]

There is some evidence to suggest that the change of kingship from Sonno-bu to Kyeru-bu took place during the second half of the first century A.D., at a time when the tribes were endeavouring to take advantage of the partial Chinese withdrawal from Korea by imposing a tributary relationship upon the Okchŏ of the east coast, and experiencing considerable problems in the process.[15] Quite possibly this early instability in the Koguryŏ kingship reflects the fact that, having lost his original connection with China, the Koguryŏ king had lost his raison d'être.

The crisis which the Koguryŏ kingship faced in the first century A.D. was faced by the Chinese nominees in southern Korea at the beginning of the fourth century. By this time, alongside the Chin king, there also appears to have been a 'lord of Ma-Han' responsible for forwarding the tribute of the various Ma-Han kuo to Tai-fang commandery. But with the wars of the Eight Princes and the collapse of Chin dynasty rule in North China, the Chinese colonies in Korea were cut off. Struggling for existence, they were no longer in a position to keep up the supply of impressive insignia to local chieftains, who in turn saw their status threatened. It is surely in this period that we have to locate the legend of the foundation of the Paekche kingship in south-west Korea, which the Samguk-sagi misdates to the first century B.C. In essence, this story tells how a so-called 'King of Ma-Han' granted land to two refugee princes from the northern kingdom of Puyŏ (in Manchuria, north of Koguryŏ); one of the two princes established himself so strongly that, within a few years, he was able to eliminate the 'King of Ma-Han' and take over the whole realm, calling his kingdom Paekche.[16] Now Paekche is mentioned in the list of 54 Ma-Han kuo given in the San-kuo-chih, but there it is not singled out from the rest in any way. In the Chin-shu and later dynastic histories, from at least the middle of the fourth century onwards, Paekche is a kingdom occupying all south-western Korea, ruled by a line of kings who were not of Han stock but traced their descent from Puyŏ, which appears as their family name. The change must evidently be dated to the first half of the fourth century, and seems to have been a response to the crisis we have suggested.

As with Koguryŏ in the first century A.D., a time of crisis is often a time of opportunity. With the collapse of Chinese rule in North China itself, where various dynasts of nomadic origin disputed power for centuries, refugee Chinese gentry swarmed into any border region that seemed to offer the promise of security. We know the names of several who sought refuge in Koguryŏ. These men were trained administrators, but their future now could only lie in taking service with non-Chinese rulers, in North China or elsewhere. Their knowledge of the mysterious art of writing made them invaluable; moreover, by employing such men, rulers like the king of Koguryŏ could gradually free themselves from total dependence upon the over-powerful tribal nobility. So also in Paekche where 'from the time of the foundation of Paekche, there were no written records until ... they obtained the scholar Ko Hŭng, and this was the beginning of their having books and records'.[17] Ko Hŭng was probably, although not certainly, a Chinese from Tai-fang commandery.

The acquisition of writing and court scribes made it possible for the kings of fourth and fifth century Korea to take a further step to bolster their originally unstable position. By compiling a definitive record of the past they could appropriate suitable heroic legends to give their status the unique sanction of the supernatural. We can see this happening most clearly in the case of Koguryŏ, where the descendants of the Kyeru-bu kings took over the legend of Tong-myŏng or Ch'u-mo, the miraculous egg-born archer who was the offspring of Heaven. Chinese authorities of the first, third and fourth centuries knew this story as the origin legend not of Koguryŏ but of Puyŏ; even in its discussion of the cults of Koguryŏ, the well-informed San-kuo-chih, aware of the story as far as Puyŏ is concerned, never connects it with Koguryŏ. Suddenly, in the stele inscription of King Kwanggaet'o set up in 414, at a time when the independence of Puyŏ had finally been destroyed, the Koguryŏ kings claim this semi-divine archer as their own ancestor; he is made to come from Puyŏ to found Koguryŏ, and from him the Koguryŏ kings are said to have descended in an unbroken line. This conflicts with what we know from earlier sources: the archer legend was originally a Puyŏ and not a Koguryŏ story, and the dynastic succession of Koguryŏ kings did not exhibit an unbroken line of descent. Nevertheless the propaganda effort was successful, and this reworked version of the legend is incorporated in most of the standard Chinese accounts of Koguryŏ written subsequently. Indications of the vital importance of this divine origin of the royal house can be found in the much later 'Lay of King Tong-myŏng', where the founder of Koguryŏ is made to rebuke a local ruler who claims to be the descendant of an immortal, with a family which had been reigning for generations; King

Tong-myŏng declares 'We are the descendant of Heaven itself. You, sir, are not even the descendant of a god, yet you usurp the royal title. Unless you come over to me, Heaven is bound to destroy you'.[18]

In the Silla foundation legend with which this essay began, presumably the same process has been at work, and the divine origin of the royal house is emphasised to set it clearly apart from the race of lesser mortals. Similar propaganda efforts in the Japanese Kojiki and Nihongi are well-known, and here also the record appears to involve 'papering over' dynastic interruptions. So it was that the new-style Korean rulers of the kingdoms of Koguryŏ, Paekche and Silla, from the late fourth century onwards, began to acquire the services of Confucian-trained bureaucrats and at the same time to justify their position in terms of very un-Confucian legendary propaganda. With this victory over the traditional tribal nobility, whose importance hereafter rapidly declined, the Korean monarchies of the fourth and fifth century entered a new phase of their existence, one in which they were in a position to respond to further opportunities rising from the importation of other new ideas with the coming of Buddhism.

NOTES

1. Samguk-sagi, Gakuto-sōsho reprint (Tokyo, 1964) of Kojŏn kanhaeng-hoe edn. of 1931, Ch.i, p. 1a.

2. Samguk-yusa, Gakuto-sōsho reprint, Kyōto, 1948, Ch.i, p. 54.

3. Shih-chi, Ch.cxv, p. 2a, translated in Burton Watson, Records of the Grand Historian of China, Columbia U.P., 1961, Vol. II, p. 258.

4. San-kuo-chih chi-chieh by Lu Pi, Peking, 1957, Ch.xxx, pp. 38a-39a. Hereinafter SKC.

5. To be distinguished from the Han dynasty or its derivative 'the men of Han' applied to the Chinese. The Chinese Han and the Korean Han are written with different characters and were apparently originally pronounced quite differently.

6. SKC Ch.xxx, p. 38a.

7. SKC Ch.xxx, p. 40b.

8. SKC Ch.xxx, p. 31a/b.

9. SKC Ch.xxx, p. 36b.

10. For a discussion of this point, see Y. Suematsu, Shiragi-shi no sho mondai, Tokyo, 1954, pp. 117-136.

11. Han-shu, Po-na edn., Ch.99 (chung), p. 20a/b. The whole passage is discussed in detail in Gardiner, 'Beyond the Archer and his son: Koguryŏ and Han China', Papers in Far Eastern History 20, Sept. 1979, pp. 57-82.

12. SKC, Ch.xxx, p. 28a. In spite of this statement, it has been suggested that Marquis Ch'u may have originally held the title 'king', since Wang Mang had lowered the rank of all foreign rulers from 'king' to 'marquis'.

13. SKC, Ch. xxx, p. 26a.

14. SKC, Ch. xxx, p. 26b. As well as the title koch'uga, SKC provides a whole series of Koguryŏ terms for various noble ranks and offices. It is noteworthy that it provides no Koguryŏ equivalent for the term 'king'.

15. See discussion in Gardiner, 'The Hou-Han-shu as a source for the early expansion of Koguryŏ', Monumenta Serica, Vol. XXVIII, 1969.

16. See Gardiner, 'Some Problems concerning the founding of Paekche', in Archiv Orientalni, 37, 1969.

17. Samguk-sagi Ch.xxiv, p. 9a. The surname Kao, read Ko in Korean, is common in China, although it is also used as the ethnikon of people coming from Koguryŏ. The fact that Ko Hŭng is described as a scholar versed in books and records is rather decisive against his being of Koguryŏ origin in the fourth century A.D.

18. See Gardiner, 'Beyond the Archer and his son', p. 81.

5 A SURVEY OF THE BACKGROUND TO THE VARIETY OF POLITICAL TRADITIONS IN SOUTH-EAST ASIA

I.W. Mabbett

There is no doubt that an approach to the traditional history of a major zone of Asia, such as India or China, is bound to distort and oversimplify at least a little to the extent that it is confined to generalizations about the whole zone. As the work of such scholars as G.W. Skinner has made clear, China possessed throughout its history a number of regions with their own internal dynamics, and in a sense the political, social and economic record is one of dialogue between centre and regions. As for India, though regional studies are now energetically prosecuted, the Aryan 'Great Tradition' of the early northern states and of Sanskrit literature was for too long (though of course the historian is constrained by the sources available) treated as a univocal statement of Indian reality. Nevertheless, such zones have a quite genuine unity of their own which arises from the sharing of a single official language, a single cultural orthodoxy, and a single political ideal. To study, through language and culture, the approximations which were made towards the political ideal is to approximate usefully towards the study of the political history of India or China.

Even this much, it must be emphasized, cannot be said of South-East Asia.

The area which has fairly recently come to be known as South-East Asia may appear, on superficial cartographical grounds, to have as much title as the other zones to be treated as a unity. Further, and less superficially, the fact that it has always been politically fragmented is not of itself an objection; India too was always politically fragmented. Again, the early South-East Asian kingdoms shared Sanskrit as official language and Indian religious lore as orthodoxy.

What such propositions may establish is that at

various stages in the past the differences between India and South-East Asia were differences only in degree; but in the long run the differences were great enough to be decisive. Aided by geography, India tended over the centuries towards cultural unity; South-East Asia similarly tended towards disunity. When the kingdoms of South-East Asia had, most of them, a single language and orthodoxy, these were Indian; when and to the extent that they ceased to be Indian and became increasingly indigenous, there was no uniting 'South-East Asian' lettered culture. In one sense there were many local traditions; in another, South-East Asians looked to metropolitan centres in India, Ceylon (for Theravada Buddhism) or the Middle East (for Islam), most of the time also looking to the court of the Son of Heaven for an ordering of the political universe. Therefore it is not possible to deal compendiously with anything that can be called 'South-East Asian kingship', and all that can be attempted here is a background survey.

But this is not to say that there are no generalizations which can be made about the zone - there are many, and they are not only negative or superficial ones. South-East Asia was not only an intermediate region between the civilizations of China and India, it was also in the ancient world a strategically placed zone straddling major trade routes, a zone with a peculiarly extravagant proportion of coastline to inhabited land area. In contrast to the densely populated world of today, this world was one in which straits and narrow seas united people. Recently, the view has been advanced, though it has by no means yet gained general acceptance, that in prehistoric times South-East Asia nurtured some of the most advanced cultural forms in the world, including a developed nautical technology that played a part in the sea traffic of the Bay of Bengal and the Indian Ocean as early as 2500 B.C.[1] Certainly some of the Malayo-Polynesians were great sailors, with marine contacts and cultural influence ranging far afield. And, in historical times, a succession of trading empires arose, taking advantage of their situation on the great trade routes (whether by coast and portage, or, later, across the oceans with the monsoons) and their ability to supply, from the subterranean wealth and the luxuriant flora of their own richly forested hinterlands, some of the ingredients for the conspicuous consumption of lords, priests, rulers and merchants in the affluent civilizations to their north and west.[2] By the sixteenth century, it appeared to the Portuguese admiral Alburquerque that, by taking the great entrepôt of Malacca, Portugal could impose an iron grip on the throat of the cherished Asian luxury trade.

Thus South-East Asia had some personality. But it was a split personality: its denizens did not consist solely of bustling merchants in the city-ports, for of course the major centres of population were the inland, rice-based agrarian kingdoms that at least by the eighth and ninth centuries grew up in the river valleys of the mainland (the Irrawaddy, the Salween, the Chao Praya, the Mekong, and the Vietnamese littoral) and the fertile interior of central and eastern Java.

But, if we are to discover anything useful about the conceptions of kingship entertained by these kingdoms, mercantile principalities and agrarian states alike, it is surely necessary at the outset to take account of the prehistoric foundations from which their political traditions grew; for it is at this basic level that we are most likely to discover a shared culture.

One possible approach would be to look more closely at the evidence of South-East Asia's claimed prehistoric advances in civilization. Did they extend to the sphere of political organization? Although there are remains of fortifications in Thailand which make it possible to speak of a process of urbanization during the last millennium B.C.,[3] it is not yet possible, and may never be, to deny that as soon as the historical record begins, with the rise of Indian-style kingdoms around the second to fourth centuries A.D., South-East Asia's written culture, centralized state organization and stone religious building borrowed heavily from elsewhere. It remains possible to argue that this court culture was merely superficial,[4] or (more plausibly) that it interacted with a still vital indigenous tradition,[5] but that is another matter: we cannot defend the total independence of South-East Asian kingship traditions.

Another approach would be, by contrast, to emphasize the deposit even in prehistoric times of culture and world-view by diffusion from outside, ultimately from the fertile crescent or even Europe. This is the sort of interpretation associated with the work of R. von Heine-Geldern, who pointed to themes in politico-religious organization and cosmology - such as the sacred mountain at the centre of the world symbolized by the official cult shrine, the ritual arrangement of the royal city to mirror the heavens, and the powerful motif of the earth god - which according to his view were spread by cultural contact from western centres of civilization as far as South-East Asia and Oceania.[6] His was pioneering work, and it will be necessary to return later to such themes here, but his diffusionist views are now far from being accepted.

In fact, some of the most fertile insights for an understanding of the evolution of traditions of kingship come from the work of P. Mus, whose view of the interaction between Hindu-Buddhist culture and prehistoric indigenous cults still has much of its instant relevance even though first embodied in an article published in 1933.[7]

What he says is that, in the pre-Aryan and pre-Hindu religions of monsoon Asia, a vast zone including southern China, South-East Asia and parts of India, earth gods were prominent. This sort of deity, though animistic in a sense, was a highly abstract and sophisticated conception. It was identical with the earth itself, not something in the earth, but it could exist on two planes: on one, inaccessible and amorphous; on the other, embodied in a sacred site or object (often a holy stone) or a sacrifice. On this plane, it could enter into a relationship with the community of men. The community's chief as priest was by his office particularly close to the spirit, and on ritual occasions he was thought to embody it. It is important to the argument that exactly this sort of cult (alongside others) existed in the India which the Aryans were later to dominate. In many ways, it is at an opposite pole from Hinduism; but Mus argues that its localism and its chthonic character exerted a powerful influence upon Hinduism's development (particularly evident in Śaivite _liṅga_ cults). Hence when Hinduism and Buddhism came to such places as Champa, the common substratum of belief meant that the imported religion, however superficially alien with its Indo-European names and universal values, could mould itself to indigenous beliefs. It was a more elaborate vocabulary, not a new grammar, and hence the Indian culture that came with it was understood - was actively 'lived' - and grew and spread. When eventually the Indian-style high culture of the Indochinese kingdoms declined, the essentially localized, shrine-oriented cult forms surfaced, but they had always been there.[8] They are there still, complete with (fairly recently) human sacrifice.[9]

Such were the cults belonging to the simple communities upon which increasingly elaborate Hindu and Buddhist cultures were superimposed early in the Christian era, after a history of trading contacts extending several centuries further back. The historical record begins with the discovery of such items as carnelian seals engraved in Indian scripts, Amarāvatī-style images, and Sanskrit stele inscriptions, along with a great variety of remains of artifacts bespeaking a developed commerce, in the coastal zone around the Gulf of Siam and down the isthmus of the Malay Peninsula.[10] These evidences of Indian-style kingdoms, further illumined by the reports of Chinese travellers who speak for example of large and revered communities of brahmans or Buddhist monks,[11] have been seen in the past by some scholars as the product of straightforward colonization by Indian warriors and settlers,[12] but, in the absence of convincing evidence, most writers have favoured various interpretations which conflict to some extent with each other but agree in seeing these states as South-East Asian kingdoms, ruled by South-East Asians (with perhaps a contributory admixture of the blood of individual Indian adventurers) who voluntarily accept Indian culture. J.C. van Leur sees the Indian element as a mere 'thin and flaking glaze' on a solid indigenous body;[13] G. Coedès postulates a process arising from commercial traffic, with initiatives on either side;[14] P. Wheatley, though he rejects J.C. van Leur's apriorism as unhistorical, stresses the initiative of indigenous chiefs in trading and agrarian communities, who may be considered to have imported Indian priests to enhance their own status with the trappings of an elaborate and magnificent foreign magico-religious system.[15] The possibilities for debate, or perhaps more accurately for differences of emphasis within an eclectic field, are endless, because devoid of evidence.

What the evidence allows us to describe with confidence is the rise of a series of kingdoms, originally perhaps small trading principalities, but including more and more inland agrarian states of the type described by van Leur (under the influence of Weber) as "patrimonial and bureaucratic", which vie with those of India in the splendour of their material culture. Whether wet-rice cultivation was developed locally in prehistoric times, was introduced by the Indians and the basis of the first 'Indianized' settlements, or a later and independent development is a question best left rigorously aside,[16] but the empires which appear from the eighth and ninth centuries onwards - most notably the Java of the Śailendras, who built the Buddhist monument Borobudur, and the Khmer kingdom of Angkor, which was responsible for mighty irrigation reservoirs or barays and numerous spectacular monuments among which Angkor Wat is only one - were relatively centralized states with highly organized manpower and a leisured élite served by armies of artisans that could only be supported by the substantial surpluses that sophisticated irrigation could afford.

In surveying these kingdoms it is thus useful to draw a line at the eighth century. From then onwards, the main political centres were the capitals of emperors commanding complex agrarian territorial administrations. Before then, despite the habit of referring to some of the earlier states as great empires, it is now becoming increasingly plausible to describe them as often very tenuously linked associations of principalities.

There is not a great deal that can be said about the features shared by political institutions in these kingdoms beyond the observation that they represent Indian models of royal aspiration, some Buddhist, some Hindu. In a recent essay on themes in South-East Asian history,[17] O.W. Wolters lays some emphasis upon the idea of 'cognatic' principles of political relationship, arguing that a relatively egalitarian dispersal of status among different branches of a royal or noble family, as opposed to a hierarchical patrilineal system, was particularly characteristic of South-East Asia. He identifies several other important themes in the region's political history - the absence of any sharp break between the personal loyalty owed to a chieftain in prehistoric communities and the rise of a 'state'; the aptness of the Indian idea of a mandala or arena of competition between great men dominated by the most successful, the overlord, as opposed to the modern idea of a sharp-edged territorial state; the absence of any constitutional limit upon the claims made by a successful ruler, which were therefore universal in scope; and the absence of any sense of gravitation towards a South-East Asian 'commonwealth'. These other themes provide valuable categories for the analysis of political relationships, but most of them can be matched in India, or indeed stem from specifically Indian inspiration.

Among the earliest was Funan, known by the name

the Chinese gave it and by the archaeology of the Mekong delta, where trade with China, India and further west was handled. Its capital was Vyādhapura, some two hundred kilometres inland. The sinicised name Funan appears to represent the old Khmer word bnam (modern phnom), 'mountain'. The kings, as lords of the mountain, embodied a tradition of the sacred mountain which echoes prehistoric cults that have persisted to modern times and which was perhaps directly linked to later kingdoms, the Śailendras of Java and the kings of Angkor. Funan is often described as an empire, but is unlikely to have exercised any real power over the largely mercantile states in the Malay peninsula that constituted the outer extensions of it. As Wolters's essay aptly reminds us, 'Funan' was probably much less like a modern 'state' than it has often been made to appear, and its rise did not mark a major discontinuity in the history of the region.[18] Rather similar considerations apply to the state of Champa to the north of it, known from the early centuries under the Chinese name of Lin Yi, which occupied a number of fragmented narrow coastal plains and river valleys around the coast of Vietnam; although, in the twelfth century, Champa was a powerful kingdom with land and naval forces capable of inflicting defeat upon Angkor, it is probably anachronistic to see the Lin Yi as more than a conglomeration of autonomous principalities with a common Malayo-Polynesian culture. To the west were a number of thriving marts, mostly known of from Chinese sources - prominent examples are P'an-p'an, Tan-tan and Tun-sun - difficult to locate by the corroboration of other sorts of evidence (P. Wheatley's study is the major synthesis in the field) but all in the area which must have been important to coastal trading routes using portage across the narrow isthmus of the peninsula. It is not surprising, if trade routes were so northerly, that the earliest records from the Indonesian archipelago should be from Borneo, where inscriptions at Kutai in East Borneo recording sacrifices and gifts of cows to brahmans by a ruler Mūlavarman have been dated to about 400 A.D; from Java, inscriptions in the Pallava grantha script, referring to pious or public works activities, have been dated variously to periods from the fifth to seventh centuries.[19]

It is striking how little can be said about what is usually regarded as a major trading empire with far-flung extensions, one of the inspiring antecedents of national Indonesian glory figuring in

Sukarno's rhetoric - namely, Śrīvijaya. This state, known chiefly by a number of Chinese versions of the name, has a very tenebrous history despite its presumed importance; various places in South-East Asia have been proposed for it;[20] it was virtually discovered by G. Coedès, and only since his work in the 1920s and 1930s have scholars generally accepted his view that the capital of Śrīvijaya was near Palembang in south-eastern Sumatra.[21] It rose in the late seventh century, taking advantage of its control of areas abutting the Malacca Straits to dominate the inter-oceanic trade that, following the increasing use of monsoon winds, was now using this route between Indian and Chinese waters, and to substitute local products for trade to China. From then on, with its naval command of both the Malacca and the Sunda Straits, it flourished on the trade of the entire region.[22] From a handful of epigraphic sources, such as the late eighth century Ligor stele and the early eleventh century inscription in southern India of Rajendra Cola, recording a raid on its ports,[23] Śrīvijaya appears to have had tentacles in the peninsula and Java, if not further afield, but problems still inhere in the reconstruction of its history, and it remains possible to suspect that it was something more like a loose association of trading principalities than an empire. The archaeological work of Janice Stargardt emphasizes the cultural heterogeneity, and the superficiality of Indian culture, in 'Śrīvijaya'.[24]

While the fertile valleys of Java saw the rise of a series of Indian-style dynasties, of which the Śailendra is among the most notable, the mainland river valleys were the bases of states built by the various peoples of the region. Among the earliest were the Mons, with a number of principalities in Lower Burma and Thailand, notably Dvāravatī on the lower Chao Phraya from the seventh century. They were absorbed politically by the empires which grew around them from the ninth century on, but transmitted much of their sophisticated Indian culture, particularly Buddhism, to these empires. Funan had been succeeded in the seventh and eighth centuries by the Khmer kingdoms known by the Chinese as Chenla;[25] these were united at the beginning of the ninth century by Jayavarman II into a powerful state, Angkor, whose rulers were able to make it the most spectacular example of a centralized 'bureaucratic' empire in South-East Asia, its remains, rescued from the jungle by the labours of the Ecole Française d'Extrême-Orient, outshining the later monuments of Pagan (eleventh century) in Burma and Siamese Sukothai (thirteenth century). It is the supreme example of the sort of rice-based centralized society that might be called a hydraulic society or an oriental despotism; its rulers and its institutions are described in detail by a substantial corpus of inscriptions,[26] and it is widely recognized as the home of the devarāja or so-called "god-king". It has been argued that increasingly great claims to divinity were made by its kings, eventually surpassing even those made by Indian rulers.[27]

It may be questioned, however, whether the name of the cult, devarāja, really means "god-king" after all. The question has recently been raised acutely by H. Kulke[28] (building in part on the work of J. Filliozat and others). It is entirely possible that it is to be construed "king of the gods", in reference to Śiva. Thus the name of the cult itself does not imply divinization.

According to H. Kulke, this cult was not the same as that of the great monuments built by the Khmer rulers. The monuments were built for glory and, in at least some sense, immortality; the devarāja was for legitimacy, and had its own separate cult object, which could be moved from place to place.

The monuments belonged to the apparatus of cosmic harmony, by which each ruler strove to make his kingdom, in all the details of its architecture, administration and ritual organization, match symbolically the world of the gods. Thus the great pyramids built by many Khmer kings represented Mount Meru, home of the gods.

The devarāja cult played its part in this apparatus; but it was not always particularly important. In the beginning it mattered a great deal to the ritual establishment of the dynasty, but in many later reigns it may well have lost its unique status as tool of legitimacy par excellence; events overtook it.

It is worth noticing that to its fortunes were linked those of a particular priestly family, to which it was entrusted. This family was required to provide cult officials generation after generation, and in return was blessed with various tracts of territory which were progressively cleared and settled, the settlements focusing upon shrines whose cult objects and appurtenances were bestowed by the ruler. (This sort of link between priesthood and colonization offers striking parallels to the development of the <u>shoēn</u> in Japan.) Such families constituted a landed court élite with whose wealth and influence rulers had to reckon. The great men of the land could not be ignored.

Such conclusions do not support a simple characterization of a type of South-East Asian 'god-kingship' consistent with 'oriental despotism'. On the contrary, they remind us that every society has to be studied on its own terms.

There are, however, lessons for the study of South-East Asian political institutions in general. The most important, probably, lies in the type of cosmology that originated the cult, a cosmology that divides the universe into an upper world of the gods, a lower surface inhabited by men, and a vividly conceived nether world of spirits, ancestors and waters; the task of the ruler is to bring about a detailed correspondence between the structure of the lower surface and that of the heavens (thus producing in some respects an <u>inversion</u> of the structure of the nether world as B. Groslier shows[29]). Now, as R. von Heine-Geldern's study, <u>inter alia</u>, amply illustrates, there is nothing uniquely Cambodian about this preoccupation with matching microcosmos to macrocosmos,[30] and it is proper to see in it the adoption of a sophisticated Indian vocabulary by a whole set of cultures grown from the traditions of simple communities that looked to the imported religion for improved ways of building bridges between themselves and their essentially territorial divinities.

The task of drawing comparisons and contrasts between this 'South-East Asian' view of political institutions and those of other Asian regions is perilous, because the scholarship of each region has its own language, translations are difficult, and generalizations are speculative. It is possible here only to mention a few areas of speculation.

The first is the question whether in ancient times South-East Asian rulers were, by divine sanction, more despotic than Indian kings. There is indeed a widespread assumption that this is the case, that in India socio-religious organization was governed by brahmanic traditions and closed to interference by the <u>kṣatriya</u> estate, while in states like Angkor rulers were god-kings without institutional limits on their power. This assumption is given considerable encouragement by L. Dumont.[31] The idea, however, is one that ought to be challenged, not because it is demonstrably false but because the evidence adduced for it, which consists pre-eminently of such institutions as the *devarāja*, does not really prove that there is a clear-cut distinction to be made. The point is not that there were no god-kings; it is that there may have been god-kings in a ritual sense whose real power was derived from their success in producing the centralization and stability thought to characterize the heavens above; cults like the *devarāja* were an *ex post facto* commemoration of this fact, and (though this is not the place to attempt a demonstration of the point) much the same holds true of India as well. As far as China is concerned, the mandate of heaven - legitimation by success, a victorious contender showing that he had heaven's support - represents a perhaps similar idea.

A point of comparison with India that offers a contrast with China may lie in the importance of patronage. The *devarāja* cult was a monopoly of a single priestly family, whose privileged position entitled its members to grants of land where they became, as it were, ecclesiastical seigneurs; this sort of (in a limited sense, 'feudal') relationship, whereby the king gathered round him a party of advisers and court dignitaries dependent on his or his ancestors' favour, is typical of the South-East Asian kingdoms and (as the *Arthaśāstra*, to say nothing of Indian epigraphy, makes clear) of India too. It is quite unlike the Chinese mandarinate, which in theory involved administration by a bureaucracy recruited on merit.

Finally, a point of contrast with India that offers a comparison with China may lie in the importance of ancestors. If the *devarāja* cult was indeed not the permanently dominant institution that it has so often been considered to be, we may well do better to seek the most valued mechanism of legitimation by the Khmer rulers in their proclivity to dedicate shrines to their royal ancestors mystically identified with gods.[32] An article by Nidhi Aeusrivongse brings out the importance of veneration for ancestors as part of the language of Angkorian culture, in which 'Indianized' kings needed legitimation by an appeal to indigenous values strong among their subjects.[33] It is true that the pre-Aryan network of cults that existed in prehistoric India probably shared something of this veneration for ancestors, in close association with the local, territorial, cults described by Mus, but it may also be true that in historical times this motif was more prominent in the culture of South-East Asian kingdoms like Java and Cambodia than in metropolitan India; and the shared heritage with Chinese traditions is too obvious to need labouring.

These comparisons and contrasts are, however, probably oversimplified. Political institutions in Asian cultures respond partly to the traffic of ideas, partly to the continuities of indigenous tradition, and partly to economic and environmental factors; the resulting kaleidoscope defies such global categories as 'South-East Asian conceptions of kingship', or even 'Indian conceptions' or 'Chinese conceptions'. Unexpectedly perhaps, one of the merits of the study of South-East Asia is that its very heterogeneity, its diversity of ecologies and its constant participation in Asia's multiform cultural commerce, cannot but keep the dangers of overgeneralization in the forefront of our attention.

NOTES

1. Such claims are particularly associated with the work of Wilhelm G. Solheim II. See, e.g., his "Northern Thailand, Southeast Asia and World Prehistory", Asian Perspectives, vol. 13 (1970), pp. 145-162. There is a substantial and ongoing literature about these revisionist findings, and the whole of South-East Asian prehistory is back in the melting-pot.

2. See, particularly, O.W. Wolters, Early Indonesian Commerce (Ithaca, 1968).

3. W.G. Solheim, op.cit., p. 158.

4. J.C. van Leur, "Early Asian Trade", in Indonesian Trade and Society (The Hague/Bandung, 1955).

5. J.R.W. Smail, "On the Possibility of an Autonomous History of Modern South-East Asia", J.S.E.A.H., vol. 2, no. 2 (1961), pp. 72-102.

6. R. von Heine-Geldern, "Conceptions of State and Kingship in Southeast Asia", F.E.Q. (November, 1942), pp. 15-30; Idem, "L'Art Prébouddhique de la Chine et de l'Asie du Sud-est et son Influence en Océanie", Revue des Arts Asiatiques, vol. XI, no. 4 (1937), pp. 177-206; Idem, "Das Tochareproblem und die Pontische Wanderung", Saeculum, vol. II, no. 2 (1951), pp. 225-255; Idem, "Weltbild und Bauform in Südostasien," Wiener Beiträge zur Kunst und Kulturgeschichte Asiens, vol. 4 (1930), pp. 28-78.

7. P. Mus, "Cultes Indiens et Indigènes au Champa", B.E.F.E.O., Vol. XXXIII (1933), pp. 367-410; Eng. trans. and ed. I.W. Mabbett and D.P. Chandler, India Seen From the East, Centre of Southeast Asian Studies, Monash University, 1975.

8. An outline of Mus's thesis is given in similar terms in the introduction to the English translation, op.cit.

9. D.P. Chandler, "Royally Sponsored Human Sacrifices in Nineteenth Century Cambodia: the cult of nak ta Me Sa (Mahiṣāsuramardinī) at Ba Phnom", J.S.S., vol. 62 pt. 2 (1974), pp. 207-222.

10. See especially L. Malleret, L'Archéologie du Delta du Mekong (4 vols., Paris, 1959), recording excavations at Oc Eo, the major port of the state known as Funan; P. Wheatley, The Golden Khersonese (Kuala Lumpur, 1961), collating and analysing primary sources bearing on the Indianized principalities, particularly in the peninsula; R.B. Smith and W. Watson, eds., Early South-East Asia: Essays in Archaeology, History and Historical Geography, London, 1979, bringing together many relatively recent archaeological studies.

11. P. Wheatley, op.cit., pp. 17, 48f.

12. See, e.g. R.C. Majumdar, Hindu Colonies in the Far East (Calcutta, 1944/1963).

13. J.C. van Leur, loc.cit.

14. G. Coedès, Les Etats Hindouisés d'Indochine et d'Indonésie (Paris, 1948/1964), ch. 2.

15. P. Wheatley, op.cit. and "Desultory Remarks on the Ancient History of the Malay Peninsula" in J. Bastin and R. Roolvink, eds., Malayan and Indonesian Studies (Oxford, 1964), pp. 33-75. See also his "Satyānṛta in Suvarṇadvīpa: from Reciprocity to Redistribution in Ancient Southeast Asia", in J.A. Sabloff and C.C. Lamberg-Karlovsky, eds., Ancient Civilization and Trade, Albuquerque, 1975, pp. 227-284, and "Presidential Address: India beyond the Ganges - Desultory Reflections on the Origins of Civilization in Southeast Asia", Journal of Asian Studies, vol. 42, No. 1 (November 1982), pp. 13-28.

16. Contrary to the received impression, the third possibility is the most likely according to R.D. Hill, Rice in Malaya: a Study in Historical Geography (New York, 1977). Many recent writers see wet rice as an Indian importation. See, e.g. B.P. Groslier, "Agriculture et religion dans l'empire angkorien", Etudes Rurales, vols. 53-56 (1974), pp. 95-117. Interestingly juxtaposed in the same volume is the prehistoric reconstruction of C.F. Gorman, 'Modèles a priori et préhistoire de la Thaïlande', ibid. pp. 42-71.

17. O.W. Wolters, History, Culture and Region in Southeast Asian Perspectives (Singapore, 1982).

18. Ibid., p. 12.

19. J.P. Vogel, "The Earliest Sanskrit Inscriptions of Java", Publicaties van der Oudheidkundigen Dienst in Nederlandsch-Indie, vol. 1 (1925), pp. 15-35.

20. The question about its location has been re-opened by Prince Chand Chirayu Rajani in "Background to the Śrī Vijaya Story", Parts I-IV, Journal of the Siam Society, vols. 62 pt. 1 (1974), pp. 174-211, pt. 2 (1974), pp. 285-324; vol. 63 pt. 1 (1975), pp. 208-256; vol. 64 pt. 1 (1976), pp. 275-325.

21. See G. Coedès, Les Etats Hindouisés, op.cit., pp. 155f.

22. O.W. Wolters, "Śrīvijayan Expansion in the Seventh Century", Artibus Asiae, vol. XXIV (1961), pp. 417-424, and Early Indonesian Commerce, op.cit.

23. See R.C. Majumdar, "The Overseas Expeditions of King Rajendra Cola", Artibus Asiae, vol. XXIV (1961), pp. 338-342.

24. See J. Stargardt, "The extent and Limitations of Indian Influences in the Protohistoric Civilizations of the Malay Peninsula," in N. Hammond, ed., South Asian Archaeology (London, 1973), pp. 279-303; and "Southern Thai Waterways: Archaeological Evidence on Agriculture, Shipping and Trade in the Śrīvijayan Period", Man, New Series vol. 8, No. 1 (1973), pp. 5-29.

25. These are as likely to have been autonomous principalities as one or two major kingdoms. See O.W. Wolters, "North-Western Cambodia in the Seventh Century", B.S.O.A.S., vol. XXXVII, no. 2 (1974), pp. 355-384; Cp. C. Jacques in R.B. Smith and W. Watson, eds., op.cit.

26. Edited by G. Coedès, Inscriptions du Cambodge, 8 vols. (Hanoi/Paris, 1937-1966).

27. See A.K. Chakravarti, "Divine Kingship in Cambodia: a study of the praśastis", in D.C. Sircar, ed., Early Indian Political and Administrative Systems (Calcutta, 1972), pp. 91-113. For a general account of the Khmer empire, see L.P. Briggs, The Ancient Khmer Empire (Philadelphia, 1951). On the circumstances of its rise, see C. Jacques, "Etudes d'Epigraphie Cambodgienne, 7: la Carrière de Jayavarman II", B.E.F.E.O., vol. LIX (1972), pp. 205-220; O.W. Wolters, "North-Western Cambodia in the Seventh century", loc.cit., and Idem, "Jayavarman II's Military Power: the Territorial Foundation of the Angkor Empire", J.R.A.S. (1973), pp. 21-30; on the circumstances of its fall, see Idem, "The Khmer King at Basan (1371-1373) and the Restoration of the Cambodian Chronology during the Fourteenth and Fifteenth Centuries", Asia Major, vol. XII, no. 1 (1966), pp. 44-89, and M. Vickery, "The z/k. 125 Fragment: A Lost Chronicle of Ayutthaya", Journal of the Siam Society, vol. 65, pt. 1 (1977), pp. 1-80.

28. H. Kulke, "Der Devarāja-Kult: Legimation und Herrscherapotheose im Angkor-Reich", Saeculum, vol. XXV, pt. 1 (1974), pp. 24-55; translated into English as The Devaraja Cult, Ithaca, N.Y. (Cornell University, Southeast Asia Program, Data Paper No. 108), 1978.

29. B.P. Groslier, 'Agriculture et religion dans l'empire angkorien,' loc.cit., p. 111.

30. See, e.g. R. von Heine-Geldern, op.cit.; A.M. Hocart, "The Four Quarters", Ceylon Journal of Sciences, Section G, I, 3 (1927), pp. 105-111; H.L. Shorto, "The 32 Myos in the Medieval Mon Kingdom", B.S.O.A.S., vol. XXVI (1963), pp. 572-591; P. Mus, op.cit., Eng. trans. p. 48, and Idem, "Has Brahma

Four Faces?", Journal of the Indian Society of Oriental Art, vol. V (1937), pp. 60-73.

31. L. Dumont, Homo Hierarchicus (Paris, 1966; Eng. trans. Chicago, 1970); see especially p. 215.

32. P. Stern, "Diversité et rythme des fondations royales khmères", B.E.F.E.O., vol. XLIV, No. 2 (1954), pp. 649-687.

33. Nidi Aeusrivongse, "Devaraja cult and Khmer kingship at Angkor", in K.R. Hall and J.K. Whitmore, eds., Explorations in Southeast Asian History: the Origins of Southeast Asian Statecraft (Ann Arbor, Michigan, 1976), pp. 107-148.

ABBREVIATIONS

B.E.F.E.O.	Bulletin de l'Ecole Francaise d'Extrême-Orient
B.S.O.A.S.	Bulletin of the School of Oriental and African Studies, London University
F.E.Q.	Far Eastern Quarterly
J.R.A.S.	Journal of the Royal Asiatic Society of Great Britain and Northern Ireland
J.S.E.A.H.	Journal of South-East Asian History
J.S.S.	Journal of the Siam Society

6 THE EARLY DEVELOPMENT OF KINGSHIP IN PRE-MUSLIM INDIA

Sarva Daman Singh

Did ancient Indian kingship originate as a primarily religious institution? How were kings seen by their subjects, and to what extent did they depend upon the consent of their subjects for their legitimacy and the exercise of their authority? What do the rituals of kingship tell us of the ways in which the king's rôle was conceptualized? What functions, military and civilian, religious and secular, did he discharge by virtue of his office? What limits were placed upon his power by scripture, tradition and custom?

The purpose of this paper is to examine the nature of kingship as it evolved in India (primarily in northern India), with attention to such questions as these, in the periods reflected by ancient literary sources. These sources were by and large the property of Indian culture as a whole and therefore exhibit Indian thought about kingship in general rather than the specific institutions of particular kingdoms. Classes of sources will be considered in turn as they bear on successive periods. This procedure will bring out the diachronics of the subject: Indian kingship was not an unchanging structure but something that evolved.

It is necessary to omit the literate Harappan or Indus civilization known to archaeology, whose teasing fragments of script have not been satisfactorily deciphered. The first period that belongs to the historical record is that spoken for by the <u>Ṛgveda</u>, the first of the four Vedas regarded as divine authority by orthodox religion. It consists of hymns largely dedicated to commemorating the attributes of gods and seeking their favour. Though not written down until later, it was composed and handed down orally during the second half of the second millennium B.C. During this period the Aryan invaders were conquering and spreading across the north of India, while their culture, originally quite distinct as it is represented in the Ṛgveda, gradually adapted itself to that of the non-Aryan indigenous inhabitants.

The evidence of the Ṛgveda indicates that the office of the king, the supreme commander in battle, grew out of warfare.[1] Indra is indeed the apotheosis of the Aryan hero elevated to royalty. Says the Ṛgveda:

> See this abundant wealth he possesses, and put your trust in Indra's hero vigour. He found the cattle and he found the horses, he found the plants, the forests and the waters.[2]

No wonder if he rises to kingship, 'the hero who in all encounters overcomes, most eminent for power, destroyer in the conflict, fierce and exceeding strong, stalwart and full of vigour'.[3] The primacy of the king's protective power is as old as the Ṛgveda. Indeed, the protection of the people is his basic responsibility inherent in the epithets that adorn him.[4] That the king fought and led his army in person is amply demonstrated by the famous battle of the ten kings in the Ṛgveda, and the warlike deeds of monarchs like Divodasa, Sudas and Trasadasyu. The concept of universal conquest was perhaps born with the battle of the ten kings; the horse-sacrifice begins as early as the Ṛgveda,[5] and becomes the symbol of paramountcy in later literature.

The requirements of a conquering people evoked not only the monarch, but also a whole military aristocracy. As smaller principalities coalesced into growing kingdoms, the dispossessed potentates joined the ranks of this aristocracy, and made war and government their chief occupation. The growing specialization of functions is clearly discernible in the Ṛgveda, where the three higher orders are specified,[6] and one famous hymn, belonging to Book X which was composed later than the rest of the Ṛgveda, contemplates the division of society into four orders of men.[7]

The Ṛgveda hints at the "election"[8] of the king by the people. Republican tribal traditions assert themselves despite the dominance of the monarch; the pre-eminence of the leader evidenced in his valour and sagacity leads all the people (viś) to "want" or "desire" him.[9] Another Ṛgvedic passage,

X. 124.8, likewise refers to the people choosing a king.[10] Vṛṇānā signifies 'choice', 'selection'; even the formal ratification of a fait accompli presupposes a persistent tradition of popular selection. Indeed, there is no proof that monarchy was sometimes not elective;[11] the later Vedic evidence corroborates the rôle of the people in the choice of their ruler.

There is no doubt that the Ṛgvedic king requires the vocal consent of the people who 'have made him the guardian of their comfort'.[12] Various classes of dignitaries are mentioned in the Ṛgveda, and figure in the later lists of ratnins (literally 'jewel-bearers') called the sustainers of kingship. Two types of assembly, the sabhā[13] and the samiti,[14] are the forums of vox populi, which serve as checks on the authority of the king. The samiti is the more important of the two, the true tribal assembly, in which common accord remains the goal of debate. "Same be their counsel, same their assembly, same their aim, in common their thought", says the Ṛgveda.[15] The king attends the samiti; indeed, 'like a true king he goes to the assembly'.[16] The growing preponderance of royal power is however clearly reflected in the late Book X, where the king goes to the assembly (samiti) as a mighty conqueror; he masters 'all your minds, your resolutions, your samiti'; he wishes to be the best (uttama) of them all, 'having gained your strength in war, your skill in peace'; his feet tread on their heads; they speak to him from beneath his feet, like frogs croaking out of the water.[17]

Both Indra and Varuna are called 'paramount lord' (samrāj),[18] which indicates the exaltation of monarchy. Some Ṛgvedic passages suggest hereditary monarchy,[19] thus emphasizing the increasing importance of the royal family without precluding the operation of the elective principle and procedure even in these cases.

We see the tribal leader turning into a territorial lord in the late tenth book of the Ṛgveda, where the monarch is charged to hold the territory (rāṣtra) in his grasp.[20] His primary function is the protection of his people, who bring tribute to him alone.[21]

The king is not yet divine. The title rājan ('king') applied to such gods as Indra, Mitra, Varuna, Soma, Yama, Agni and Bṛhaspati, serves only in these contexts to stress the similarity of their function.[22] King Purukutsa is styled as a demi-god (ardhadeva),[23] which stops short of conferring divinity. As Varuṇa is likened to a mighty monarch surrounded by his spies, imposing the rule of ṛta or eternal law on the world below,[24] the earthly king should also be credited with a wide criminal jurisdiction,[25] an inference supported by the clear testimony of later texts. Here we see an assimilation of the king's rôle to divine function, not an ascription of divinity to the ruler's person.

The status of the royal chaplain (purohita) is proof of his usefulness to the monarch. He accompanies the king and his army to the field of battle, and prays with charms and spells to ensure his master's success.[26] The separation of priestly and royal functions is as old as the Ṛgveda, and becomes a basic feature of Indian polity.

Now we turn to the period of the later Vedic literature, which was composed from around the end of the second millennium B.C. to about the eighth and seventh centuries B.C. The sixth century florescence of heterodoxies such as Buddhism coincided with the tail-end of the Vedic period, and the sectarian teachers addressed themselves to some of the same questions as the contemporary brahmanical metaphysicians. Over the late Vedic period as a whole, society became more settled and agricultural, and the relatively centralized kingdoms of the North-East began to arise. The literature consists of the texts (saṁhitas), handed down by various brahmanical schools, of the Yajur Veda; the Sāma-Veda and the Atharva Veda (sacred liturgical texts); the Brāhmaṇas (exegetical works related to ritual and sacrifice); and the Upaniṣads (esoteric doctrines purporting to explain the secret meanings of the Veda).

The later Vedic literature suggests as strongly as the Ṛgveda that the office of the king grew out of warfare.[27] The Atharva Veda stresses the martial obligations of the monarch when it says: 'Of lion aspect do thou devour all the clans (viś); of tiger-aspect do thou beat down the foes; sole chief, having Indra as companion, having conquered, seize thou on the enjoyments of them that play the foe'.[28] In the rājasūya ceremony the king is called the 'sacker of forts'.[29] The Kuru-Pañcāla kings conduct regular raids in the season of dues, i.e., in winter after the rains.[30] King Pratardana meets his death on the field of battle.[31] The Aryan invasion of India led to the growth of the monarchic element, just as it did also in the case of Greece.[32]

Late Vedic texts assert the pre-eminence of the warrior-aristocratic element (kṣatra). The

Bṛhadāraṇyaka Upaniṣad asserts that kṣatra is life-breath (prāṇah); the breath of life protects (trāyate) one from being hurt (kṣaṇitoḥ).[33] The well-nourished condition of the community is attributable to the operation of kṣatra in society.[34] Says the Taittirīya Saṁhitā:[35] 'Indra shall conquer, he shall not be conquered; overlord among kings shall he rule; in all conflicts shall he be a protector, that he may be reverenced and honoured.'

To what extent did rulers in this period depend for their power upon their subjects? One Atharvavedic passage speaks of a ruler re-elected by the people, though he had been earlier driven out.[36] The fact that the people are described as 'choosing' or 'desiring' a king in a number of Vedic passages cannot be ignored or satisfactorily explained away. That a banished ruler is reinstated clearly shows the exercise of choice by at least some subjects.

The later Vedic literature refers to the king-makers (called ratnins), who offer a symbolic amulet or maṇi to the king on his accession to the throne. The king takes the jewel of authority from all the people present in an Atharvavedic hymn: 'The skilful builders of chariots and the ingenious workers of metal, the folk about me all, do thou, O Parna, make my aids. The kings and king-makers, the charioteers and leaders of hosts, the folk about me do thou, O Parna, make my aids.'[37]

The people and the professions thus invest their ruler with authority. The ratnins are the sustainers of the king's realm; they are characterized as the 'givers and takers of a kingdom'.[38] We come across fifteen ratnins in all, though all the names do not figure in all the texts.[39] 'Limbs of the ruling power',[40] as they are called, their role in the ratnahaviṁṣi ritual of the rājasūya ceremony is vital to a proper comprehension of the later Vedic polity. Their importance to the king and his realm is dramatically displayed by the king's visits to their houses for the performance of the requisite ritual. They represent all the four varṇas of the Aryan society, presumably also the non-Aryans, all the important professions, and even the women of the realm. They emphasize the power of the people notwithstanding the king's gain in status and stability at their expense; they remind the king of past procedures, of royal obligations, of common expectations. Their allegiance adds to the allure of monarchy.[41]

The assemblies (the sabhā and the samiti) remained important. The Atharva Veda tells us that royal prosperity depends on concord between the king and the assembly.[42] Indeed, the king prays for the cooperation of both the sabhā and the samiti: 'May the sabhā and the samiti, the two daughters of Prajapati, concurrently aid me. May he with whom I shall meet cooperate with me; may I, O Ye Fathers, speak agreeably to those assembled.'[43]

The king ascends the throne for life.[44] Kingship is often hereditary, as is suggested for example by a reference to a kingdom of ten generations, daśapurusam rājya.[45] One Brāhmana text speaks of the birth of an heir to the throne;[46] and of the king as the father of the realm.[47] The principle of selection by others, though, is neither forgotten nor in abeyance.[48] That the choice was usually limited to the members of the royal family is indicated in the legend of Devāpi and Samtanu;[49] and the king normally came from the ranks of the kṣatriyas, as the brāhmaṇa is called unsuitable for kingship.[50] The Aitareya Brāhmaṇa, however, visualizes the possibility of a brāhmaṇa monarchy;[51] and the other Vedic texts refer to śūdra and even non-Aryan rulers.[52]

The king was certainly no despot riding roughshod over the susceptibilities of his people. If he did, he came to grief. We hear of many kings deposed by their people;[53] the Śatapatha Brāhmaṇa for example refers to Dustarītu Pauṁsāyana being banished from his kingdom, though it had come to him through ten generations.[54]

The king's obligation to his subjects is conspicuous in the oath he takes before the consecrating priest in the aindramahābhiṣeka ceremony. "From the night of my birth," says he, "to that of my death, for the space between these two, my sacrifice and my gifts, my place, my good deeds, my life and my offspring, mayest thou take if I play thee false."[55]

Is this oath addressed to the priest alone or to the community as a whole? K.P. Jayaswal thought that the priest stood for the community; U.N. Ghoshal and R.S. Sharma tended to identify him more narrowly with his own class.[56] There is much to be said for Jayaswal's point of view. The role of the ratnins in royal consecration exhibits broad-based participation in the legitimation of the king's authority; and the priest is only one of them. The priest in the present context stands neither for himself nor for his class, but for dharma, law or the sacred order of things in relation to the whole people. Dharma is higher than the four orders of society, which depend upon it. The priest and the king are as subordinate to it as the others. The king takes the vow to fulfil his duty before he sits on the throne.[57] He is therefore called dharmasya-goptā,[58] the 'protector of dharma'; and dhṛtavrata,[59] the 'upholder of the sacred law.' The monarch is the embodiment of the moral law, matched only by the learned brāhmaṇa who is not above it; and the administration of a solemn obligatory oath by the latter to the former would be meaningless and farcical without reference to the people.[60] Tyranny is incompatible with the dictates of dharma.

The interdependence of the priest and king comes out clearly in so many Vedic passages;[61] and the kṣatriya does well to have a royal chaplain (purohita) to help guard the kingdom:

> .... For him are his people in harmony, with one aspect and one mind, who has for his purohita to guard the kingdom a brāhmaṇa with this knowledge.[62]

They serve as checks on each other. The 'lordly power' guards the people against the oppressive greed of the 'holy power'; and the 'holy power' protects the people from the exactions of the 'lordly power'.[63] The purohita is half the self of the kṣatriya.[64] But the lower ritual status of the brāhmaṇa is clearly reflected in the Aitareya - Brāhmaṇa,[65] where it is said that the kṣatriya sacrificer should desist from taking soma or curds or water, the food, respectively, of the brāhmaṇa, the vaiśya and the śūdra, the other three orders of society besides the ksatriya nobility. If he eats their food, his offspring will be like a brāhmaṇa, vaiśya and śūdra; and the second or third from him may indeed become a brāhmaṇa, vaiśya or śūdra. The consequences would be far from desirable.[66]

In material terms and in mundane reckoning, the king was always superior to the priest, who managed to harmonise his theoretical spiritual superiority with often obsequious obedience to the will of his master. There never was a class war between the brāhmaṇas and the kṣatriyas in the modern Marxist sense. The dichotomy between the supposed brāhmaṇa supremacy in matters of spirit and religion, and his subservience to the rich in real life, has been an enduring feature of the Indian social situation.

The interdependence of the royal and priestly

orders is implied in texts, notably the Brāhmaṇas, detailing consecration rituals administered by priests to kings. These rituals tell us something about the way in which kingship was evolving in the period of the Brāhmaṇa texts, for they mention many epithets which are applied to rulers and which, though their precise meanings are unclear, manifest the rise of imperial ambitions. Kings seek to subordinate other kings to themselves. One consecration ritual is said to ensure 'superiority, pre-eminence and supremacy over all kings', and the status of a 'sole ruler' 'from the one end up to the further side of the earth bounded by the ocean'.[67] The concepts of universal monarchy and paramount sovereignty are prominent. The proclamation expresses all the characteristics of Indian kingship: sovereignty and the state; the power of taxation; military might and victory; the bond between the king and the priests; and the burden of administration for the protection of the laws (dharma), for the furtherance of common welfare.

All the kings anointed with the aindramahābhiṣeka 'go round the earth completely, conquering on every side, and offering the horse in sacrifice'.[68] The horse sacrifice (aśvamedha) is the acme of Aryan aspiration for dominion.[69]

Both tribal and territorial traits are in evidence in the later Vedic monarchy. The vision of universal rule stretching up to the oceans portends the pursuit of the universal emperor (cakravartin) ideal by the would-be conquerors of a later day.

Before we move on to the period of established peasant-based kingdoms and empires, it is necessary to take some notice of a large question: is the later Vedic ruler the owner of the land of his realm? Unambiguous authoritative statements are far to seek, but there are many passages in the literature that have been sifted to support one interpretation or another. These passages occur in ritual contexts, and it is uncertain what lessons should be drawn from them about actual practice.

The expression grāma-kāma, occurring not infrequently in the later saṁhitās, points to the king's grant of his royal prerogatives over villages to his favourites, so far as fiscal matters were concerned. The cultivators were reduced to tenancy, and the Śatapatha Brāhmaṇa speaks of the kṣatriya's right to apportion land.[70]

The Jaiminīya Brāhmaṇa,[71] however, observes that the king cannot make a gift of the entire earth in the viśvajit sacrifice, when he has to give everything that belongs to him. The earth is common, and does not belong to the sovereign alone. And the Śatapatha Brāhmaṇa,[72] too, tells of Viśvakarman Bhauvana, who, intent on giving the earth to his priest Kaśyapa after a sacrifice, was reproved by the Earth herself: 'No mortal must give me away....' But even these passages perhaps prove the contrary to be true, if they are construed as protests against the arbitrary gifts of land by kings. These scriptural injunctions may only have been dictated by the necessity to call a halt to the king's commands ever impinging on the rights of subjects.

In the Bṛhadāraṇyaka Upaniṣad we find king Janaka claiming the power of giving his kingdom away to whomsoever he likes.[73] Another text indicates that the brāhmaṇa, the rājanya or the vaiśya begs the sacrificial ground from the kṣatriya,[74] which perhaps means the king's ownership of the unappropriated land.

Individual ownership of land for purposes of cultivation is clearly reflected in a number of passages.[75] And in the Chāndogya Upaniṣad,[76] fields and houses are mentioned as examples of wealth.

Royal ownership of land did not thus mean the negation of the people's right in land. It was a gradation of ownership; the rights of the king were superimposed over those of the people without undue hindrance to their right to till, to sow and reap their harvest, to inherit and to partition their land.

From the end of the Vedic period onwards, many of the patterns of political authority are set. Sources for the following period, from the sixth century B.C. onwards, represent an arena of competing kingdoms with the centre of gravity in the North-East. They constantly waged war upon each other, engaged in trade, formed dynastic alliances, and progressively evolved relatively centralized bureaucratic structures.

Sources for the early part of this following period include the Dharma Sūtras, treatises on customary law. In them there is emphasis upon the organic unity of society together with the sovereignty of dharma, the sacred order which determined laws and duties. The human king upholds dharma under the authority of the sacred canon (the Vedas), the law as codified in texts, and custom.[77] He must be learned; he must be an accomplished warrior; and he must be unimpeachable in his acts and speech. His main duties include the protection of society and of all created beings; patronage of the learned brāhmaṇas; provision for the indigent regardless of class; and the banishment of hunger, sickness and suffering from the community. He should wipe out thefts altogether; and should pay the value of unrecovered stolen property out of his treasury. Protection of life and property is his primary function. He should be just and impartial; there are penalties for tyrants both in this world and the next.[78]

He should not encroach upon the property of his people, and should be content with his legal dues[79] regarded as his remuneration for protection. They amount to one-sixth of his people's production in terms of income or spiritual merit.[80]

The royal chaplain (purohita) and the assembly (pariṣad)[81] restrain the monarch, who is hereditary. The king personally dispenses civil and criminal justice; he is the embodiment of daṇḍa, the power of the state to punish, coerce or sanction.[82] Heirless property goes to the king, who is also considered the master of treasure trove. All interest on lent capital ceases to accrue on the death of the king until the consecration of his successor.[83] The king, then, is the main sustainer of all legal and economic processes.

The most complete extant set of Buddhist sacred scriptures is the Pāli canon of the Sthaviravādin (Theravāda) school. Though it was not finally written down until centuries later in Ceylon, portions of it speak for conditions in the period of the rise of the faith in Northern India (from the sixth century B.C. onwards). It adumbrates an ideal state of nature in which man lives a life of blameless bliss on an immaterial plane.[84] Fall from virtue makes man earthbound; class and caste, private property, theft, deceit and violence lead to the creation of the state to repair and restrain human behaviour. People meet to appoint a man to maintain law and order; and the "Great Chosen One" (mahāsammata) is charged with the obligation of protection in return for a share of the people's produce. He is called rājā, because he pleases his people.[85] (This is a fanciful etymology.) Social contract serves or seeks to remedy the loss of selfless joys of the original millennium now no more.[86]

The Jātakas, stories of former lives of the Buddha, also echo the theory of a social contract, and refer to the election of kings.[87] The stories of tyrants banished or killed abound.[88]

The king commands his army, and is an active participant in battle. He usually comes from the ranks of the warrior class.[89] He is duly trained in the art of handling elephants, horses and chariots, and weapons such as the bow and the sword.[90] Courage and leadership are the pre-requisites of royalty. The king protects and conquers. But he must conform to his ordained duty. Dharma is the king of king emperors.[91] The khattiya (Pāli equivalent of kṣatriya, the aristocratic order) is called the best of men by the Buddha, higher than the brāhmaṇa.[92]

The Sanskrit epics are another class of literature containing evidence of political conditions early in the classical period, but cannot be reliably dated. The Mahābhārata is a huge and loosely integrated encyclopaedia of narrative, didactic and legendary matter some of which tells stories handed down from early in the Vedic period, the compilation of which did not begin before the fourth century B.C. Many of its didactic passages roughly date from the beginning of the Christian era.

The epics recognise that military function is inseparable from the royal obligation to protect the people from the threat of invasion or anarchy.[93] Royal status is claimed by men of blue blood, generals of armies and warriors of distinction.[94] Might is the prime qualification of the kṣatriya.[95] The chief commander's selection by the kings and warriors present on the field of battle, ratified by the shouts and acclamation of the whole army, reminds one of an earlier epoch when the outstanding military leader was chosen king and commander.[96] The election of the general (senāpati) and his consecration bring back vivid memories of the coronation of the Vedic monarch.[97]

The hero restores order and authority whenever society is threatened by the dark forces of destruction. The avatāra exalts the authority of the monarch. The kṣatriya is reminded of his inexorable obligation to vindicate the rule of dharma by recourse to arms. An elaborate code of military ethics is at least theoretically incumbent upon warriors.

These prescriptions overlap with those of other types of literature, the manuals or texts (śāstra) of dharma and of politics (artha). They are best considered all together, for strict chronological sequence is not easy to observe. The Arthaśāstra, for example, is a Machiavellian text on political management traditionally attributed to Kauṭilya at the end of the fourth century B.C., but in fact it is at least as likely to represent the teachings of a school compiled at some time in several following centuries. The lawbooks, smṛtis or dharmaśāstras, date in general from early in the Christian era.

One culturally important myth that serves to legitimize the institution of royal power is commemorated in most of our texts - the mātsyanyāya myth. This postulates a remote age of unalloyed bliss, in which truth and virtue reign supreme. The ideal state needs no laws to impose upon the unwavering virtues of the people. But an inescapable deterioration in the standards of behaviour dethrones both truth and virtue; law and legal procedure become essential for the regulation of erring humanity; and the king comes into being to administer and chastise. The utopian fantasy of the ideal age yields place to the reality of the state as we know it under a human ruler charged with the prime task of preserving dharma. Such a supposition bemoans the fallibility of man and pleads for the institution of the law-state as an instrument of deliverance.[98]

The state is regarded as an organic unity, consisting as it does of seven limbs or constituents.[99] The king, the minister, the country, the fort, the treasury, the army and the ally indicate its unity in terms of a common ruler, a settled administration, a definite system of revenue, the strength of the state, a settled territory, and freedom from external control.

The king is the keystone of the arch of polity. He may occasionally be drawn from any of the three higher orders; but as a king he represents kṣatra implying protection. The king's failure to protect would lead to total perdition; and the brahmanical authorities cannot foresee anything but calamitous chaos in the event of the king's disappearance. Royal incompetence would lead to a loss of direction comparable to a boat without a helmsman. People's prosperity and the king's contentment alike depend on the latter's protective function.

Authority invariably attracts veneration in India, and the king is called a deva; which, however, means a divine being rather than the Lord of Creation. To quote Manu:

> When the world was without a king and dispersed in fear in all directions, the Lord created a king for the protection of all. He made him of eternal particles of Indra and the Wind, Yama, the Sun and Fire, Varuṇa, the Moon, and the

> Lord of Wealth. And because he has been formed of fragments of all those gods, the king surpasses all other beings in splendour. Even an infant king must not be despised, as though a mere mortal, for he is a great god in human form.[100]

Nārada speaks of kings gifted with the powers of the gods Agni, Indra, Soma, Yama and Kubera.[101] The expression of these divine forms in the king's person ensures the fulfilment of five distinctive functions.

But royal divinity does not make the king infallible. He is not above good and evil like the devas themselves, who are by no means paragons of virtue. The functional similarity between the king on the one hand and the different deities on the other attracts the attention of Hindu theorists and leads to the formulation of ideas suggestive of divinity. But to say that the royal person is totally innocent of the divinity attributed to royal functions is not altogether true. Never absolute, always qualified, the divinity of the monarch depends on the fulfilment of his functions, and remains liable to unequivocal repudiation in cases of incurable remissness. Bāṇa decries the divine airs of kings puffed up by flattery.[102]

Nārada alone holds even a wicked king inviolable owing to his divinity.[103] The view fails to win common approval, however. This is illustrated by the story of the tyrant Vena killed for mouthing the impious presumption of royal divinity as a ground for exemption from punishment.[104] The elevation of the ruler to a divine status by the writers on dharma simply suggests the need for a strong king to preserve the social order, and cannot serve to extenuate his guilt or baseness. Taxation constitutes the king's wages for protection. The subjects like cattle should be milked only at the proper time, if they were tended with loving care.[105] The king should defend all orders in accordance with the dictates of the canon, and then alone claim his share of the agricultural produce as his fee for protective exertion.[106] Aryadeva mocks the false pride of the king who is no better than a slave of his people living on one-sixth share of their crops.[107] Popular sovereignty is stressed by this spirited reiteration of the king's compact with his people.

The king cannot hope to protect or conquer without mastering himself. Discipline must bridle self-indulgence. The king upholds dharma, which comprehends individual caste obligations. He is exhorted and expected to command and compel his subjects to follow their respective dharmas and do everything in conformity with righteousness. Society is regulated by the king's rod of punishment; but the power of daṇḍa, coercion or punishment, does not allow him to act arbitrarily. The monarch is himself an element of the social order; daṇḍa is the means, dharma the end of human striving. Rājadharma binds the king to conformity.[108]

The eternal vigilance of daṇḍa is the price of social order; and the king uses the scriptures as his eyes to discharge the subtle demands of duty. He studies the śāstras, philosophy and logic; the three Vedas and vārtā (agriculture and commerce); and the art of government.[109] Hence his ability to investigate suits and dispense justice in accordance with the canon. But he also respects the conventions of different castes and regions, which he can flout only at his own peril.[110] Thus the informed king's daṇḍa restrains the evil propensities of human nature; and the fear of retribution keeps society on an even keel. He is the guardian of law rather than its creator, but cannot altogether help assuming a legislative function as an inescapable concomitant of royal responsibility. Royal edicts must however conform to custom and canon in matters pertaining to religion, even if reason and equity dictate terms in the realm of secular activity. This tolerance stresses the need to accommodate varying religious experience in a land of many creeds. The codes relate law and norm to the incessant process of social evolution. The judicial procedure rests on dharma and rational law, and according to Kauṭilya and Nārada, on royal decree.[111] The relationship of punishment to caste is calculated to pamper the privileged at the expense of the poor; and the preservation of the hierarchical order by daṇḍa ensures uninterrupted production by the lower classes for the benefit of those higher placed.

The king constitutes the highest court of appeal; but the judges appointed by him usually come from the brāhmaṇa class. Daṇḍa is a two-edged sword; its appropriate exercise exalts the king, as 'If the king did not inflict punishment untiringly on evil-doers the stronger would roast the weaker like fish upon a spit ...'[112]

The rivalry between brahma and kṣatra prompts

the brāhmanas to propound the doctrine of dharma's pre-eminence in terms of kṣatra's subservience to the former. The kṣatriya not infrequently grows impatient of brāhmaṇic interference in the exercise of his sweeping secular authority; and some brāhmaṇas oblige their master by recognizing a fundamental antagonism between politics and ethics. It is considered alike impolitic and calamitous for kings to follow dharma, sacred duty, to the detriment of the other ends of life. Kauṭilya and Kāmandaka call for compromise between ethics and expediency in their statement that the behaviour of kings differs from that of ordinary men. Political necessity makes theoretical morality expendable. The interests of the king and community take precedence over considerations of ethics. Kāmandaka manifests a robust realism in identifying the approval or opinion of enlightened men with dharma.[113] Bṛhaspati equivocates: at one place he regards the pursuit of wealth as all-important,[114] while at another he seeks to subordinate material ends to virtue.[115] Bāṇa refers to the policies of worldly-wise kings based on gross materialism compounded by cruelty and ignoble superstitions.[116] And Māgha fails altogether to distinguish between politics and unrepentant self-interest.[117]

The earthly king conquers to extend the borders of his realm; territorial agglomeration assures adequate Lebensraum for his people. The conquest of new lands is the driving ambition of the would-be conqueror. He is defined as a king 'who is endowed with personality, luck and the requisite attributes, who is the basis of traditional power and forceful heroism (krama vikrama).'[118] Vijaya or victory is closely connected with śrī, welfare, fortune and majesty.[119] The kṣatriya adds to his śrī by his prowess and heroism summed up in the word vikrama, which also suggests the strides of Viṣṇu which encompassed the universe. The conqueror ideal comprehends the basic assumption of Hindu thought that all foreign powers are potentially unfriendly, if not categorically inimical. Hence the need for conquest and the devious diplomacy which makes friendships as precarious as they are variable in the context of constant geopolitical manoeuvre. The dream of world conquest beckons. In the theory of diplomacy offered by Kauṭilya and others,[120] neighbours are automatically enemies, while the kingdom beyond a neighbour is a natural ally.

The ideals of universal conquest (digvijaya) and righteous conquest (dharmavijaya) find clear enunciation in the Epics.[121] The fruit of victory is homage and tribute to the superior power pursued by many heroes of the Epics, and later by rulers of undoubted historicity, like Samudragupta of the Gupta dynasty. But the will to survive is often more imperious than precept; and departures from dharma in war are condoned in no uncertain terms by later writers.[122]

The paramount ruler reduces his rivals to vassalage without depriving them of their possessions; and the performance of a proper sacrifice proclaims a successful bid for the glory of the universal emperor. The realm of the king performing the horse sacrifice knows no bounds; he drives a 'chariot of unchecked course (apratirathaḥ) up to the end of directions'.[123] One umbrella and one king is the idea of a universal ruler.[124] Kālidāsa, the famous fifth-century poet, clearly speaks of natural boundaries 'extending up to the seas'.[125] Indeed, the universal ruler partakes of the characteristics of Viṣṇu himself in a partial incarnation.[126]

The term cakravartin, universal emperor, is often explained as signifying a ruler whose chariot wheels roll unimpeded in all directions. But the symbolism of the wheel, cakra, seems to be a derivation from the orb of the sun, whose rays find their way to every corner of the earth. In the earliest Indian tradition and legend the term cakravartin referred to the great heroes of the solar race. The cakra also stands alike for time and space, for dominion, with the king at its centre. It is a symbol of the king's conquering efficacy.[127]

Burrow derives rājan, king, from the word rajas belonging to the root rāj meaning 'to stretch out'. The king stretches himself out to protect and conquer with his long arms, as also to enforce obedience.[128] Conquest is an inescapable function of royalty. We believe that the idea can be best understood as an idealistic vision and an invitation to the vijigīṣu, the would-be conqueror, to do and dare in his bid to give a semblance of political unity to a country crying for unity; to reconcile the diversity of particularisms with the grandiose concept of an overriding authority.

Righteous rule invokes the bounty of nature; tyranny provokes her blight.[129] The king's pious vow, says Kauṭilya, is his readiness in action; the discharge of his duty constitutes his sacrifice. His happiness lies in the happiness of his subjects; his welfare in their welfare. Whatever pleases his subjects is good for him, not exactly what pleases him. He should therefore be ever active and striving for people's prosperity, which depends on exertion; failure on the reverse.[130] Aśoka gives evidence of ceaseless exertion; for there is no higher duty than the welfare of the whole world; and what little effort he makes is in order that he may be free from his debt to all beings. The paternal concept of kingship finds a noble votary.[131]

Such lofty ideals as these represent to us something of what people thought, and of how rulers wished to be seen, but the degree to which the thoughts and images were veridical is of course to some extent a matter of surmise. Prescription is not description.

It is to the literary sources that this discussion has been primarily addressed, but it cannot be said that a study of inscriptions would necessarily provide a 'corrective' or a different picture. Inscriptions such as Aśoka's represent ideals in much the same way as do the texts. Epigraphic and numismatic evidence can however supplement that of literature in important ways. The records reveal rulers devoted to the welfare of the entire sentient world; kings brave and boastful, given to conquest and territorial gains; royal intellectuals patronising arts and letters; pomp and circumstance; the notion of royal divinity; the obligation to uphold dharma; as well as pettiness hiding beneath grandiloquent titles. As the ancient period draws to a close, conceit waxes and strife spreads. Profligacy soars, as evidenced in the carnal revelry of the temple sculptures commissioned by the kings. Besides the influence of tradition, there are no effective checks against royal excess and tyranny. Gifts of land to priests and brāhmaṇas, nobles and officials, side by side with the presence of jealous feudatories, inject feudal elements into the body-politic that ultimately lead to disunity, balkanization and foreign conquest.

NOTES

1. See my Ancient Indian Warfare with Special Reference to the Vedic Period, Leiden, 1965, pp. 135ff.
2. RV.1.103.5.
3. RV.VIII.35.17; cf. SV.IV.II.4.1; AB.VIII. 4.12. For Indra as the prototype and guardian of kingship, see R.N. Dandekar, "Vṛtrahā Indra" ABORI, vol. 31, 1950, p. 53, f.n. 2.
4. RV.III.43.5. Gopā - janasya; IX.35.5 janasya gopatiḥ.
5. Ibid., 1.162; 163.
6. Ibid., VIII.35.16-18.
7. Ibid., X.90.12. Compare the patrician gentes of Rome, the eupatridae of Athens, the nobles of early Germany, the earls of the Anglo-Saxons, and the athravas and rathaesthas of ancient Iran. cf. CHI, I, p. 125.
8. There is no need to take the word "election" in its twentieth century sense.
9. RV.X.173.1, viśas tvā sarvā vāñchantu. The word gaṇa in RV.IV.35.3 and elsewhere seems to indicate a republican form of government. Cf. also TB. II.8.6.4; ŚB. XIII.2.8.4. See R.S. Sharma, Aspects of Political Ideas and Institutions in Ancient India, Delhi, 1959, p. 91ff. J.P. Sharma, Republics in Ancient India, c.1500 B.C.-500 B.C., Leiden, 1968, pp. 15-80, recognizes many forms of non-monarchical governments in Vedic India.
10. ta īm viśo na rājānam vṛṇānā. Zimmer translates: 'wie die Gaue sich den König küren,'. Cf. Altindisches Leben, Berlin, 1879, pp. 162 ff. Cf. also Barnett, Antiquities of India, London, 1913, p. 97; Weber, Indische Studien, XVII, 88; Geldner, Vedische Studien, II, 303; Monier Williams explains vṛ in Ṛgveda as meaning 'to choose, select, choose for one's self, choose as or for'.
11. Cf. Vedic Index, II, p. 211.
12. RV.1.100.7.
13. The sabhā figures often in the Ṛgveda; cf. II.24.13; VI. 28.6; VII. 1.4; VIII.4.9; X. 34.6. It is 'a more select body, less popular and political in character'. Cf. Ghoshal, Studies in Indian History and Culture, pp. 349 ff.; Vedic Index, II, pp. 426-7.
14. The samiti, the assembly of the Vedic tribe, occurs in RV. 1.95.8; IX. 92.6; X. 97.6; 166.4; 191.3. According to Ludwig, Translation of the Rigveda, 3, 253 et seq., the samiti included all the people, the viśaḥ. Cf. Vedic Index, II, 430-31.

K.P. Jayaswal, Hindu Polity, 3rd ed., Bangalore, 1955, p. 12, calls samiti 'the national assembly of the whole people or viśaḥ'.

15. RV. X. 191.3; Bloomfield, SBE, XLII, 136.

16. RV. IX. 92.6, rājā na satyaḥ samitīriyānaḥ. Despite the clear reference to 'Soma ... like a wild bull in the wood', J.P. Sharma, op.cit., p. 51, takes this passage to mean a non-monarchical government; sedulous search for originality sometimes contributes to the dubious quality of conclusions.

17. RV. X.166.4-5. Verse 1 contains his prayer: ṛṣabhaṁ mā samānānāṁ sapatnānāṁ viśāsahiṁ/ hantāraṁ śatrūṇāṁ kṛdhi virājaṁ gopatiṁ gavāṁ. 'Make me a bull among peers, make me my rivals conquer. Make me a slayer of foes, a sovereign ruler, a lord of kine.' The third verse addressed to Vacaspati voices the wish that his rivals may speak to him humbly. The pride of power is still tentative, and seeks divine sanction for self-assertion.

18. RV. 1.25.10; VI. 68.9; VIII. 16.1; cf. also IV. 21.2; VI. 27.8; VIII. 19.32.

19. Cf. The Vedic Age, 1965, p. 356; Vedic Index, II, p. 211.

20. RV. X.173.2. cf. AV. VI. 27.2.

21. RV. X. 173.6; bali-hṛt; VII. 6.5.

22. Cf. Index to Griffith's RV, vols. I-II; RV. I. 67.1; IV. 4.1; VII. 18.2; I. 130.1.

23. RV. IV. 42.8-9.

24. Cf. A.L. Basham, The Wonder that was India, London, 1961, pp. 236, 237. He is called dhṛtavrata, the upholder of the sacred law, which becomes a common epithet of later kings. Cf. RV. I.25.8-10; 44.14; 141.9; II. 1.4; X. 65.5.

25. Cf. Vedic Index, II. p. 213.

26. RV. VII. 18.13; AV. III.19; cf. RV. III. 33.3 ff.; VII. 18; cf. Hopkins, JAOS, XV, p. 260 et seq.

27. TS. II. 42.1; cf. KS. X.10; MS. II. 5.10; AV. I. 29.6; AB. I. 14.

28. AV. IV. 22.7.

29. purām bhettā, cf. Vedic Index, s.v. rājan.

30. TB. I. 8.4.1-2.

31. Kauṣ. Up. III. 1.

32. According to Aristotle, kingship in the heroic age was limited to leadership in war and to certain religious observances. Cf. S.H. Hooke (ed.), Myth, Ritual and Kingship, Oxford, 1958, p. 28.

33. Bṛ. U. V. 13.4; cr. ŚB. XIV. 8.14.4.

34. *AB*. VIII. 7.10, *kṣatra rūpaṁ tat*; cf. *TB*. III. 8.23.3, *rājanyo bāhubalī bhāvukaḥ*.
35. *TS*. II. 4.14.2.
36. *AV*. III. 4.2 *tvām viśo vṛṇatāṁ rājyāya* ...
37. *AV*. III. 5.6-7. *ye dhīvāno rathakārāḥ karmārā ye manīṣiṇaḥ/upastīn parṇa mahyaṁ tvaṁ sarvān kṛṇvabhito janañ //6// ye rājāno rājakṛtaḥ sūtā grāmaṇyasca ye/upastīn parṇa mahyaṁ tvaṁ sarvañ kṛṇvabhito janān //7//* Cf. Bloomfield, *SBE* XLII. 114; Jayaswal, *op.cit*., pp. 188-189.
38. *rāṣṭrasya pradātāraḥ, ete pādātāraḥ*, cf. *TB*. I. 7.3.
39. *TS*. I. 8.9; *MS*. II. 6.5; IV. 3; *KS*. XV. 4; *TB*. I. 7.3 ff.; *SB*. V. 3.1.ff. Cf. Jayaswal, *op.cit*., pp. 192 ff.; R.S. Sharma, *op.cit*., pp. 103ff. They include such people as the priest, the noble, the chief queen, the commander, the charioteer, the village headman, the metal-worker, the courier and others - the retinue of a royal household.
40. *MS*. IV. 3.8, *Kṣatrasya etyaṅgāni*.
41. Cf. U.N. Ghoshal, *The Beginnings of Indian Historiography and Other Essays*, Calcutta, 1944, pp. 249ff.
42. *AV*. VI. 88.3; Cf. III. 4.
43. *Ibid*., VII. 13, 1, *Sabhā ca mā Samitiścāvatāṁ prajāpaterduhitarau samvidāne/yenā samgacchā upa mā sa śikṣāccāru vadāni pitaraḥ samgateṣu*.
44. *AV*. III. 4.7.
45. *ŚB*. XII. 9.3.1-3.
46. *AB*. VIII. 9.
47. *Ibid*., VIII. 17. *rājapitā*.
48. See above; cf. also Raychaudhuri, *op.cit*., pp. 160-61, and n. 8 on p. 160.
49. *Nirukta*, II.10; *Vedic Index*, II, p. 211.
50. *ŚB*. V. 1.1.12.
51. *AB*. VIII.23.
52. *Ch.U*. IV. 2.1-5; *ŚB*. XIII. 5.4.6; *Jaim Up. Br*, I. 4.5.
53. *Vedic Index*, s.v. *rājan*; Cf. *AV*. III. 3.4; *KS*. XXVIII, 1; *TS*. II. 3.1; *MS*. II. 2.1; *PB*. XII. 9.3.3; *Kauśika Sūtra*, XVI. 30.
54. *ŚB*. XII. 9.3.1 *et seq*.; cf. *AB*. VIII. 10.
55. *AB*. VIII. 15.
56. K.P. Jayaswal, *op.cit*., pp. 202, 203; U.N. Ghoshal, *The Beginnings of Indian Historiography and Other Essays*, Calcutta, 1944; pp. 281, 282; R.S. Sharma, *op.cit*., p. 127.
57. Cf. Raychaudhuri, *op.cit*., p. 168.
58. *AB*. VIII. 12; 17-18.
59. *VS*. X. 27; *TS*. I. 8.16; *TB*. I. 7.10.2; *ŚB*. V. 4.4.5.

60. The brāhmaṇa could never afford to antagonize the people, who remained his principal benefactors in day-to-day life.

61. cf. AV. III. 19; Muir, OST., I, p. 283.

62. AB. VIII. 27. Does this mean that the people were otherwise incited to violence by disgruntled brāhmaṇas?

63. Ibid., VII. 22.

64. Ibid., VII. 26.

65. Ibid., VII. 27-34.

66. Ibid., VII. 29, ādāyyāpāyyāvasāyī yathākāmaprayāpyaḥ ... anyasya balikṛdanyasyā'dyo yathākāmajyeyaḥ ... anyasyu preṣyaḥ kāmotthāpyo yathākāmavadhyaḥ.

67. AB. VIII. 12-23.

68. samantam sarvataḥ pṛthivīṃ jayan parīyāyāśvena ca medhyeneje.

69. Drekmeier, Kingship and Community in Early India, p. 22, thinks that the aśvamedha harks back to an age when the grazing area of the herds was the limit of the tribal leader's claim to territory.

70. ŚB. VII. 1.1.8.

71. JB. VI. 7.3.

72. ŚB. XIII. 7.1.14-15.

73. Br. U. IV. 4.23, So 'ham bhagavate videhān dadāmi māñcāpi saha dāsyāyeti.

74. AB. VII. 20.

75. cf. RV. I. 110.5; VIII.91.5; IV. 41.6; TS. III. 2.8.5; KS. V.2; MS. IV. 12.3.

76. Ch. U. VII. 24.2.

77. Gautama, I. 1-2.

78. See Gautama, X, XI; Āpastamba, II, 10-25.

79. Vasiṣṭha, XIX. 14.

80. Baudhāyana, I. 10, 18, 19.

81. Pāṇiṇi, V. 2. 112, calls the king pariṣad-bala.

82. Gautama, XII. 43.

83. Vasiṣṭha, II. 49.50.

84. Dīgha Nikāya, III, pp. 61-77, 84-95.

85. cf. Basham, The Wonder that was India, p. 82.

86. Later Buddhist writers present a similar picture of the original social contract. Cf. Buddhaghosa, Visuddhimagga, Ch. XIII; Vasubandhu, Abhidharmakośa, III, 98.

87. Tittira Jātaka, no. 37; Ulūka Jātaka, no. 270; Saccaṁkira Jātaka, no. 73; Padakusalamānava Jātaka, no. 432; Mahāsutasoma Jātaka, No. 537.

88. Cf. Raychaudhuri, op.cit., pp. 176-177.

89. Ang, III, 76, 152.
90. Majjh, II, 69, 94; Ang, III, 152.
91. Ibid., III, 147, dhammo rañño cakkavattissa rājā.
92. Dīgha, I, 99, khattiyā va seṭṭhā hīnā brāhmaṇā; Ang., V. 328.
93. See my Ancient Indian Warfare, pp. 146ff.
94. Mbh. I. 126.34.
95. Ibid., I. 127.11.
96. Ibid., V. 153.1 ff; VII. 5.38 ff.
97. Ibid., VIII. 6.5 ff.
98. Cf. Mbh., XII. 59.14-27; Ghoshal, A History of Indian Political Ideas, p. 399; Kautilya, I, XII, 26 gives his version of a social contract.
99. Kauṭilya, VI. 1; Manu, IX. 297; Bṛhaspati, 84.5; Kāmandaka, IV. 1.
100. Manu, VII, 3-5, 8. Translation from Basham, op.cit., pp. 84, 85.
101. XVIII. 26ff.
102. Kādambarī, pp. 177-78.
103. Nārada, XVIII. 31.
104. Mbh., XII. 59.
105. Kāmandaka, V. 84.
106. Nārada, XVIII. 5.17; Kātyāyana, 15.
107. Catuḥśataka, V. 77, gaṇadāsa.
108. Cf. Nārada, XVIII. 14-16.
109. See Hillebrandt, Altindische Politik, pp. 20 ff.
110. Bṛhaspati, I. 1.126-31.
111. Kauṭilya, IV. 1; Nārada, I. 10.
112. Manu, VII, 39, Translation by Basham, op.cit., p. 114.
113. Nītisāra, II.37; VI. 7.
114. VI. 7.ff.
115. II. 55ff.
116. Kādambarī, pp. 177-78.
117. Śiśupālavadha, II. 30.
118. Nītivākyāmṛta, 114.15 ff.
119. Nītisāra, I. 1.
120. Kauṭilya, VI. 2; Nītisāra, VIII.
121. Mbh., XII. 97.1-2.
122. Nītisāra, IX.5-7.
123. Raghu, III.4.
124. Ibid., IV, 15, 30, 39.
125. Ibid., I, 30.
126. Cf. Brahmāṇḍa Purāṇa, I. 29, 78. The word cakravartin occurs as early as the Maitrī Upaniṣad, I. 4.
127. Gonda, Ancient Indian Kingship from the Religious Point of View, pp. 123-25.
128. Cf. BSOAS, XII, London, 1948, pp. 645 ff.

129. Rāmāyaṇa, II, 57.

130. Kauṭilya, I. 16. prajāsukhe sukhaṁ rājñah prajānāṁca hite hitaṁ/nātmapriyaṁ hitaṁ rājñaḥ prajānāṁ tu priyaṁ hitam. cf. ātmatyāgaḥ sarvabhūtānukampā of Mbh.

131. See especially Dhauli and Jaugada Sep. Edict 1 in, e.g., A. Cunningham, ed., Inscriptions of Āsoka, Varanasi, 1961.

ABBREVIATIONS

AB	Aitareya Brāhmaṇa
ABORI	Annals of the Bhandarkar Oriental Institute
Ang.	Anguttara Nikāya
AV	Atharva Veda
Br.U.	Bṛhad Āraṇyaka Upaniṣad
BSOAS	Bulletin of the School of Oriental and African Studies, London
Ch.U.	Chāndogya Upaniṣad
Jaim. Br.	Jaiminīya Brāhmaṇa
Jaim. Up.	Jaiminīya Upaniṣad
JAOS	Journal of the American Oriental Society
JB	Jaiminīya Brāhmaṇa
Kaus Up	Kauṣītaki Upaniṣad
KS	Kauśika Sūtra
Mbh	Mahābhārata
OST	Original Sanskrit Texts on the Origin and History of the People of India, 4 vols., 2nd ed., London, 1872.
RV	Ṛg Veda
ŚB	Śatapatha Brāhmaṇa
SBE	Sacred Books of the East
TB	Taittirīya Brāhmaṇa
TS	Taittirīya Saṃhitā
VS	Vājasaneyi Saṃhitā

7 KINGSHIP IN ISLAM: ISLAMIC UNIVERSALISM THROUGH THE CALIPHATE

S.A.A. Rizvi

> Say: Oh Allah! Owner of Sovereignty (mulk)! Thou givest sovereignty (mulk) unto whom Thou wilt, and Thou withdrawest sovereignty (mulk) from whom Thou wilt. Thou exaltest whom Thou wilt and Thou abasest whom Thou wilt. In Thy hand is the good. Lo! Thou art Able to do all good things.[1]

This verse from the Qur'ān tends to indicate that the supreme authority in Islam is vested in Allāh. The umma or Islamic community is the ummat Allāh (Allāh's community) and as such is the legitimating instrument in Islamic government. Enemies of the umma are accordingly 'aduww Allāh (Allāh's enemy).

Muḥammad was the final messenger of Allāh in a long chain of prophets and after him this process of deputation ended. The Qur'ān affirms:

> Muḥammad is not the father of any man among you, but he is the messenger of Allāh and the Seal of the Prophets; and Allāh is Aware of all things.

According to the Qur'ān the prophetic office is not opposed to that of kingship. It says:

> (And it was said unto him): Oh David! Lo! We have set thee as a viceroy (khalifatan fi'l ardi) in the earth; therefore judge aright between mankind, and follow not desire that it beguile thee from the way of Allah. Lo! those who wander from the way of Allah have an awful doom, forasmuch as they forget the Day of Reckoning....[3]

> And verily We tried Solomon, and set upon his throne a (mere) body. Then did he repent.
> He said: My Lord! Forgive me and bestow on me sovereignty such as shall not belong to any after me. Lo! Thou art the Bestower.
> So We made the wind subservient unto him, setting fair by his command whithersoever he intended.
> And the unruly, every builder and diver (made We subservient).[4]

After his call to this office in 610 A.D. Muḥammad's concern was not merely with the establishment of his new religion but it was also imperative for the nascent umma to overcome the economic, political and social challenges which the growing conflicts between the mercantile and nomadic economies of Mecca had posed. God's messenger (Rasūl Allāh) was also required to find methods to defend the umma from persecution and harassment by its enemies. In accordance with pre-Islamic Arab traditions Muslims recognized Muḥammad as a Saiyid or head, who presided over the councils of tribal notables. Muḥammad's position as Saiyid of the umma transcended limited tribal boundaries and his status as God's Messenger added a new dimension to his political authority. His emigration or hijra in September 622 to the fertile oasis of Medina was not in fact a flight but a planned migration based on an agreement between Muḥammad and the war-torn tribes of Medina. Between 622 and 627 other agreements were made by Muḥammad among the emigrants (Muhājirūn), their supporters in Medina (Anṣār) and the town's Jewish community. In its present form the basic agreement, known as the Constitution of Medina, is a conflation of at least two other documents and may be dated sometime between 622 and 627. Its main articles are as follows:

1. The believers and their dependents constitute a single community (umma).
2. Each clan or subdivision of the community is responsible for blood-money and ransoms on behalf of its members (arts.2-11).
3. The members of the community are to show complete solidarity against crime and not to support a criminal even when he is a near kinsman, where the crime is against another member of the community (arts.13,21).
4. The members of the community are to show complete solidarity against unbelievers in

peace and war (arts.14, 17, 19, 44), and also solidarity in the granting of 'neighbourly protection' (art.15).

5. The Jews of various groups belong to the community, and are to retain their own religion; they and the Muslims are to render 'help' (including military aid) to one another when it is needed (arts. 24-25, 37, 38, 46).[5]

Naturally the agreement enhanced the scope of Muḥammad's personal, political, economic and social responsibilities. In war and peace, victory and defeat, the initiation and control of political policies, the collection of dues and taxes, the promulgation of legal statutes and the deliverance of judgments in civil and criminal disputes, Muḥammad acted as a God's vicegerent receiving commands directly from Allāh, which were communicated through the archangel, Gabriel, or his own intuition (guided by Divine Will). Muḥammad's rôle as God's Messenger made distinctions between divinely revealed laws and those which he himself devised, superfluous. Both the Qur'ān and the Sunna (the record of the Prophet's life in thought and action) were absolute, unchallengeable and not to be arbitrarily interpreted. The agreement of recognized religious authorities (ijmā') on a regulation (hukm) imposed by God was the only basis of orthodox law (Sharī'a). The Sharī'a went a long way towards maintaining the unity of the umma in its religious and ethical attitudes; the principal duty of the Muslim government was to enforce obedience to the Sharī'a. The concept of dīn, conventionally translated as religion in the western sense of the word, was not exclusive; dīn and dawla (kingship) were two sides to the same coin. Islam was both a religious and political community, non-conformity and rebellion were thus interchangeable. Unlike Jesus, Muḥammad had not instructed, 'render unto Caesar the things which are Caesar's and unto God the things which are God's'. Bernard Lewis writes:

> During three centuries of struggle and persecution, this distinction (between Caesar and God) was firmly established in Christian doctrine and practice, and the Christian religion created its own institutional structure, separate from that of the state - the Christian Church, law and hierarchy. The great change came with the conversion to Christianity of the Roman Emperor Constantine and the beginning of

> the uneasy linkage in Christendom between Church and state.... In Islam, God is Caesar, and the head of the Muslim community is His vicegerent on earth.[6]

The death of Muḥammad on 8 June 632 produced great consternation among the Muslims of Medina, but Abū Bakr, his most senior friend and a leader of the community, pacified them with these succinct lines, 'If one worships Muḥammad, Muḥammad has died; but if one worships God, God is living and does not die', and then to 'Umar he added, 'stretch forth thy hand that I may swear allegiance to thee!'[7] Muḥammad's mission as a messenger of Allāh had ended, but his political, economic, social and religious leadership of the umma needed a replacement. A Qur'ānic verse had already divinely sanctioned such a procedure; it said:

> Oh ye who believe! Obey Allah, and obey the messenger and those of you who are in authority; and if ye have a dispute concerning any matter, refer it to Allah and the messenger if ye are (in truth) believers in Allah and the Last Day. That is better and more seemly in the end.[8]

Soon Muslims were divided among themselves regarding the rules for the appointment of those 'in authority'; however the need for a successor to Muḥammad was never questioned.

While 'Alī, Muḥammad's cousin and son-in-law, prepared for the burial of his body, the Prophet's leading companions hurriedly convened a council in a roofed enclosure known as the Saqīfa of Banu Sā'ida. A heated discussion ensued between the Muhājirūn and the Anṣār which led to the election of Abū Bakr as successor. He called his new role, the 'Successor of the Messenger of Allāh' (Khalīfat Rasūl Allāh), while strictly forbidding that he be addressed as 'Caliph of God'. A modern authority rightly states:

> Abū Bakr thus became the successor (khalifa) of the Messenger of God and in this way the caliphate was founded, an institution which had no equivalent - and was destined never to have any - outside the Muslim world. The caliphate lasted for centuries, and many things were subsequently changed, but the idea that the appointment of the caliph was a kind of contract imposing reciprocal obligations on the

> man elected and on his subjects gained ground, and became a fundamental concept once the Muslims had developed a juridical mentality. The fortuitous circumstance that the first man to be elected to this high office was a Qurayshite became, for all except the heterodox, a principle - the caliph had to be a member of the Prophet's tribe, and the Prophet was a Qurayshite. Since the men who elected Abū Bakr, while the populace waited outside to hear the result, had been Muḥammad's closest associates, it became the privilege of the leading figures in the community (the 'men who release and bind') to have the right of choosing, and the populace had only to ratify their decision.[9]

Abū Bakr managed to crush firmly the religio-political uprisings of the Islamicized tribes in the peninsula which refused to pay taxes to the Caliph in Medina. However he was not destined to see the consummation of the success of the military expeditions to the lands beyond Arabia, as he died on 23 August 634. During the tenure of the caliphate of 'Umar, whom the Companions of the Prophet elected at the initiation of their first Caliph, the Sasanid empire of Iran and Iraq was conquered, the armies of Heraclieus in Syria were defeated, Damascus and Jerusalem were annexed, Egypt surrendered and the Arab empire extended as far as Tunisia and part of Algeria.

The establishment both of the dīwān (literally, register), to organize salaries and to maintain a record of the stipends to the army and the people of Medina, and of the bayt al-māl (the treasury of the Muslim state) were among new administrative measures based on analogies of past actions by the Prophet or on injunctions in the Qur'ān. 'Alī opposed the creation of the dīwān and recommended that nothing be held in reserve, all revenue being distributed in accordance with Muḥammad's practice.[10] Bilāl and some others among the Companions urged 'Umar to distribute the lands acquired in Iraq and Syria, in the manner that the spoils of the army were divided; however, 'Umar overruled them with the argument that 'Allāh has given a share in these lands to those who shall come after you'.[11] 'Umar's decision was marked by both political realism and profound foresight for it helped evolve the basic framework of the new Islamic administrative system. Theoretically the original rights of ownership of land were

God's, Muḥammad's and the community's.[12] Under Muḥammad, however, there was little land or revenue of which to dispose. The pre-Islamic custom of sharing movable booty (ghanīma) with either one-fourth or fifth going to the leader, was continued. As specified in the Qur'ān the Prophet was free to dispose of four per cent of the booty (khums al-khums) according to his own discretion, and, after the Battle of Badr in March 624, one fifth of the prophet's share in the booty was recorded in the financial accounts. In 628-29 the fertile Jewish oasis of Khaybar was conquered and Muḥammad allowed the Jews to migrate to a neighbouring settlement known as Fadak, which the Muslims had acquired without battle. The vanquished Jews were required to surrender half their lands and produce which the Muslims were to share amongst themselves annually. The revenue from Fadak allocated to Muḥammad was given by him to travellers in need and the poorer members of his own Hāshimite clan.

The vast conquests of 'Umar called for a new basis of revenue administration. The divergent interests of the desert tribesmen and the town dwellers of Mecca and Medina soon became all too clear. The town dwellers wished to exploit the new resources commercially, while the tribesmen hankered after the land, wishing to convert it into pasture, as was subsequently done by the Mongol hordes. Trade prospects for urban dwellers in the conquered countries were effortlessly developed and zakāt (alms tax) and ṣadaqa (alms) were paid on the property, in accordance with Qur'ānic injunctions and the practice at the time of Muḥammad. However, the problem of land ownership and its administration was a formidable one. There were vast tracts of land in the conquered countries whose owners had either died in war or fled to other territories, their land coming under the category of mawāt or uncultivated. On the basis of a tradition of Muḥammad, 'Umar argued that 'mawāt land belongs to whoever restores it to life' (hyā').'[13] He assigned these lands as permanent, irrevocable grants to enterprising leaders and they were taxed on the basis of Muḥammad's ruling that 'a tenth ('ushr) is to be paid on all lands irrigated by running streams and a half-tenth on the lands artificially irrigated'.[14] The protected people (ahl al-dhimma, dhimma or dhimmis), that is, non-Muslims who did not abscond and who cultivated their lands, were ordered to pay kharāj (yield of the fields) in addition to jizya. The de jure basis for the realization of both jizya and kharāj was the fact that all land was owned by God and His Prophet; therefore the right of ownership accrued through conquest was a de facto one.

'Umar, however, did not intend to transform the caliphate into an empire according to the Persian model. He was known to have such simple habits as a preference for plain food and for the wearing of coarse and patched clothing. However, his sternness extended to patrolling the streets of Medina secretly, carrying a hide whip with which he inflicted punishment on those he caught violating the Sharī'a. When he visited Syria, Mu'āwiya, the governor, received him in full royal splendour. 'Umar's shocked question was, 'Are these royal Persian manners?' Mu'āwiya replied, 'Oh Commander of the Faithful, I am in a border region with (the enemy) in military equipment'. 'Umar did not dissent. Ibn Khaldūn defends both 'Umar and Mu'āwiya this way:

> He ('Umar) had used an argument that was in agreement with the intentions of the truth and of Islam. If the intention (implied in 'Umar's remark) had been to eradicate royal authority as such, 'Umar would not have been silenced by the answer with which Mu'āwiya (excused) his assumption of royal Persian manners. He would have insisted that Mu'āwiya give them up altogether. 'Umar meant by "royal Persian manners" the attitude of the Persian rulers, which consisted in doing worthless things, constantly practising oppression, and neglecting God. Mu'āwiya replied that he was not interested in royal Persian manners as such, or in the worthlessness connected with them, but his intention was to serve God. Therefore, ('Umar) was silent.

Ibn Khaldūn did not ignore the fact that Muḥammad censured royal authority, but adds that the Prophet disapproved of

> ....royal authority for achieving superiority through worthless means and for employing human beings for indulgence in (selfish) purposes and desires... . If royal authority would sincerely exercise its superiority over men for the sake of God and so as to cause those men to worship God and to wage war against His enemies, there would not be anything reprehensible in it.[15]

On 3 November 633 'Umar, then aged only fifty-three, was killed in Medina by a Persian slave. Before he died he managed to appoint a committee of six senior Qurayshites to elect one of their number to the caliphate. 'Uthmān, one of Muḥammad's fathers-in-law, was elected. However during the tenure of his caliphate opposition sprang up over a number of different issues, including economic and administrative mismanagement and charges of nepotism. A group of Egyptian Muslims marched against Medina to force the Caliph to introduce reforms and a riot broke out. 'Uthmān was besieged in his house where, in June 656, the rioters assassinated him in cold blood. The Caliph's Umayyad kinsmen fled from Medina and a number of leading Companions in Medina, unwilling to elevate 'Alī to the post of caliph, also left the capital; thereafter members of the groups who had opposed 'Uthmān invited 'Ālī to become caliph. Mu'āwiya, the Syrian Governor, and also 'Uthmān's cousin, refused to recognize the validity of such an election. Meanwhile, 'Ā'isha, the cherished wife of Muḥammad, who was also the daughter of Abū Bakr, supported by Ṭalha and al-Zubayr, two of Muḥammad's leading Companions, became vocal in demanding reprisals against the Caliph's assassins. Several hundred troops rallied under 'Ā'isha's banner; however, 'Ālī foiled their attempt to seize Iraq. On 9 December 656 in a battle near Baṣra, after launching her army's attack, seated in a litter on the back of a camel, the valiant 'Ā'isha was defeated at what was later somewhat predictably known as the Battle of the Camel (al-Jamal). Ṭalha and al-Zubayr were killed and 'Ā'isha retreated to Medina.

'Ālī's war against Mu'āwiya proved a protracted struggle which resulted in the crystallization of a group of his loyal supporters into a sect known as the Shī'īs. Those among 'Ālī's supporters who deserted him were called Khārijites. In July 658 'Ālī defeated and killed many leading Khārijites; however, the process of defection remained unstemmed. Even Mecca and Medina became hotbeds of rebellion. In January 661 'Ālī was assassinated in Kufa by a Khārijite and his supporters, led by the Prophet's cousin, 'Ubayd Allāh ibn Abbās, elected 'Ālī's son, Ḥasan, as Caliph. Mu'āwiya again challenged the election, managing to split Ḥasan's supporters, and proceeded to march against his adversary. Finding his supporters lukewarm and divided Ḥasan abdicated. An agreement between the two leaders was reached but the peace terms featured in most sources are confusing. According to some, Mu'āwiya pledged himself to leave the choice of successor to a shūra or committee decision. Ḥasan retired to Medina, living there quietly until his death in 669-70. Although disillusioned and frustrated the Shī'īs could find no alternative in view of Ḥasan's firm decision to honour the agreement.

Before his death sometime in April 680 Mu'āwiya managed to persuade the élite in the important towns of the empire to recognize his son, Yazīd, as successor. Ḥusain, Ḥasan's brother, and four other notables, refused to accept the principle of hereditary succession to the caliphate. After Yazīd's accession in Damascus Ḥusain rejected the invitation of Medina's Umayyad Governor to make bay'a (a pledge of allegiance) to Yazīd. He left for Mecca. Some of Ḥusain's followers in Medina rallied around him but while he was travelling from Mecca to Iraq the new Governor in Kūfa managed to turn public opinion in favour of Yazīd. On 10 Muḥarram 61/10 October 680 Ḥusain, his followers and family (estimated as numbering about 72), died martyrs' deaths in battle against a large army sent to cut off their march to Kūfa.

Yazīd's reign marked the beginning of the dynasty of Umayyad caliphs. Although in general Ḥusain's descendants withdrew from political activity, as early as 685 a revolt against the Umayyads was launched in the name of Muḥammad, a son of 'Ālī by a Ḥanafī woman. From time to time other adventurers also organized uprisings against the Umayyads, ostensibly to revenge 'Ālī. H.A.R. Gibb says:

> The establishment of the Umayyad Caliphate of Damascus (661) was thus the outcome of a coalition or compromise between those who represented the Islamic ideal of a religious community, united by common allegiance to the heritage of the Prophet, and the Meccan secular interpretation of unity, against the threat of anarchy implicit in tribalism. But this was only a modus vivendi reinstating a central authority over the loosely bound provinces of the Arab empire.[16]

In 749 a new dynasty descending from Muḥammad's uncle, al-'Abbās bin 'Abd al-Muṭṭalib (d.653) crushed the Umayyads and shifted the centre of political authority of the Muslim world from

Syria to Iraq. The early 'Abbāsid propagandists took the oath of allegiance in the name of al-riḍa min al Muḥammad (a mutually agreed upon member of Muḥammad's family) and promised the umma to restore its revenue rights (fai'), charitable taxes and plunder, illegally usurped by the Umayyads for their own personal aggrandizement.[17] Between 750 and 945 the new 'Abbāsid dynasty firmly established its rule in the regions under their control, although from as early as the eighth century independent dynasties were established in Spain, Morocco and western Algeria. Of these the most important were the Umayyads in Spain, who ruled from 756 to 1031, and the Shī'ī Fāṭimids, who first dominated North Africa and later Egypt and Syria between 909 and 1171. From 945 onwards 'Abbāsid power began to decline rapidly and between the eleventh century and 1258 the 'Abbāsid caliphs were ruling in name only.

From the time of Mu'āwiya's reign the growing influence of the centralized monarchical institution of the Sasanians and the Byzantines had transformed the patriarchal caliphate of the first four caliphs (known as 'the Rightly Guided') into a universal empire. However the new elective system introduced by Mu'āwiya (to raise his son to the throne), and pursued by his Umayyad and 'Abbāsid successors, retained a contractual element which imposed reciprocal obligations. The custom of bay'a had also helped to make the elevation of the caliph into a contractual agreement; on the one side there was the will of the umma (expressed in the designation of the candidate), who constituted the offer, and on the other there was the will of the elected person constituting acceptance.

Bay'a was very much a pre-Islamic Arab institution. At a place in the Arabian peninsula called 'Aqaba, between Mina and Mecca, before his departure to Medina the Prophet had accepted bay'a from seventy-two men of Medina who had pledged themselves to defend him while a guest in their city. The assembly of Saqīfa declared the election of Abū Bakr by taking a pledge of bay'a. Bay'a promised by the shūra was followed by a similar pledge of the people as a whole. Bay'a was always concluded between two parties with a hand clasp and, according to Ibn Khaldūn, 'This (bay'a) was considered to be something like the action of buyer and seller (after concluding a sale)'.[18]

It was not the election to the caliphate itself but the procedure and validity of the process which remained a hotly disputed question. 'Abbās, the

Prophet's uncle, and Ṭalha, Zubayr and 'Alī, who were absent from the Saqīfa of Banu Sā'ida debate, did not immediately offer their allegiance to Abū Bakr. It is said that Abu Sufyān, the father of Mu'āwiya, tried to persuade 'Alī to rise against Abū Bakr offering him forceful military backing. Other dissenting leaders gradually gave their bay'a; however 'Alī held out for six months. The controversy over the validity of bay'a was rekindled during 'Alī's election and Mu'āwiya affirmed that as only a minority had participated it was therefore invalid. Although 'Alī replied that 'the election of the caliph was a right of (Anṣār, Muhājirūn or Badr combatants) who were present in Medina at the relevant time',[19] the dispute over the validity of 'Alī's bay'a was never resolved.

At the time of the bay'a with Ḥasan bin 'Alī, Qays bin Sa'd bin 'Ubāda al-Anṣārī, who had first initiated it, proposed that the bay'a should be, 'on the Book of God, the Sunna of the Prophet and the war (qitāl) against those who declared licit that which is illicit (al-muḥillun)'.[20] But Mu'āwiya continued to refuse to recognize the validity of Ḥasan's election and his right to bay'a.

Mu'āwiya's precedent of nominating his own son as successor and eliciting bay'a from the élite throughout the empire became general practice under both the Umayyads and the 'Abbāsids. The two dynasties did not however nominate only sons as successors. Of the fourteen Umayyad caliphs four alone nominated their sons, and of thirty-seven 'Abbāsids, sixteen did the same, the rest specifying their brothers or other close relatives as successors. However the practice initiated by the Umayyads of obtaining bay'a for their heirs-apparent or having it renewed for themselves after their accessions to the throne, was perpetuated by the 'Abbāsids.

From the earliest times bay'a to a caliph neither involved blind obedience nor precluded the right to register opposition. Abū Dharr al-Ghifārī, a distinguished Companion of Muḥammad, and a noted ascetic, openly opposed 'Uthmān's political policies, incurring banishment for his pains. Although 'Uthmān had forbidden the people of Medina to associate with Abū Dharr, 'Alī and his sons extended to the exile a touching farewell.[21]

'Ā'isha remained strongly opposed to 'Uthmān's policies, although she remained aloof from the insurgents who had assassinated him and did not support the cause of 'Alī. After 'Alī became caliph 'Ā'isha left Mecca for Baṣra and quickly succeeded in organizing a movement to revenge Uthmān's death. After her defeat she retired from active political life, remaining neutral in the war between Mu'āwiya and 'Alī. Sunnī opinion refrained from passing judgment on either 'Alī, 'Ā'isha or Mu'āwiya, ascribing their mistakes to faulty reasoning (ijthihād) rather than their own sins.

Under the Umayyads Ḥasan of Baṣra (642-728), one of the great intellectuals of early Islam and the father of a number of Islamic movements such as ṣufism, futūwwa (chivalric orders) and the Mu'tazila,[22] proclaimed that 'the violent actions of tyrants were a punishment sent by God which could not be opposed by the sword but must be endured with patience'.[23] Nevertheless he himself fearlessly criticized the policies of contemporary rulers when he considered them detrimental to Islam and between 705 and 714 was forced to hide from the authorities after openly censuring the policies of Ḥajjāj bin Yūsuf, the Governor of Iraq.[24]

Following the example of Abū Dharr and Ḥasan many ṣūfīs unhesitatingly admonished rulers and governors for what they believed to be un-Islamic policies. One ṣūfī reportedly gave the following advice to the pious Umayyad Caliph, 'Umar bin 'Abd al-'Aziz (717-720):

> If thou wouldst be saved tomorrow from the Divine punishment, regard the elders of thy Moslems as the fathers, and their young men as thy brothers, and their children as thy children. The whole territory of Islam is thy house, and its people are thy family. Visit thy father, and honour thy brother, and deal kindly with thy children.[25]

The principle of consultation was not confined to the election of a caliph alone but was also projected into the administrative institutions of Islam. In fact even the pre-Islamic inhabitants of Mecca, as well as the nomadic tribesmen in the Arabian peninsula, had had their own councils which had produced crucial decisions relating to nearly every aspect of life. An early chapter in the Qur'ān revealed in Mecca, entitled al-Shūra (counsel), exhorts Muslims to resolve problems through consultation (amruhum shūra);[26] the fact is also underlined in verses revealed at Medina. Muḥammad himself did not hesitate to consult his companions for advice.

The Rightly Guided Caliphs made decisions after

thorough discussion with ahl al-ra'y (competent to give opinion) although they often issued orders entirely on their own initiative. Abū Bakr ran his administration with mutual consultation but was obliged to suppress firmly those tribes who refused to send taxes to Medina and those whose members turned apostate, against all counsels of leniency and caution. About the same time, despite threats of rebellion in Arabia, Abū Bakr persisted with Muḥammad's original plan to despatch a large army under Usāma towards Syria, overruling the views of his advisers. In both cases his personal judgment was farsighted and ultimately vindicated. The government by consultation under 'Umar was also a success. Frequently he conferred with the leading Companions of the Prophet who were considered ahl al-ra'y (competent to give an opinion) and on important occasions would summon the entire population of Medina to express their opinions in an assembly for prayer.[27] However he also made many important decisions which rejected the views of the more prominent Companions, although a number, such as the question of land management in Iraq and Syria, were later ratified by the people of Medina.

'Uthmān's principal advisers were his own kinsmen and the governors of provinces he himself had appointed. Naturally this policy proved disastrous and also scandalized the people of Medina. It was paid for dearly by the Caliph with his life.

In July 657 Mu'āwiya, engaged in battle against 'Alī, ordered his troops to hoist copies of the Qur'ān onto their lances in the hope of gaining a respite from the heat of battle. His ruse was intended also, however, as an invitation to the parties to resolve the dispute by referring to the Qur'ān. Although 'Alī was forced by his supporters to agree to this form of arbitration, curiously enough another group of supporters asserted that the battle should be a decisive one in accordance with the following Qur'ānic verse, frequently quoted by 'Alī himself to rally allegiance:

> And if two parties of believers fall to fighting, then make peace between them. And if one party of them doeth wrong to the other, fight ye that which doeth wrong till it return unto the ordinance of Allāh; then, if it return, make peace between them justly, and act equitably. Lo! Allāh loveth the equitable.[28]

The dissidents' cry was, 'no decision but God's (lā ḥukm illā li-llāh)', and they later formed a sect known as Khawarij or Kharijites (Seceders) which introduced a policy of blood and iron into the politics of Islam. Only Abu Bakr and 'Umar, they believed, could be listed among the Rightly Guided Caliphs, for towards the end of his reign 'Uthman had deviated from the truth and both 'Ali and Mu'awiya (and their supporters who had agreed to arbitration) were sinners. Sin, to the Kharijites, was identified with infidelity to Islam. They upheld the elective principle for the office of caliph but unlike the Sunnis asserted that incumbents need not be Qurayshites (members of Muhammad's tribe). Some even went to the extent of denying the very need for a state. They also believed that an unjust caliph and his supporters were infidels and their Muslim associates could no longer be counted among the faithful. The right of revolt against an unjust caliph was upheld. However Muslims who did not unequivocally follow such just caliphs as Abu Bakr, or 'Umar, were also kafirs or infidels.[29]

The Shī'īs developed their own political theories surrounding the personality of 'Alī. Firstly they claimed that the Qur'ān firmly endorsed 'Alī as Muḥammad's successor. Moreover, returning from his Farewell Pilgrimage in March 632 Muḥammad had stopped at a pool between Mecca and Medina (the Ghadīr Khumm) where he had taken 'Alī's hand, declaring 'He of whom I am the mawla (patron) of him 'Alī is also the mawla (man kuntu mawlahu fa 'Alī mawlahu)'.[30] According to the Shī'īs this statement explicitly designated 'Alī as Muḥammad's successor and therefore the first Imām (supreme leader or successor of the Prophet Muḥammad). Sunnī authorities did not generally dispute the accuracy of this incident although they interpreted it differently. According to the Shī'īs the first three caliphs were usurpers to whom 'Alī did not make bay'a but merely refrained from provoking bloodshed among the early Muslims.

The principal tenets of Shī'ī jurisprudence were reinforced under the guidance of the sixth Shī'ī Imām, Ja'far al-Ṣādiq (b.699-700 or 702-703, d.765), who was even consulted by the great Sunnī jurists Abū Hanīfa (699-767) and Mālik bin Anas (715-794). The first six Imāms were recognized by the important branches of Shī'īs as rightful successors of 'Alī through his daughter Fāṭima. To the Shī'īs the institution of the imamate was a pillar and fundamental article of faith in Islam, second only to the prophethood, and was the consummation and fulfilment of that office. Therefore the choice of imāms should not be the prerogative of the umma. Like a prophet an imām was divinely appointed, the only distinction between the two being that the latter did not receive Divine revelation through the intermediary of an angel. He was infallible and immune from sin (mā'ṣūm) and disobedience to an imām amounted to infidelity. The office of the Shī'ī Imām was subject to the Divine command. Only a small sect of Shī'īs (the Zaydiyya or supporters of Zayd, a great-grandson of 'Alī) differed from both the Ismā'īlīs and the Ithnā'ashariyya; they refused to recognize a hereditary line of imāms and believed that descendants of 'Alī's wife, Fāṭima, could rise against an illegitimate ruler to become imāms. However, a section of the Zaydiyya regarded Abū Bakr and 'Umar as legitimate caliphs.

The political theories of the various Islamic sects were generally justified by their jurists. The earliest available rationalization of the Sunnī theories was produced by Abū Ḥanīfa al-Nu'mān bin Thābit and his talented disciple, Abū Yūsuf (b.731, d.798). According to Abū Ḥanīfa only ahl al-rā'y could choose a caliph through mutual consultation and the exacting of allegiance under duress was not a legitimate method of election. He also endorsed the view of his predecessors that the caliph should be a Qurayshite. To him an unjust and cruel caliph was not fit for office; however, under such a rule, duties performed by Muslims in fulfilment of the laws of the Sharī'a were not invalidated.[31] The Caliph, advocated Abū Ḥanīfa, was neither entitled recklessly to spend money from the treasury nor to appropriate gifts offered to him or his family in his position as head of state. Some traditionalists held the view that while Muslims could protest against tyranny, they could not legitimately rise in rebellion; however, Abū Ḥanīfa advocated that rebellion against a tyrant was obligatory, provided that it aimed at replacing him with a just ruler and not plunging the country into bloodshed and chaos.[32]

Abū Ḥanīfa did not accept the office of qādī offered him by the later Umayyad and early 'Abbāsid rulers although his disciple, Abū Yūsuf, did. He wrote a work entitled the Kitāb al-Kharāj, a title used by twenty other authors[33] who all offered details of an Islamic framework for taxation. The appearance of a number of works on this subject was intended as a reminder to the early 'Abbāsids of their promise to share the revenues with the umma. Abū Yūsuf called on Hārūn ar-Rashīd (786-809) to follow in the footsteps of the Rightly Guided Caliphs and those of the Umayyad, 'Umar ibn 'Abd al-'Azīz. In an exhortation addressed to Hārūn ar-Rashid in the preface of his work Abū Yūsuf wrote that God had appointed him (the Caliph) a shepherd and trustee and it was therefore imperative that he should spare no pains in discharging his duties. Rulers, added Abū Yūsuf, were responsible to their Creator, just as a shepherd was to his master, and the happiest of shepherds before God on Judgment Day was he whose subjects were content. The Caliph should dispense justice, refrain from issuing arbitrary orders and avoid inflicting punishment in anger. He did not own his kingdom but was a deputy of the real Owner (God).[34] It is extraordinary that 'Abbāsid propagandists raised insurrection in the later Umayyad period on the grounds that they would right the wrong inflicted on the 'Alīds or descendants of 'Alī; and the 'Abbāsid caliphs and their jurists began to claim that they were deputies of God, a concept which Abū Bakr had strongly repudiated. Abū Yūsuf, however, warned Hārūn:

> Beware of losing any of your flock, lest the owner of the flock collect its value from you and deduct from your wages the price of what you have lost. The building must be propped before it collapses. Everything you do for those entrusted to your care is for your good, and everything you lose is to your detriment. Do not forget to look after the affairs of those committed to your charge, lest you be forgotten. And do not neglect them and their interest, lest you be neglected. You will not lose your share in this world during the days and nights when your tongue is busy mentioning God in psalms of praise, glorification and thanksgiving and in prayers for His Messenger, the prophet of mercy and leader on the straight path, peace be upon him. Yea, God in His grace and mercy has appointed the rulers to be His vicegerents on earth and has granted them the light of wisdom to illuminate the eyes of their subjects as to their confused affairs and to make clear to them the rights as to which they are doubtful.[35]

Conversely Abū Yūsuf advised Muslims to obey their rulers, not to reproach them unnecessarily and to show forbearance towards any arbitrary behaviour. They should, however, attempt to check them humbly for evil practices.[36] In principle amr bi al-ma'ruf w-al-nahi'an al munkar (enjoining what is right and forbidding what is wrong) was the right which the Muslim religious élite (ahl al-ra'y) could expect to enjoy.

Abū Yūsuf repeatedly reminded rulers to refrain from violating agreements made with non-Muslims and argued that the latter should not be assigned responsibility for the defence of the state, while excessive jizya (poll tax) and kharāj (land revenue) should not be imposed on them.[37]

The jurists of the four recognized schools of Sunnī fiqh (jurisprudence) and the principal compilers of Ḥadīth all flourished during the early period of 'Abbāsid rule. At that time the power of the 'Abbāsids was at the height of its glory and naturally their main concern was to protect the interests of a God-centred rule which promoted the laws of the Sharī'a. However, a number of significant political theorists who were also jurists wrote during the period of rapid disintegration of the 'Abbāsid caliphate. From 945 to 1055 the Buwayhids or Būyids of the Iranian plateau obtained from the caliphs the title Amīr al-Umarā' (Grand Emir or Supreme Commander), thus becoming de facto rulers and rendering the Abbāsid caliphs mere figureheads through the control of their appointments and dismissals. Although they themselves were Shī'īs they managed to retain the overlordship of the caliphate while furthering their own political interests. The caliphs invested the Amīr al-Umarā' with legitimacy, thus saving them from the political hazards of confrontation with the overwhelming Sunnī majority of the caliphate. Later the rise of Yamīn al-Dawla Maḥmūd of Ghazna (998-1030), who had originally paid allegiance to the Abbāsid Caliph al-Qādir (991-1031) and who in 1029 had delivered a crushing blow to Būyid power in western Iran, aroused new hope, both among the Sunnī caliphs and their political theorists. Encouraged by the decline of Shī'ī power, two such theorists, al-Māwardī (b.974, d.1058) and his contemporary Ibn al-Farrā', popularly known as Abū Ya'lā (b.990, d.1065), wrote books on political concepts and the law. Although independently they compiled works called al-Aḥkam al-Sulṭāniyya (Ordinances of Government), the two texts are remarkably similar. What distinctions there are stem from the authors' affiliations to different schools of jurisprudence - al-Māwardī was a Shāfi'ī and Abū Ya'lā a Hanbalī. Of the two works al-Māwardī's became the more famous.

Al-Māwardī underlined the theory that the imāmat (an alternative name for the caliphate favoured by Sunnī jurists) was indispensable to the Sharī'a and not to reason, as believed by the Mu'tazila, and the consensus of the community was the appointing authority of the imām. The élite or ahl al-ḥall wa'l-'aqd [possessor of (the power of) loosening and binding] numbering five, three or even one, could form a body of qualified electors. They believed the most important condition for a candidate to the office of caliph was his Qurayshite descent. Six other qualifications were : 1. justice, 2. knowledge of the Sharī'a, 3. sound sight, hearing and speech, 4. healthy limbs, 5. administrative competence and 6. courage and energy in war.[38] The following were the duties and functions of the imām:

1. To enforce the laws of the Sharī'a and to protect Muslims from the evil influence of heresy.
2. To dispense justice and protect the weak against the high-handedness of the strong.
3. To maintain law and order and promote measures for peaceful economic activity and travel.
4. To promote the application of Qur'ānic penalties for offences.
5. To garrison the frontiers and ensure the security of the life and property of both Muslims and non-Muslims alike.
6. To establish the supremacy of Islam over all religions and faiths and to wage war against non-Muslims who oppose Islam and refuse its protection.
7. To collect taxes authorized by the Sharī'a without resorting to extortion.
8. To regularly allot allowances and stipends from the treasury to those entitled to receive them.
9. To appoint honest and trustworthy officials to the treasury and other government posts.
10. To personally supervise governmental and religious activities.[39]

On the whole al-Māwardī believed that the duties and functions of an imām were not only the protection of the Sharī'a; he was also called on to streamline the administration and promote public welfare (maṣalih 'āmma) by which of course was meant that of orthodox Sunnīs.

Al-Māwardī asserted that once an imām was elected he could not normally lose his title or authority and could only be deposed for the following reasons:

1. If the imām had become licentious and openly violated the Sharī'a or held such views as amounted to the abrogation of the accepted religious law.
2. Loss of physical senses or bodily organs, making the caliph disabled and incapable of personally governing the empire.
3. A blind[40] and insane candidate could neither be elected as a caliph nor could continue to rule.
4. If a counsellor or governor of the imām obtained domination over the caliph or usurped his rights he could only be tolerated as long as he adhered to Sunnī law. Should the governor or counsellor violate Sunnī law, the imām had to seek the assistance of others to oust the counsellor.[41]

The last condition was emphasized by al-Māwardī in order to rationalize the domination of the Būyid amirs over the now helpless incumbents of the caliphate. However Sunnī Ghaznavid power also proved to be ephemeral, and the burden of liberating the Sunnī caliphate from the tutelage of the Shī'ī Būyids fell to the shoulders of the Sunnī Saljūqs, who in 1055 obtained the title of sultan from Caliph al-Qā'im (1031-1075). The greatest protagonist of sultanate power was Niẓām al-Mulk Tūsī (b.1018, d.1092), vizier to the Saljuqid Sultans, Alp-Arslān (1063-1072) and Malik-Shāh I (1072-1092). The Siyāsat-Nāma which Niẓām-al Mulk completed in 1092 contained a detailed rationalization of the power of sultans and the basis of their administration. In it he stressed the point, 'a kingdom may last while there is irreligion, but it will not endure when there is oppression'.[42] His contemporary al-Ghazālī (1058-1111) advocated that the caliphate symbolized the collective unity of the Islamic Sunnī community and its historical continuity, deriving its functional and institutional authority from the Sharī'a and therefore constituting the only legitimate form of Islamic government. While he endorsed the qualifications for caliphs prescribed by earlier jurists he added that the compelling necessity for the position of imām to be filled demanded an alteration of the traditional qualifications.[43] He also noted that de facto rulers were in fact sultans, the validity of their governments depending on an oath of allegiance to the caliph. In turn the sultan was the leading member of the ahl al-ḥall wa'l-'aqd and was the constituted authority to nominate a caliph. Emphatically al-Ghazālī wrote:

> An evildoing and barbarous sultan, so long as he is supported by military force, so that he can only with difficulty be deposed and that the attempt to depose him would cause unendurable civil strife, must of necessity be left in possession and obedience must be rendered to him, exactly as obedience must be rendered to emīrs... . We consider that the Caliphate is contractually assumed by that person of the 'Abbāsid house who is charged with it, and that the function of government in the various lands is carried out by means of Sulṭāns, who owe allegiance to the Caliph .... Government in these days is a consequence solely of military power, and whosoever he may be to whom the holder of military power gives his allegiance, that person is the Caliph. And whosoever exercises independent authority, so long as he shows allegiance to the Caliph in the matter of his prerogatives of the Khuṭba and the Sikka, the same is a sultān, whose commands and judgments are valid in the several parts of the earth.[44]

In 1258 Hulāgu (1256-1265) conquered Baghdād and the farsighted 'ulama' hastily signed a ruling that 'a just infidel emperor was preferable to a believing unjust emperor'.[45] In subsequent centuries justice came to be regarded as the cornerstone of royal authority; thus Ibn Khaldūn (1333-1379) could write: 'Royal authority is an institution that is natural to mankind ... People cannot persist in a state of anarchy and without a ruler'.[46]

NOTES

1. Qur'ān, III, 26, English translation by M.M. Pickthall; The Meaning of the Glorious Koran, Mentor Book, 14th printing.

2. Qur'ān, XXXIII, 40.

3. Qur'ān, XXXVIII, 27.

4. Qur'ān, XXXVIII, 35-38.

5. W.M. Watt, Islamic Political Thought (Edinburgh, 1968), pp. 5, 130-134.

6. B. Lewis (ed.), The World of Islam (London, 1975), p. 12.

7. Richard J. McCarthy, The Theology of Al-Ash'arī (Beyrouth, 1953), pp. 115-116. Rejecting the view of those who believed that Abū Bakr was explicitly designated to be Imām (Caliph) Abu'l Ḥasan 'Alī bin Ismā'īl al-Ash'arī (b.873-74, d.935-36) says, 'For if the Apostle of God had designated Abū Bakr's Imāmate (succession) the latter could not have said, "stretch forth thy hand that I may swear allegiance to thee!"', p. 116.

8. Qur'ān, IV, 59.

9. Laura veccia Vaglieri, 'The Patriarchal and Umayyad Caliphates' in the Cambridge History of Islam, Vol. I, P.M. Holt, A.K.S. Lambton, B. Lewis, editors (Cambridge, 1970), pp. 57-58.

10. L. Caetani, Annali del' Islam (Milano, 1905-26), Vol. IX, p. 275.

11. Abū Yūsuf, Kitāb al-Kharādj (Cairo 1302/ 1884-85), p. 24.

12. Yaḥyā Ben Ādam's Kitāb al-Kharāj in A. Ben Shemesh, Taxation in Islam, Vol. I (Leiden and London, 1958), pp.65, 67.

13. Al-Bukhārī, Saḥīh II, Bāb man aḥya arḍan mawatan.

14. A. Ben Shemesh, Taxation in Islam, Vol. I, pp. 28-39.

15. F. Rosenthal, Ibn Khaldūn, The Muqaddimah (New York, 1958), Vol. I, pp. 416-17.

16. H.A.R. Gibb, An Interpretation of Islamic History (Lahore, 1957), p. 9.

17. Ṭabarī, Ta'rīkh al-rusul wa'l mulūk (Leiden, 1964), Tertia Series I, pp. 29-33.

18. F. Rosenthal, The Muqaddimah, Vol. I, pp. 428-29.

19. Encyclopaedia of Islam, Vol. I, pp. 381-83.

20. Encyclopaedia of Islam, Vol. III, p. 241.

21. Alī ibn Ḥusain, al Mas'ūdī, Murūj al-Dhahab (Paris, 1861-77); Vol. IV, pp. 268-74.

22. A theological sect which devised the speculative dogmatics in Islam. Like the Shī'īs and the Khārijīs the Mu'tazilas owed their development to the political tensions over the caliphate of 'Alī. They advocated that the caliphate of Abū Bakr was legitimate but was not based on divine revelation. Mu'tazila held a middle-of-the-road policy in regard to wars between 'Alī and his rivals, 'Ā'isha and Mu'āwiya, maintaining that one of the parties was in error, while never venturing a definite verdict. See Jāhiz of Basra (b.767-68, d.868-69); Kitāb Istihqāq al-Imāma in the Rasā'il al-Jāḥiz (Cairo, 1933), pp. 247-58.

23. H. Ritter, Studien zur Geschichte der Islamischen. Frommigkeit, 1, Hasan el-Baṣri in Der Islam XXI (1933) p. 51.

24. Encyclopaedia of Islam, Vol. III, p. 247.

25. R.A. Nicholson, Kashf al-Mahjūb by 'Alī bin 'Uthmān al-Jullābī al-Hujwirī, (London, 1967, new edition), p. 99.

26. Qur'ān, XLII, 38.

27. Abū Yūsuf, Kitāb al-Kharāj (Cairo, 1933, 2nd. ed.) pp. 116-117.

28. Qur'ān, XLIX, 369.

29. 'Abd al-Qāhir Baghdādī, Al-Farq bain al-Firaq (Cairo, n.d.), pp. 55, 61, 63-68, 82-83, 99, 313, 315.

30. Shaikh 'Alī al-Muttaqī, Kanz al-'Ummāl fi sunan al-aqwāl wa'l-af'āl (Hyderabad, India 1894-96), Vol. VI, pp. 152, 390.

31. Ibn al-Bazzāz al-Kardari, Manaqib al-Imām al-Ā'ẓam (Hyderabad, 1903), pp. 15-16.

32. Abu'l 'Alā'Maudoodi, 'Abū Ḥanīfah and Abū Yūsuf' in M.M. Sharīf; A History of Muslim Philosophy (Pakistan Philosophical Congress, 1963), Vol. I, pp. 685-89.

33. Of the twenty-one books bearing the title Kitāb al Kharāj or Kitāb Risāla fi al-Kharāj three are extant. The first of these was by Mu'āwiya bin 'Ubayd Allāh bin Yasār al-Ash'arī (d.170/760). A minister of al-Mahdī (775-785), Shemesh, writes, 'Now what is the meaning of "Kharāj", with which these twenty-one books deal? The root of this name is Aramaic "halak", and it was used in the Persian empire to denote a tax in the general sense...'. Though it is sometimes used to designate tax on landed property, as distinct from poll-tax levied on the heads of persons (Jizya), we find all Muslim authors using it also in its original meaning of a general tax... . Abū Yūsuf, Abū 'Ubayd, Qudāma, Khatīb and Yahyā (see notes) use "Tasq", "'Ushr",

"Jizya" and "Kharāj" as synonyms: Taxation in Islam, Vol. I, p. 6; Yahyā ben Adam's Kitāb al-Kharāj. Yahyā's book, written in Ma'mūn's reign (813833) is a collection of traditions surrounding the subject of land taxation.

34. Abū Yūsuf, Kitāb al-Kharāj, p. 5.

35. Abū Yūsuf, ibid., pp. 3-4, extract translated by A. Ben Shemesh, Taxation in Islam, Vol. II (Leiden and London, 1965), pp. 72-73.

36. Kitāb al-Kharāj, pp. 9, 12.

37. Ibid., pp. 14, 37, 125.

38. 'Alī ibn Muḥammad, al-Māwardī, Al Aḥkām al-Sulṭāniyya, (Cairo, 1881), p. 7.

39. Ibid., p. 16.

40. This disability was responsible for the practice of the blinding, by their rivals, of about twenty Abbāsid caliphs and a large number of sultans in order to debar them from holding the office of head of state.

41. Al-Aḥkām al-Sulṭāniyya, p. 33.

42. Hubert Darke, The Book of Government or Rules for Kings, The Siyāsat-nāma (London, 1960), p. 12.

43. Leonard Binder, 'Al-Ghazālī', in A History of Muslim Philosophy, Vol. I, pp. 782-83.

44. Ghazālī, Iḥyā' 'Ulūm al-Dīn; Vol. II, p. 124; extract translated in H. Gibb and H. Bowen; Islamic Society and the West (Oxford, reprint 1960), p. 31.

45. C.E.J. Whitting, Al-Fakhrī (London, 1947), p. 14.

46. Franz Rosenthal, Ibn Khaldūn, The Muqadimah, Vol. I, pp. 380-81.

8 ANCIENT AFRO-ASIAN KINGSHIP

Brian Colless

The oldest knowledge we have concerning kingship comes from the writings and inscriptions of the Hamitic Egyptians of the River Nile and the Sumerian and Semitic Mesopotamians of the Tigris and Euphrates Rivers. Variously called the Fertile Crescent, the Near East, or Western Asia (and though Egypt lies on the continent of Africa its language and people are Afro-Asian, belonging to the Hamito-Semitic family), this entire region has a long tradition of monarchy which extends over five millennia.[1] Here we shall focus our attention on the second millennium B.C. and on three significant civilizations, namely Mesopotamia, Egypt, and Israel. Each had a distinct type of kingship in that era: the Mesopotamian king was a human agent of the gods; the Egyptian king was a divine agent of the gods; the Israelite God was also King of Israel. In Mesopotamia the king was a mortal man; in Egypt the pharaoh was an incarnate god; in Israel the King was the eternal God Yahweh. It needs to be added that in the Israelite case, after a few centuries of absolute theocracy (the period of Moses, Joshua, and the Judges), the God-King Yahweh began to govern through an earthly king (Saul, then David and his dynasty) in the Mesopotamian manner, with considerable borrowing from the Egyptian and Canaanite styles.

Broadly speaking the cardinal functions of kingship were the same in each of these three Hamito-Semitic systems: administering law internally; waging war externally; promoting economic welfare.[2] These basic tasks are actually set forth in the prologue to the Sumerian lawcode of the Mesopotamian king Lipit-Ishtar early in the second millennium before Christ: he was "the wise shepherd" of his people who had been called by the great gods Anu and Enlil

> to establish justice in the land and to banish complaints, to turn back enmity and rebellion by the force of arms, to bring well-being to the Sumerians and Akkadians.[3]

More precisely, the following functions were ascribed to Yahweh the God-King of Israel, pharaoh the god-king of Egypt, and the gods and king of Mesopotamia:

(1) Creator	(2) Sustainer	(3) Redeemer
(4) Saviour	(5) Ruler	(6) Lawgiver
(7) Manager	(8) Designer	(9) Recorder
(10) Rewarder	(11) Arbiter	(12) Healer
(13) Teacher	(14) Mediator	

The ramifications of these roles will be explored here, in an endeavour to synthesize and systematize recent research findings in Hamitic, Semitic, and Biblical studies.[4] It must be emphasized at the outset that in the following pages the king's own view of his statuses and roles will be presented, as recorded in his own words, or in speeches of his sycophants, or in utterances attributed to deities.

1. CREATOR

The creation of the universe seems a massive task for an earthly king to undertake, especially since the world is already in existence when he comes on the scene. In Israel, of course, this was no problem, because Israel's King was the eternal God Yahweh, and he was clearly the one who had made the heavens and the earth "in the beginning" (Genesis 1-2).

In Egypt likewise the gods were credited with constructing the universe, but, as we shall see, the pharaohs also had a part to play in the process. Naturally the sun-god is prominent in creation, variously appearing as Re, Khepri, or Atum, and in this respect he is the prototype of the pharaoh. Thutmose III, for example, occupied "the throne of Atum" and carried out the divine creator's role: on the one hand he achieved "what had not been done since the time of Re" (the commencement of time), and on the other hand he restored conditions "as they were in the beginning".[5] This paradox can be resolved by invoking the Egyptians' static view of the universe, whereby the original world order was eternally normative, and thus any seeming innovations were in fact merely manifestations of things implicit in the divine plan from the beginning. The pharaoh's creative function, like that of the sun-god, was regarded as a continuous round of producing cosmos out of chaos.[6] And as the successor of Re on the throne of Egypt, the pharaoh was in some mysterious way the creator of the Egyptians,[7] "the begetter who creates the people".[8]

Turning now to Mesopotamia, in the eighteenth century B.C. we find King Hammurabi of Babylon designated as "creator of the land"; furthermore, in the prologue to his celebrated lawcode he appears as one who "gives life", whom the gods made "to rise like the sun over the black-headed people and to light up the land", he being "the powerful king, the sun (or sun-god) of Babylon, who causes light to go forth over the lands of Sumer and Akkad".[9] This does not seem to indicate the same kind of relationship between Hammurabi and the Babylonian sun-god Shamash as existed between the Egyptian Re and the pharaoh.[10] Nor can we heap up overwhelming evidence for the Mesopotamian king's creatorship, for although as "King of the Land" and "King of the Four Quarters" he was the earthly ruler of Creation, the gods alone were generally held to be the creators of the universe and the human race.[11] Nevertheless, it is important to notice that the sovereign took a leading part in the New Year Festival, when chaos was reduced to order through ritual enactment of the Babylonian Epic of Creation (Enuma Elish), whereby Marduk, king of the gods, won his primeval victory over the dragon Tiamat once more.[12]

2. SUSTAINER

In Mesopotamia it was acknowledged that "the king is he who maintains the life of his country".[13] Accordingly, on the stele that bears his laws, Hammurabi is praised as "the shepherd ... who makes affluence and plenty abound, who provides in abundance ..., the one who extended the cultivated land ..., who stores up grain".[14] All these life-sustaining activities are also attributed to Marduk, the God-King of the Babylonian pantheon;[15] and when Hammurabi calls himself "god among kings" and "the sun of Babylon" in this same context, it would seem that he is claiming to be, like Marduk, a solar deity of fertility. Nevertheless it is better to refrain from drawing this conclusion and accept the view that the Mesopotamian ruler was never regarded as an incarnation of the sun-god; and no matter how superhuman his powers may have been, plenteous abundance in nature and healthful prosperity among mankind were only signs that he had served the gods with the obedience and faithfulness required of him as their chosen representative, whereas, it is claimed, the Egyptian pharaoh was able to dispense "life, prosperity, and health" by his own divine sovereignty.[16]

This contrast needs to be made, even though at times the line of separation appears very thin indeed. The benediction "Life! Prosperity! Health!" had to be constantly pronounced on the pharaoh himself by those who surrounded him; moreover, the frequent epithet accorded to him, di ankh, can be understood either as "endowed with life" or as "giver of life".[17] Both ideas are in fact applicable, for "maintenance of life" or "giving life" was "the usual term applied to that peculiar influence exercised by the gods over the king and by the king over his subjects".[18]

Whatever fine distinctions are made, the fact remains that in both Egypt and Mesopotamia gods and kings alike provided sustenance for their people. And it is interesting to see Yahweh of Israel exploiting the granaries of Egypt to keep his people alive in the days of his (and the pharaoh's) faithful servant Joseph (Genesis 41:53-57; 45:4-8; 50:19-21), and subsequently, in the wilderness, sending them bread and fowl from heaven (Exodus 16; Numbers 11). "Yahweh is my shepherd, I shall not want," sang the grateful Israelite, "he makes me lie down in green pastures. He leads me beside still waters; he restores my life.... Thou preparest a table before me ..., my cup overflows; ... and I shall dwell in the house of Yahweh forever" (Psalm 23). And as an Egyptian father similarly pointed out to his children, with reference to King Amenemhet III:

> He gives food to those who are in his service,
> And he supplies those who tread his path.
> The king is a ka (vital force),
> And (the command of) his mouth is increase (of provisions).[19]

3. REDEEMER

The word "redeemer" has acquired a theological aura around it and therefore seems more appropriate to Yahweh "the King of Israel and his Redeemer" (Isaiah 44:6) than to the rulers of ancient Egypt and Mesopotamia. Nevertheless kings were sometimes called upon to practise redemption in a literal sense, by ransoming prisoners of war or releasing slaves and prisoners. Certainly a statement on liberation from oppression and slavery is contained in the prologue to the Sumerian lawcode of Lipit-Ishtar, though unfortunately the text is damaged: "I procured ... the freedom of the sons and daughters of ... Sumer and Akkad upon whom ... slaveship ... had been imposed".[20] And in an Egyptian hymn of joy at the accession of Ramses IV there is mention of amnesty and liberation: "They who were fled have come back to their towns; they who were hidden have come forth again... . They who were in prison are set free; they who were fettered are in joy".[21]

In Israelite family custom the redeemer (go'el) was the kinsman who protected and defended the rights and interests of the individual and the group. One of his functions was to redeem a near relative from slavery (Leviticus 25:47-49). The term redeemer is applied to Yahweh, for at the Exodus he ransomed and rescued Israel from servitude and oppression in Egypt: "I am Yahweh, and I will release you from the burdens of the Egyptians and deliver you from their bondage; I will redeem you with an outstretched arm and with great acts of judgement" (Exodus 6:6). "You shall say to Pharaoh: Thus says Yahweh, Israel is my first-born son, and I say to you, release my son so that he may serve me" (Exodus 4:22-23).

It is known that Mesopotamian kings made a practice of bringing in social reforms at the beginning of their reign: they issued remissive proclamations, termed acts of mīsharum (equity), thereby granting release from slavery and debt to needy members of the population.[22] This bears a close likeness to the situation in the accession hymn to Ramses IV of Egypt, quoted above. It also finds a parallel in the redemption of Israel by Yahweh at the Exodus; and an Israelite hymn-writer understood the kingship of Yahweh in this light: "Yahweh reigns... . He will judge the peoples with equity" (Psalm 96:10).

4. SAVIOUR

The term "saviour", like "redeemer", sounds more religious than political; and yet even in the Bible the Hebrew word for "save" (yasha') has warlike connotations, involving victory over enemies and occupation of territory. As Divine Saviour Yahweh is called upon to play a warrior's role, fighting for the Israelites against their foes, and establishing his chosen nation in the land of Canaan (Exodus 14; Deuteronomy 31:3-6).

> Yahweh is my strength and my song
> and he has been my salvation....
> Yahweh is a man of war,
> Yahweh is his name.
> Pharaoh's chariots and army
> he has hurled into the sea.

So sang Moses and Israel, it is said, after their God's signal victory over the Egyptians at the Sea of Reeds at the time of the Exodus (Ex. 15: 2-4). "Stand firm and watch the salvation (or victory) of Yahweh, which he will win for you today... . Yahweh will fight for you, and you will only have to stand still", Moses had declared (Ex. 14: 13-14).

It is widely held that the pharaoh who was worsted in this clash was Ramses II, and this divine warrior-king had allegedly performed a similar single-handed feat in a battle with the Hittites, at Qadesh in Syria. He too was afterwards praised by his men as one "who saves his army on the day of fighting",[23] and he had likewise called out to his hosts: "Stand firm, steady your hearts, my army, that you may behold my victory, I being alone".[24] In the event, the god Amon-Re was given the ultimate glory for this military success, for Ramses goes on to say "Amon will be my protector" and "Amon has given me his victory, no infantry being with me and no chariotry". Nevertheless the comparison between this pharaoh and Yahweh is striking, even down to the details of their respective exploits.[25]

For one thing, Ramses dealt with the Hittites in the same way as Yahweh treated the Egyptians (Ex. 15: 4, cited above): "he hurled them headlong, one upon the other, into the waters of the Orontes".[26] Furthermore, the divinity of both these kings brought the same sort of panic on the enemy, such that the Hittites reportedly exclaimed, "He is no man who is in our midst, but Sutekh great of strength, Ba'al in person...; let us come quickly and flee before him, and seek for ourselves life";[27] while the Egyptians, in their encounter with Yahweh, cried out in dismay, "Let us flee away from Israel, since Yahweh is fighting for them against Egypt" (Ex. 14: 25).

The pattern was similar in Mesopotamian warfare. In the case of Assyrian kings, the discomfiture of the enemy was generally attributed to their god Ashur. As witness we may call Shalmaneser III (ninth century B.C.), who affirmed: "The terror and the glamor of Ashur my lord, overwhelmed them ... and they dispersed".[28] But sometimes we find them extolling their own might and majesty, as when Sennacherib of the eighth century boasted: "Luli, king of Sidon, whom the terror-inspiring glamor of my lordship had overwhelmed, fled far overseas".[29] For a Babylonian example we may take Hammurabi: although it is stated in one place that he "called up his army, marched against Rim-Sin, king of Ur, and personally conquered Ur and Larsa",[30] elsewhere the proper procedure is set forth: "(Encouraged) by an oracle (given) by Anu and Enlil who advance in front of his army, and through the mighty power which the great gods had given to him, he was a match for the army of Emutbal and its king Rim-Sin".[31] Immediately after this Hammurabi is significantly styled "the hero who proclaims the triumphs of Marduk".

The wars of Yahweh followed the same pattern as elsewhere in the Near East.[32] As the gods of Egypt and Mesopotamia, represented by their standards, preceded the king and his army on their campaigns, so Yahweh as both God and King led the hosts of Israel through Sinai into Canaan, striking terror into his antagonists in every encounter and granting possession of Canaanite territory to the Israelite tribes. His victories, or acts of salvation, brought peace and security, and it is surely significant that the Hebrew root for "save" (yasha') is cognate with Arabic wasi'a, "be spacious", and therefore has strong overtones of giving room and relieving anxiety.[33]

The idea of security and room to move being restored to the dominions of the king is found in Egyptian texts. "And so it was that [after the Battle of Qadesh] if a man or a woman proceeded on their mission to Djahi [Syria-Palestine], they could reach the land of Hatti without fear around about their hearts, because of the greatness of the victories of his majesty" [Ramses II].[34] Similarly,

Hammurabi was "the saviour of his people from distress, who establishes in security their portion in the midst of Babylon".[35]

As the prophet Zephaniah sang to Israel in the seventh century B.C (3: 15-17):

> Yahweh the King of Israel is in your midst,
> you shall fear evil no more....
> Have no fear, Zion,
> let not your hands fall slack,
> Yahweh your God is in your midst,
> a Warrior who saves you.

5. RULER

We have now come to the very core of kingship: the sovereign rule that the king bears over his subjects or vassals. Here the basic motif or rôle appears to be "election"; yet not so much election of the king by his people as election of his people or vassals by the king. If there is an election to choose the king, it will of course be the gods who hold it.

This idea of the king as the chosen representative of the gods is certainly true of Mesopotamia, as Esarhaddon of Assyria shows when he says "In the gladness of their hearts the gods, lifting their eyes to me, had chosen me to be truly and rightly king";[36] or when he styles himself "Esarhaddon, great king, legitimate king, king of the world, king of Assyria, regent of Babylon, king of Sumer and Akkad, king of the four rims (of the earth), the true shepherd, favourite of the great gods, whom Ashur, Shamash, Bel and Nabu, the Ishtar of Nineveh and the Ishtar of Arbela have pronounced king of Assyria ever since he was a youngster".[37] For his part, Hammurabi indicates at the beginning of his lawcode that the supreme gods Anu and Enlil had named Marduk as divine king of Babylon and Hammurabi as the earthly ruler. Then in his epilogue he avers: "I, Hammurabi, the perfect king, was not careless or neglectful of the black-headed people, whom Enlil had presented to me, and whose shepherding Marduk had committed to me".[38] It is therefore not the people who elect the king but their gods. The nation and its leaders merely take an oath of allegiance.[39]

It was the practice of the Egyptian, Mesopotamian, and Hittite imperial suzerain to impose a treaty on his vassals, whereby they owed their overlord loyalty, tribute, and service, in return for his protection. This was the model for the covenant between Yahweh and Israel at Mount Sinai (Exodus 19-24): the "Ten Commandments" demanding undivided allegiance and obedient service correspond to the stipulations laid down in suzerain-vassal treaties.[40] When Israel came to appoint earthly regents as representatives of Yahweh, the covenant was made in a triangular way between God, king, and nation, as may be seen in the case of the seven-year old Jehoash (2 Kings 11): he was crowned and anointed by Jehoiada the priest, was proclaimed king by public acclamation (11:11), and a covenant was made by the priest "between Yahweh and the king and the people, that they should be Yahweh's people" (11:17).

It does not seem possible to find evidence for all fourteen of our kingship roles being applied to the earthly ruler in ancient Israel. This may be because the Old Testament contains only writings which emphasized the kingship of Yahweh, whereas some of the kings of Israel and Judah may well have seen themselves cast in the same mould as the mighty pharaohs. Nevertheless a number of the hymns in the Psalter are recognized as "royal psalms", involving the earthly king. Psalm 2, for example, has "the kings of the earth" rising up "against Yahweh and his anointed"; Yahweh laughs in derision and says "I have set my king on Zion, my holy hill" (in Jerusalem) and "You are my son, I have begotten you today". This striking claim to Divine parentage for the king is offset by the fact that the whole of Israel was likewise held to be the son of Yahweh, "the Rock" that "begot" and "bore" Yeshurun (Israel) (Deuteronomy 32:18). However, this vivid language indicates Divine adoption rather than Divine procreation.[41]

In the preamble to his laws, Hammurabi of Babylon is called variously son of the moon god Sin, son of (the grain god) Dagan, and brother of the god Zababa (and thus "a son of Enlil").[42] Ashurbanipal of Assyria named as his mother not only the goddess Ninlil but also Belit of Nineveh and Ishtar of Arbela; moreover he stated in one place that he, the eldest prince in the line of succession to the throne, was the offspring of Ashur and Belit and that Ashur and Sin had formed him "in his mother's womb, for the rulership of Assyria". Yet it seems that the many cases where a Mesopotamian king is called the "son" of a god or goddess do not indicate divinity but merely divine election.[43]

In Egypt, by contrast, divinity in some sense was customarily attributed to the pharaohs. A striking reference occurs at the beginning of a text of Ramses II:

> Utterance of Ptah-Tatenen, of lofty plumes and ready horns, begetter of the gods, to his son, his beloved, firstborn of his body, the divine god, sovereign of the gods, great in royal jubilees like Tatenen, King Ramses II, given life... . I am thy father who begat thee as the gods... . I make thy heart divine like me, I chose thee.[44]

Here we have an assertion of the king's divinity as well as his election by the gods; and with regard to the pharaoh's role of ruler, Ptah is represented as saying further:

> I have set thee as everlasting king, ruler established forever.... I have given to thee the divine office, that thou mayest rule the Two Lands like the King of Upper and Lower Egypt.[45]

In Egypt there was a covenant between ruler and vassal as the wise father reminded his children: "Be scrupulous in the oath to him, that you may be free from a taint of disloyalty".[46]

6. LAWGIVER

It is a well-known fact that Hammurabi of Babylon issued a code of laws on an impressive stone column, and this has made him the foremost example of the ancient West Asian legislator-king. Early in the prologue to his laws he states that the gods (at this point naming in particular Anu and Enlil) had chosen him to make justice shine in the land";[47] and in the epilogue he declares, "I, Hammurabi, am the king of justice, to whom Shamash committed law".[48] The sun-god Shamash is pictured with Hammurabi at the top of the famous stele, and as the all-seeing eye of heaven Shamash is naturally concerned with justice in the world.[49]

In Egypt it was the moon-god Thoth who had the major interest in this field: he was "the lord of the laws", "the legislator in heaven and on earth",[50] and thus the model for the pharaoh, of whom it was said "he lays down laws like Thoth" and "speaks justice like Thoth".[51] Menes, the first king of Egypt, was held to have received his laws from Thoth.[52]

The Israelites hailed Yahweh as being at once their judge, lawgiver, and king (Isaiah 32:22). Yahweh handed down his laws or ordinances through Moses (Exodus 21:1), who is also accorded the title "lawgiver".[53] Israel's first code of laws is found in Exodus 21-23, where it appears to form part of the covenant stipulations laid down by Yahweh, since Moses presents "all the words of Yahweh and all the ordinances" before the people for acceptance with their oath of allegiance (Exodus 26:3).[54]

The recording and promulgating of law collections was an established practice in the world of the Bible, as the many Sumerian, Akkadian, Hittite, and Hebrew codifications indicate. Surprisingly, however, not a single law-code has survived from Egypt, although edicts of various pharaohs concerning specific circumstances are extant; but this can not lead us to the conclusion that the Egyptian kings ruled solely by decree, for it is only by an unfortunate accident that all the rolls of papyrus or leather containing the laws of the Egyptians have perished.[55]

7. MANAGER

Administration of the realm was the king's responsibility, though naturally he had the assistance of a trained bureaucracy. From the records and correspondence of Hammurabi and his dynasty we learn that the Mesopotamian ruler supervised the collection of taxes and rents, the care of herds and lands, the maintenance and extension of canals, the transport of timber and other commodities, the employment of labour, and the regulating of the calendar.[56] Hammurabi explicitly styles himself as "the administrator" in the prologue to his laws, as also "director of the temple of Emah".[57] So the king was likewise the manager of the gods' earthly estates.

In Egypt the brief reign of Tutankhamen saw "his majesty in his palace ... conducting the affairs of this land and the daily needs of the Two Banks" and this rôle included "making monuments for the gods..., building their sanctuaries anew..., setting for them divine offerings as a regular daily observance..., inducting priests and prophets..., consecrating male and female slaves, women singers and dancers...".[58] In fact it was the pharaoh's deputy, the vizier, who controlled the affairs of Egypt, in his capacity of "Steward of the Whole Land", but important administrative decisions were certainly submitted for the king's approval.[59]

Similarly, in Israel's theocracy Moses was virtually the vizier of Yahweh, the God and King of Israel. As Divine Lord, Yahweh was owner of the land of Israel and required tithes and offerings from his people; he managed his estates with the assistance of judges, priests, prophets, scribes, and workmen. During the reign of David and Solomon, in the tenth century B.C., Israel began to look like the rest of the kingdoms of its era, with a monarch sitting in his capital city (Jerusalem) and administering affairs of church and state.

Dossiers of administrative directions to the personnel of palace and temple are attested for the whole ancient Near East. An interesting collection of royal instructions to officers, craftsmen, priests, and servants has survived from the empire of the Hittites.[60] We also know of prescriptions for officials, priests, soldiers, and workers in Egypt.[61] From Mesopotamia we have Middle Assyrian documents on the duties of royal harem officials, and a text defining the responsibilities of the mayor of the city-state Nuzi.[62]

In the case of Israel, we find Yahweh giving directions through Moses (Exodus 25:1 - 31:11) on the constructing, furnishing, staffing, and daily routine of the Tabernacle, the cult centre of itinerant Israel and in a sense the house or portable palace of Yahweh (29:45, "I will dwell among the people of Israel"). Aaron and his sons were to be consecrated to the priesthood and to take charge of the service of Yahweh (27:20 - 29:44), while Bezalel and Oholiab would be the artistic directors (31:1-11).

8. DESIGNER

Not only did kings build temples and cities, they were also credited with designing them, or else with having received the architectural plans from the gods. Thus Hammurabi described himself as "the designer of the temple of Ebabbar ... the one who rebuilt Ebabbar for Shamash ... who laid out the plans for Kesh";[63] while Gudea of Lagash had the specifications revealed to him for the temple of the god Ningirsu that he intended to rebuild.[64]

In Egypt the pharaoh characteristically built "according to the design of his own heart", as may be seen in Queen Hatshepsut's words inscribed on a temple she rebuilt: "I have done this according to the design of my heart ... I have restored that which was in ruins".[65] At the same time, however, it could be said: "It was according to the ancient plan. Never was done the like since the beginning".[66] This paradox would have to be resolved in the same way as in the case of the pharaoh's creator rôle, noted above.[67]

In theory, then, the pharaoh was his own architect, but once again we find him authorizing a deputy to oversee the work. The procedure is set forth in a building inscription of Sesostris I of the twentieth century B.C.[68] The king summons his court together and announces his plan to erect a temple; this is applauded by the courtiers in a responding speech; then the king turns to his chief architect and commits the execution of the plan to him: "It is your counsel that carries out all the works that my majesty desires to bring about ... order the workmen to do according to your design." Finally the king directs the founding ceremony, in which he is imagined as working with the goddess Seshat in the ritual of "the stretching of the cord" on the building site.

We should note, however, the existence of ancient Egyptian manuals on temple construction: included in a register of books kept in the library of the late Ptolemaic temple at Edfu was one entitled "Book on the plan of the temple", and its reputed author was the ancient vizier Imhotep, architect of the early Zoser complex of pyramids.[69]

Yahweh was the designer of his own sanctuaries, for he is said to have handed down to Moses a pattern for the Tabernacle and its furnishings (Exodus 25:9) and a plan of the Jerusalem Temple to David (I Chronicles 28:11-19).[70]

9. RECORDER

The literate societies of the ancient world were accustomed to keeping written records: the king made decisions and his scribe recorded them in writing. A similar situation applied in the heavenly realm, for in Mesopotamia we find Marduk's son Nabu acting as divine recorder "who organizes the whole of heaven and earth, who directs everything, who ordains kingship",[71] while in Egypt it was the ibis-headed Thoth who carried out this function.[72]

Names and decrees were the main things preserved in records. A useful example is found in the Bible, originating from the chancellery of the Persian Empire: "Memorandum. In the first year of Cyrus the King, Cyrus the King issued a decree: Concerning the house of God at Jerusalem, let the house be rebuilt...." (Ezra 6:2-5). In like manner Yahweh said to his scribe Moses: "Write this down as a record in a book....: I will completely erase the memory of Amalek from under heaven" (Exodus 17:14).

In Egypt the vizier was ordered by the king to keep records and documents. In this connection we hear of "the criminal docket" (or register of malefactors), "property-lists" (or wills), "depositions", "petitions in writing", "name records", "edicts", "reports", and so on. These appear in the instructions from the pharaoh to the vizier.[73] Scribes carried out this work of recording and their patron deity was Thoth, the secretary of the sun-god Re. With the assistance of the goddess Sheshat, Thoth recorded the number of years allotted to the pharaoh. He also played a major part in the judgement of the dead as recorder of the verdict.[74]

It thus appears that the recorder's rôle was chiefly one of ordination, and this involved the issuing of edicts and the determining of destinies (as Nabu was wont to do at the New Year Festival in Mesopotamia). The recording of fates sometimes meant that Nabu actually blotted out or erased certain names from his registers, as stated in the cursing section of a treaty drawn up by Esarhaddon of Assyria: "May Nabu, who holds the tablets of fate of the gods, erase your name and make your descendants disappear from the land".[75] This is what Yahweh intended for the Amalekites in the edict cited above, and as he says elsewhere to Moses (Exodus 32:33): "Whoever has sinned against me, him will I blot out of my book". This would be a convenient point to mention that in Egypt the names of Pharaoh's actual or potential foes were inscribed on pots and then smashed, in a ritual of magical execration.[76]

10. REWARDER

Loyal servants of the king expected to be rewarded for their service, just as the disloyal received their deserts. In the parable of the talents, Jesus has a lord saying "Well done, you good and faithful servant" to the two stewards who had invested his money wisely for him, but words of rebuke and dismissal to the lazy one who had betrayed his trust (Matthew 25:14-30). The rewarder's rôle, it should be noted, is one of retribution, either for good or for ill.

The ancient Near Eastern king would make royal grants in return for (or as an inducement to) faithful service. To war veterans or to vassal kings the ruler would give a grant of land. A boundary marker inscribed with details of the grant would usually be set up on the site. Gifts would be presented to diligent officials as an act of royal benevolence.[77] An Assyrian grant of Ashurbanipal to his servant Baltaya characterizes the recipient as one who served his master with his whole heart, while the king "returns kindness to the one who serves in obedience and keeps his royal command".[78] Such language finds parallels in Yahweh's bestowal of the promised land on Abraham and his descendants as a reward for Abraham's faithfulness (Genesis 15 and 17); and his establishing of a "house" or dynasty for David (2 Samuel 7:15-16; 1 Kings 3:6).

Another form of royal grant in Egypt and Mesopotamia was the charter of immunity, whereby a temple was granted exemption from civil obligations, such as taxation and forced labour.[79] In Israel the Levites were placed in a position of priestly privilege, to serve Yahweh at the Tabernacle and the Temple (Numbers 18).

11. ARBITER

The royal role of arbitration is aptly illustrated by the famous case of the two harlots who brought their case of disputed ownership of an infant to King Solomon (I Kings 3:16-28). In Israel and Mesopotamia it was customary for the king to sit in the city gate to dispense justice.[80] In Egypt every one of the pharaoh's subjects had the right to appeal to him, but as in other administrative matters his vizier deputized for him; as Chief Justice the vizier attended to lawsuits and petitions.[81] Moses stood in the same relationship to Yahweh, and like the Egyptian vizier he had a staff of subordinate magistrates (Exodus 18:13-23).

In the Biblical setting petitions presented directly to Yahweh are the basis for the Judeo-Christian practice of prayer. This kind of prayerful lawsuit was often a call for "vindication" in the face of oppressors (e.g. Jeremiah 11:20): "O Yahweh of Hosts, a just judge..., let me see your vindication against them, for to you I have submitted my lawsuit". Vindication meant taking physical action by force when an innocent party was threatened or wronged. Numerous examples of such pleas are contained in the Amarna correspondence in which Canaanite vassal-kings seek military assistance from Pharaoh Akhnaten to deliver them from the attacks of their enemies. These fall into the category of "defensive vindication".[82]

But there were times when the king himself had to sue for breach of contract. In this case we should speak of "punitive vindication". Thus in Deuteronomy 32 we find Yahweh threatening to issue a lawsuit against his people Israel for breaking the covenant through disobedience and disloyalty. This is an example of the "covenant lawsuit" by means of which the prophets of Yahweh indicted Israel for transgression of the covenant (e.g. Isaiah 1:1-20; Jeremiah 2:1-37; Micah 6:1-8). In such situations Yahweh was both plaintiff (the offended party) and judge (who pronounced judgement and gained redress for the breach of covenant). "I will smite you sevenfold for your sins," he says; "I will bring a sword upon you, which will execute vindication of the covenant" (Leviticus 26:24-25).

When we look at the Mesopotamian counterpart of this action we see why Yahweh is both plaintiff and judge: because he is both King and God he is playing the rôle of the offended suzerain on the one hand and on the other hand the rôle of the god of justice. When treaties were made between kings (whether treaties of parity with allies, or of suzerainty with vassals) the gods were called to witness the oathtaking ceremony, and they were expected to activate the curses written into the contract if it was ever broken. In particular the Mesopotamian sun-deity Shamash, whose department was justice, intervened to grant legal redress and vindication to the plaintiff by declaring war on the guilty transgressor and decreeing his defeat in the ensuing battle (which therefore amounted to a kind of trial by ordeal). Accordingly, in "The Epic of Tukulti-Ninurta", we observe the Assyrian king Tukulti-Ninurta I (1244-1208 B.C.) issuing a formal prosecution against a treaty violator, namely Kastiliash, the Kassite king of Babylonia. The sun-god Shamash is invoked to pass judgement on the offender; this done, the Mesopotamian gods declare war on him and fight on Assyria's behalf in a vengeful exercise designed to restore the order of justice.[83]

In Egypt the pharaoh himself was often found venting his wrath against rebellious vassals at home and abroad. The wise father who exhorted his children to be scrupulous in their oath to Amenemhet III added a warning: "He is Sekhmet (a fierce lion-goddess) against him who transgresses his command; he whom he hates will bear woes".[84]

12. HEALER

The power of "the king's touch" as a healing agent is known throughout world history.[85] However, it was usual for Egyptian and Mesopotamian kings to have physicians attached to their court rather than to function as physicians themselves.

Healing was the province of many Hamito-Semitic gods, and Yahweh was certainly thought to be concerned with health. At the Exodus the God of Israel declared (Exodus 15:26): "... I will inflict none of the diseases on you that I inflicted on Egypt, for I am Yahweh your Healer". In a treaty-curse of the Assyrian king Esarhaddon we meet a Mesopotamian goddess of healing: "May Gula, the great physician, put illness, weariness, and an unhealing sore in your body".[86]

In Egypt the deity Thoth was the patron of physicians and supervisor of their House of Life in which knowledge of medicine and magic was conserved.[87] Amon-Re is hailed in a hymn as, among many other things, divine physician; he is praised as a dissolver of evils and a dispeller of ailments, who restores eyesight without having recourse to remedies.[88] The god Ptah was considered to have endowed Ramses II with "health and joy of heart".[89]

Ancient medical observations and prescriptions have been preserved on Egyptian papyri and Akkadian clay tablets.[90] The Israelite medical code is found in Leviticus, which has elaborate instructions on hygiene and sacrifices aimed at restoring a wholesome relationship between man and God.

13. TEACHER

Education was a vital concept in the ancient Near East and schools were regularly attached to the palace and the temple.[91] As both these establishments required ethically and technically trained officers, it was in the king's interest to promote public instruction. In Egypt the pharaohs themselves were highly educated; some are credited with composing a "book of instruction", or else directing their vizier to produce one. Such are "The Instruction of King Amenemhet" and "The Instruction of the Vizier Ptah-hotep".[92] Mesopotamia had its text books and school literature too, and its kings were given to boasting of their literacy and proficiency in the scribal art.

In the Bible, although the Book of Deuteronomy exhibits aspects of the covenant and lawcode forms, its ultimate form is that of "book of instruction" (31:24-26) presented by the Divine King of Yahweh to his "son" Israel through his aged "vizier" Moses.[93]

14. MEDIATOR

The king stood in an intermediary position between his people and the gods, a mediator between the human and the divine. In Mesopotamia the later Assyrian kings boasted of their priestly rôle. Adad-Nirari III (810-783), for example, called himself "high priest, tireless caretaker of the temple Esarra, who keeps up the rites of the sanctuary".[94] In Egypt it was the king's task to lead the daily cult in all the temples of the land, an impossibility even for a divine pharaoh. As might be expected he frequently deputized this rôle. Nevertheless there were pictures on the sanctuary walls showing the pharaoh performing the rituals, and the officiating priest (as at the Theban temple of Amon) would say: "I am the priest; it is the king who has sent me to behold the god".[95] The same was true of Assyrian kings and their priests.[96]

In the words of Henri Frankfort the ancient Near Eastern king was "instrumental in the integration of society and nature", for his "principal task lay in the maintenance of the harmony with the gods in nature".[97] As he then points out, the earthly king of Israel could not take this sacerdotal function upon himself, for he was certainly not the leader in the cult, although he did create the conditions that made the worship of God possible.[98] And so King Uzziah (Azariah) of Judah was stricken with leprosy as a punishment for offering up incense to Yahweh in the Jerusalem temple, since this was the sacred prerogative of "the priests, the sons of Aaron" (2 Chronicles 26: 16-21).

Of course it would be nonsense to apply the terms "priest", "mediator", or "intermediary" to the God Yahweh. Aaron was his high priest; and Moses also acted as mediator on occasions, notably after the apostasy of Israel in the Golden Calf episode (Exodus 32-33). The kings of West Asia might likewise appeal to their gods on behalf of their subjects, and even undergo rites of penitence to conciliate the gods,[99] but their role of bridegroom to a goddess in fertility rituals[100] was abhorrent to Yahweh himself and considered an abomination in his eyes if practised in any form in Israel. Such sexual rites would imply that the divine was immanent in nature; but Israel believed that Yahweh transcended nature, as universal King and Lord of creation (Psalm 95-96):

> For Yahweh is a great God,
> a great King over all gods;
> the ends of the earth are in his hands,
> and the heights of the hills are his also;
> the sea is his, he is the one who made it,
> and likewise the dry land, formed by his hands.
> ... for all the gods of the nations are idols,
> but Yahweh constructed the heavens.

Moses and his successors the prophets were always there to remind Israel of this fundamental doctrine.

CONCLUSION

These were the beginnings of kingship in Africa and Asia. For the ancients themselves the archetype of kingship was with the supreme gods in heaven. For a modern scientific view an analogical model for monarchy may be found in the insect world, notably in the bee hive, the termite colony, and the camps of soldier ants on the march. The queen termite, for example, is protected and pampered by her subjects so as to enable her to carry out her primary function of giving life to them all: without her the whole kingdom will die. This was likewise the cardinal task of the ancient Afro-Asian monarch, to impart life to the people as their creator and sustainer. Indeed, in certain African kingdoms of more recent times the king has lived in seclusion, concentrating on his role as divine life-giver; such a king would leave administration to others and he would certainly not go out to war, even though all his nation's victories would be attributed to his personal valour.[101] This might sometimes have been the case in ancient Egypt, the probable source of later African kingship. Nevertheless it would be hard to deny that Pharaoh Ramses II took part in the Battle of Qadesh in the thirteenth century B.C., even though we reject his claim to have defeated the Hittite army single-handedly. And who could doubt that the Assyrian Sennacherib and the Babylonian Nebuchadnezzar were themselves in attendance at their respective sieges of Jerusalem (II Kings 18-19 and 24-25)?

We have here isolated fourteen typical kingship roles. Basically these can be reduced to four main concerns: law, war, welfare, worship. All of these are seen in a four-thousand-year-old statement of the Mesopotamian King Lipit-Ishtar, cited in our opening section above. These judicial, military, managerial, and sacerdotal rôles constitute a pattern for Afro-Asian royalty in succeeding millennia, a model to be copied or modified at various times and in various places, and in modern times in most places to be completely rejected.

NOTES

1. General works on this subject are S.H. Hooke (ed.), Myth, Ritual, and Kingship: Essays on the Theory and Practice of Kingship in the Ancient Near East and in Israel (Oxford, 1958); C.J. Gadd, Ideas of Divine Rule in the Ancient Near East, Schweich Lectures 1945 (London, 1948); The Sacral Kingship: Contributions to the Central Theme of the VIIth International Congress for the History of Religions, Rome, April 1955 (Leiden, 1959); Henri Frankfort, Kingship and the Gods: A Study of Ancient Near Eastern Religion as the Integration of Society and Nature (Chicago, 1948); Ivan Engnell, Studies in Divine Kingship in the Ancient Near East, 1st. Edn. (Uppsala, 1943), 2nd. Edn. (Oxford, 1967). Engnell goes too far in attributing divinity to kings; Georges Posener, De la divinité du Pharaon, Cahiers de la Société Asiatique, XV (Paris, 1960), plays down divine kingship even in Egypt. Note that ancient Egyptian culture was neither truly Hamitic nor Semitic, as pointed out by Frankfort, KAG, 348, n.4. Certainly the Egyptians distinguished themselves from the "Asiatics" of their empire.

2. This is affirmed by George E. Mendenhall, TTG, 29 (in his chapter on "Early Israel as the Kingdom of Yahweh", 1-31): "Yahweh was the one who exclusively exercised the classic functions of the king, as described in the prologue to the Code of Hammurabi and in other early codes as well ... The administration of law internally, the waging of war, and the economic well-being of the diverse population are here already the three prime functions of the king, and they correspond to the modern functions of a state as a monopoly of force."

3. ANET, 159; also cited by Mendenhall, TTG, 29.

4. This is therefore a preliminary endeavour to summarize a vast subject in a way that has never been attempted before. Our chief representatives for Egypt and Mesopotamia will be the thirteenth-century Pharaoh Ramses II (or Ramesses II) and Babylon's King Hammurabi (or Hammurapi) of the eighteenth century before Christ. However, we may sometimes need to look to other kings for illustrations of particular rôles, and we shall not always confine the search to the second millennium B.C. It must be admitted, moreover, that the fourteen terms used for the performers of each rôle have not been investigated thoroughly to determine whether they have a counterpart in the language of each region

(Egyptian, Akkadian, Hebrew). Nevertheless it is hoped that the English designations will cover adequately the complex of terms, ideals, and actions that make up each of the rôles identified here.

Note that the translations of excerpts from the Bible are my own. Minor alterations have sometimes been made to the translations of Egyptian and Mesopotamian extracts (usually from ARE and ANET, but sometimes as cited by other authors when no other edition or translation of the text is available to me).

5. Frankfort, KAG, 148-149. See also ARE, III, 175-182, esp. par. 411, for a similar statement by Ramses II.

6. KAG, 149-150. Cf the "restoration inscription" of Tutankhamen, who "drove out disorder from the Two Lands ... and the land is as it was at the first time" (Morenz, ER, 114, in preference to J.A. Wilson's version in ANET, 251).

7. Frankfort, KAG, 148.

8. ANET, 431.

9. ANET, 164-165.

10. Frankfort, KAG, 307-309.

11. KAG, 227-228; these titles were also applied to the gods Anu, Enlil, and Shamash (Utu).

12. KAG, 326-330.

13. Cited by Frankfort, 309 (and 408, n.61) from Oxford Editions of Cuneiform Texts, III, 11.

14. ANET, 164-165.

15. Engnell, Studies (see n.1 above), 191-193, has a useful comparative table of titles shared by gods and kings but his conclusions, 23-24, go too far.

16. Frankfort, KAG, 309-310.

17. Frankfort, KAG, 57-59.

18. Frankfort, KAG, 89.

19. ANET, 431.

20. ANET, 159 underlining indicates uncertain meaning).

21. ANET, 379.

22. For a summary of recent discussion on royal remissive acts in Mesopotamia see Weinfeld, DDS, 149-155. For examples see ANET, 526 (The Edict of Ammisaduqa) and 627 (A Royal Decree of Equity, by the son and successor of Hammurabi, namely Samsu-iluna).

23. See Alan Gardiner, The Kadesh Inscriptions of Ramesses II (Oxford, 1960), 8; cf. AEL, II, 63.

24. Gardiner, 11; cf. AEL, II, 67.

25. These comparisons, which do not seem to have been noticed before now, may indicate a deliberate Israelite imitation of Egyptian royal style. It remains to be proved that Ramses II was the pharaoh of the Exodus; his son and successor Merneptah has also been suggested. But one of the cities built by the Hebrews was named Ramses (Exodus 1:11), and Ramses II is known to have employed "Apiru" in his building projects, while Merneptah mentions Israel as one of his enemies. A plausible hypothesis, therefore, is that Ramses II was the pharaoh who oppressed the Hebrews while Merneptah was the king who let Israel leave Egypt.

26. Breasted's translation, ARE, III, par.326; cf. Gardiner, 30 (B104).

27. Gardiner, 10; cf. AEL, II, 67.

28. ANET, 277. The "terror and glamor" of gods that threw enemy armies into panic is to be connected with the winged sun disk depicted in Egyptian, Hittite, Mesopotamian, and Iranian reliefs. See TTG, 32-66. Compare Yahweh's "pillar of fire and cloud" (Exodus 14:24).

29. ANET, 287. Sennacherib goes on to say: "The awe-inspiring splendor of the Weapon of Ashur, my lord, overwhelmed his strong cities". For Assyrian reliefs showing Ashur wielding a bow and arrow in a fiery winged sun disk, see Mendenhall, TTG, 45-47.

30. ANET, 267.

31. ANET, 270.

32. See further Manfred Weippert, "Heiliger Krieg in Israel und Assyrien", Zeitschrift für die alttestamentliche Wissenschaft, 84 (1972), 460-493.

33. John F. Sawyer, Semantics in Biblical Research: New Methods of Defining Hebrew Words for Salvation (London, 1972). Compare Indian kingship, AIK, 100-105.

34. ANET, 258.

35. ANET, 165.

36. Cited by Frankfort in his section "The Choice of the Gods", KAG, 238-240.

37. ANET, 289.

38. ANET, 164 (Prologue) and 177 (Epilogue).

39. ANET, 289-290. The beginning of this text was cited above at n. 37. For Israel see I Samuel 10 and I Kings 12.

40. G.E Mendenhall, Law and Covenant in Israel and the Ancient Near East (Pittsburgh, 1955) and J.A. Thompson, The Ancient Near Eastern Treaties and the Old Testament (London, 1964) are two of a large number of studies on this subject. For a summary of

the progress in this research see D.J. McCarthy, Old Testament Covenant: A survey of Current Opinions (Oxford, 1972).

41. Cf. Deuteronomy 14:1-2, addressed to Israel: "You are the sons of Yahweh your God ... and Yahweh has chosen you to be his special possession..."

42. ANET, 164-165.

43. For the sources of the Ashurbanipal examples, and other instances also, see Frankfort, KAG, 299-301.

44. ARE, III, par. 399, 400, 402.

45. ARE, III, par. 403.

46. ANET, 431; Oppenheim, AM, 285, refers to oaths of loyalty taken by high Assyrian officials.

47. ANET, 164.

48. ANET, 178.

49. See the impressive hymn to Shamash, ANET, 387-389; BWL, 121-138.

50. Bleeker, HAT, 136, 137.

51. Bleeker, HAT, 145.

52. Bleeker, HAT, 145; Lurje, SAR, 126. This tradition was recorded by Diodorus Siculus.

53. Moses is undoubtedly the lawgiver (or "commander") mentioned in Deuteronomy 33:21; see Weinfeld, DDS, 153.

54. The "words" of Yahweh were probably the commands (apodictic laws), while the "ordinances" would be the clauses beginning with "if" or "when" (casuistic laws), as on the stele of Hammurabi. Both these types of formulation are also found in covenant documents, it should be noted. See further Paul, SBC.

55. Lurje, SAR, 126-129, gives evidence indicating the use of lawcodes in ancient Egypt and also references to unpublished fragments of Egyptian law books. For a royal edict see ARE, 3, 22-33 (par. 45-67), inscribed on a tall pillar by Horemheb in the fourteenth century.

56. Frankfort, KAG, 251.

57. ANET, 165.

58. ANET, 251-252.

59. Frankfort, KAG, 53, who further states that "the king was kept at one remove from the details of government by the vizierate, which was the true center of the country's administration. But ... the vizier was instructed to have an audience with the king each morning to report on the state of the nation."

60. ANET, 207-211.
61. Lurje, SAR, 131.
62. Oppenheim, AM, 286.
63. ANET, 164.
64. Frankfort, KAG, 255-258 and 267-274 on the Mesopotamian pattern of royal procedure for the setting up of sanctuaries.
65. ARE, II, par. 303; Frankfort, KAG, 268.
66. ARE, II, par. 339; Frankfort, KAG, 271.
67. See above, at n. 5.
68. AEL, I, 115-118; ARE, I, par. 498-506.
69. Morenz, ER, 85.
70. See Weinfeld, DDS, 246, 254, for the Biblical traditions set alongside Egyptian and Mesopotamian accounts of revelations to kings regarding sanctuary building.
71. BWL, 112-113.
72. Bleeker, HAT, 119-123.
73. ARE, II, 273-281.
74. Bleeker, HAT, 143-150.
75. ANET, 541.
76. Examples of Egyptian execration texts from the Middle Kingdom period may be found in ANET, 328-329; for other curses and threats see 326-328.
77. See Frankfort, KAG, 360, n. 21, for Egyptian royal endowment of land, a tomb, and an inscribed monument.
78. See further Weinfeld, DDS, 70-81, for this and other examples, as also detailed comparisons with the grants made by Yahweh to his servants.
79. For an early Egyptian example of such a charter see ANET, 212 (and 672 for a revised translation); for Mesopotamia, L. Oppenheim, AM, 120-123 and 285, on the granting of privileges to cities.
80. Examples from Israel are found in 2 Samuel 15: 2-6 (Absalom); 19:8 (David). City gates were used for trading, trials, and political assemblies in Mesopotamia.
81. ANET, 213-214; ARE, II, par. 663-711.
82. See the important study of Mendenhall, "The 'Vengeance' of Yahweh", TTG, 69-104.
83. H.B. Huffmon, "The Covenant Lawsuit in the Prophets", Journal of Biblical Literature, 78 (1959), 285-295; J. Harvey, "Le 'Rîb-Pattern', réquisitoire prophétique sur la rupture de l'alliance", Biblica, 43, 2 (1962), 172-196.
84. ANET, 431. See above also, at n. 8 and n. 46.
85. Gonda, AIK, 10; Frankfort, KAG, 36 and 354, n. 1 (Charles II of England and scrofula).

86. ANET, 539.
87. Bleeker, HAT, 141-143.
88. ANET, 369.
89. ARE, III, 177 (par. 401).
90. See Henry Sigerist, A History of Medicine, Vol. I (1951).
91. L. Dürr, Das Erziehungswesen im Alten Testament und im antiken Orient (Leipzig, 1932); C.J. Gadd, Teachers and Students in the Oldest Schools (London, 1956); H. Brunner, Altägyptische Erziehung (Wiesbaden, 1957).
92. For these and other examples of the "book of instruction" genre, see ANET, 412-424.
93. This is my personal view; the case for it will have to be presented elsewhere; but it must be emphasized that Deuteronomy 31:26 needs to be translated "Take this book of instruction" (torah) rather than "Take this book of the law".
94. ANET, 281.
95. Frankfort, KAG, 55.
96. Frankfort, KAG, 260, in his section on "Representation of the People": "The daily cult of the gods, for which the king was responsible, was left to the priests, who acted as his representatives except on the none-too-rare occasions when his presence was imperative."
97. Frankfort, KAG, 343.
98. KAG, 342. Thus Solomon built the Temple of Yahweh in Jerusalem. However, he did lead the assembly of Israel in prayer at the altar (1 Chronicles 6:12-42) and then "the king and all the people offered sacrifice before Yahweh" (7:47).
99. KAG, 258-261.
100. KAG, 330-331, "The Sacred Marriage". Such fertility rites were borrowed by the Israelites from the Canaanites, of course.
101. See Eva L.R. Meyerowitz, The Divine Kingship in Ghana and Ancient Egypt (London, 1960).

* * * * *

ABBREVIATIONS

AEL Miriam Lichtheim, Ancient Egyptian Literature, I (Berkeley, 1973), II (Berkeley, 1976).

AIK J. Gonda, Ancient Indian Kingship from the Religious Point of View (Leiden, 1969).

AM L. Oppenheim, Ancient Mesopotamia: Portrait of a Dead Civilization (Chicago, 1964).

ANET James B. Pritchard (Ed.), Ancient Near Eastern Texts relating to the Old Testament, 3rd. Edn. (Princeton, 1969).

ARE James Henry Breasted, Ancient Records of Egypt, Vols. I-V (Chicago, 1906-1907), reprinted 1962).

BWL W.G. Lambert, Babylonian Wisdom Literature (Oxford, 1960).

DDS Moshe Weinfeld, Deuteronomy and the Deuteronomic School (Oxford, 1972).

ER Siegfried Morenz, Egyptian Religion, English Edn. translated by Ann E. Keep (London, 1973).

HAT C.J. Bleeker, Hathor and Thoth: Two Key Figures of the Ancient Egyptian Religion (London, 1973).

KAG Henri Frankfort, Kingship and the Gods: A Study of Ancient Near Eastern Religion as the Integration of Society and Nature (Chicago, 1948).

SAR I.M. Lurje, Studien zum altägyptischen Recht des 16. bis 10. Jahrhunderts v.u.Z., Forschungen zum Römischen Recht, 30. Abhandlung (Weimar, 1971), first published in Russian (Leningrad, 1960).

SBC Shalom M. Paul, Studies in the Book of the Covenant in the Light of Cuneiform and Biblical Law (Leiden, 1970).

TTG George E. Mendenhall, The Tenth Generation: The Origins of the Biblical Tradition (Baltimore, 1973).

9 MALAY KINGSHIP IN A BURMESE PERSPECTIVE

A.C. Milner

What is the significance of monarchy in the modern history of South-East Asia? In this essay, I do not examine the administrative details of government or the variety of Indian and Islamic ideological elements which are connected with kingship. I am concerned with the conception of monarchy and with the way in which that conception influenced Malay and Burmese experience and behaviour in the colonial period. The idea of kingship, I suggest, has been underestimated as a force in the indigenous societies of South-East Asia. In particular, there is evidence that kingship was capable of mediating the impact of colonial rule. My principal interest is Malaya, but it is the situation in colonial Burma which provokes me to inquire into the rôle played by kingship in the last century of Malay social history. In Burma, the British abolished monarchy, and the dramatic consequences of this act suggest the need to re-examine the implications of the retention of kingship in 'British Malaya'.

The contrasts between Muslim Malaya and the Theravadin Buddhist kingdoms of mainland Southeast Asia are obvious. Such large, land-based states as Burma and Thailand are a far cry from the petty river-based Sultanates on the Peninsula. In their early encounters with Southeast Asia, European travellers were as impressed by the power and civilization of these Buddhist polities as they were scornful of the fragmentation and military recklessness in the Malay world. Yet there are indications that, on the eve of European colonization, the Malay and Buddhist polities possessed in their kingship

---

* I should like to thank Professor J.A.C. Mackie for his generous advice on several matters related to this paper.

systems certain structural features common to both.

To a remarkable extent - particularly if viewed against Indian monarchy - the historical sources depict Southeast Asian kingship as a lynch-pin in political and social life: while the Indian ruler performed prescribed duties within a system articulated around the classifications of caste and dominated by a priestly class, the Southeast Asian ruler was himself the focus of his system.[1]

To emphasise the centrality of kingship in the pre-colonial period is not to say that Southeast Asian rulers always possessed a monopoly of power in their polities. Individual kings may well have been influenced or even dominated by certain courtiers or territorial chiefs. The play of power, however, took place within the idiom of kingship. Those residing in Malay polities, for instance, considered themselves to be living not so much in territorially defined states as under Rajas. One lived in a kerajaan, a term defined literally as "the condition of having a Raja," and this did not merely describe a person's political situation. The kerajaan was a religious and moral system. It had what we would call an ideological and psychological significance.[2]

Law, for instance, was defined in relation to rajaship. When the British-influenced traveller, Munshi Abdullah, visited Pahang in the 1830's he was told that any attempt to alter the adat or customary law of the state would be punished by the divine wrath of the late rulers.[3] The Malay legal digest, the Undang-Undang Melaka, also links law to rajaship. The preamble proclaims that the laws had been "handed down" from ruler to ruler. It was the Raja who administered the "customs and laws" and those reading or listening to the texts are warned that transgression of the undang undang was considered treason to the ruler.[4] By contrast, in the last century or so there has been a growing demand that Malay law be grounded in Islamic law, the sharia. The old Malay code certainly displays the influence of Muslim law, yet it has as its reference point, not the divinely ordained sharia, but the Raja.

In presenting Malay law and custom as being - to use an expression employed in a Malay text from Sumatra - "in the hands" of the Raja,[5] Malay writings made broad claims for the significance of the monarch. It is difficult to overstate the comprehensiveness of the adat system 'held' by the Raja. All action was determined by customary law. Each person had a status or rank, often encapsulated in a title, and the duties and privileges accompanying that position were carefully defined. Malay legal texts and chronicles give particular attention to describing the sumptuary laws which governed behaviour, dress and house styles.[6]

As one might expect, these court writings discuss court ceremony in great detail, but they also convey the impression that life at every level had a ceremonial or ritualistic character. To the outside observer there seemed little spontaneity in human relations. When Munshi Abdullah left the British colony of Singapore in the 1830's to travel in the Malay states he was horrified at the power of the sumptuary laws. So completely did they control or formalize Malay life that, in the states under Malay government, people, he believed, could not "lift their heads" or enjoy themselves. They were afraid to wear fine clothing or build a handsomely decorated house. Malays were not able to produce anything novel.[7]

To Abdullah and other observers these laws governing behaviour and life style presented a picture of a thoroughgoing and oppressive system. The people, it was remarked, "never thought anything was right or wrong, advantageous to them personally or otherwise; it was simply, 'What is the Raja's order?'"[8] What is more, Malay government, if the word could be used at all, appeared to be preoccupied with the trivia of ritual rather than the real material needs of the community. Such judgements, however, were made by men who judged the Malay world from a modern perspective. Abdullah himself viewed men as individuals whose minds and characters developed over time. For him and other modern thinking observers, the kerajaan system with its comprehensive array of sumptuary and behavioural laws would necessarily suffocate the evolution of individuality. By contrast, in the traditional Malay world, men were not perceived as private individuals but as public men and sumptuary laws did not so much oppress as define them. To modern observers social life in that world might indeed have seemed ceremonial in character but for Malays it was perhaps a comfort rather than a burden to believe that, in the words of a Malay saying, mens lives are "contained within custom."[9]

It is not a minor matter, therefore, that this powerful legal and customary structure lay "in the hands of the raja." Equally, the significance of the ruler in the essentially "public" life of the Malay subject was revealed when he bestowed titles and ranks which defined a subject's rights, obligations and even identity, and when the ruler's physical presence formed the focal point of a vast ceremony of state.

Not merely social life, however, operated in the idiom of the kerajaan. The subjection of religious matters to rulership in the early Malay world is striking to an observer of Islamic developments in the 1980's. An emphasis among Malay Muslims today on the believers' equality before God and, in particular, an impatience with the spiritual pretensions of rulers, must not blinker our perceptions of the medieval Malay world. Malays did not have to dilute or distort Islamic teaching to assimilate that religion into their own king-based ideology.[10] Islam was adopted by Malays at a time when the Muslim lands could be described as a galaxy of monarchs who adopted lofty titles and claimed spiritual leadership. Medieval Islam did not, as a consequence, threaten the Malay rulers. It is not merely that conversion was generally accomplished without the overthrow of reigning dynasties; also, formerly pagan rulers are actually described as having propagated and defended Islam. The Malay Annals, for instance, describe the Melaka raja, Sultan Mohammed Shah, as the first to be converted in his state and they relate that he "commanded" all the people of Melaka, "whether of high or low degree," to become Muslim.[11]

In the Malayo-Muslim kingdoms or kerajaan which emerged after the adoption of the new faith, the ruler appears to have been as central to the religious concerns of his subjects as to any other aspects of their lives. The Raja came to be described as "God's Shadow on Earth" and sometimes as "caliph." A Portuguese account of seventeenth century Pasai, in North Sumatra, remarked that the people of that country believed their ruler "governed on earth in place of God",[12] and this theme is carefully developed in a range of Malay writings. The Malay Annals for instance, explain that a "just prince is joined with the Prophet of God like two jewels in one ring. Moreover, the Raja is as it were the deputy of God. When you do your duty to the Prophet of God it is as though you were doing your duty to God himself."[13] A legal code from Pahang and a seventeenth-century text from Sumatra also invoke the "two jewels in one ring" formula to describe the position of the Raja.[14]

In explaining the spiritual significance of the kerajaan it must not be assumed that this was a static system. The dynamic potential is revealed, for instance, in the Malay romance, the Hikayat Hang Tuah, when its "hero" remarks that "we who live under Rajas do whatever work we have to do as diligently as possible, for, as the old people say, 'it is good to die with a nama (name or reputation) which is good'."[15] Hang Tuah is emphasising that working for the ruler brings rewards in the hereafter. A text from Sumatra puts the point differently. It reminds its readers that the ranks obtained in this world have implications in the next.[16] What is suggested in both these texts is that just as progress in this life was "contained" within a web of customary obligations and rules considered to be grounded in the raja, so a person's death status can be enhanced through serving the raja.

In mainland Southeast Asia, also, there are indications that both social and spiritual life were considered to have been oriented around kingship. Accounts of Burma and Thailand in the centuries before European colonial intervention present the monarch as the articulating principle in the social system of his polity. No less than in the Malay case this social system is characterised by a preoccupation with ceremony. The "golden court" of Burma has been described as "largely tinsel".[17] The "principal expenditure" of the ruler was on "trinkets and golden vessels bestowed on public officers on their elevation to various grades of nobility..."[18] The seventeenth-century Thai court - where, according to one observer, one neither "walks, speaks, eats or wakes without some kind of ceremony"[19] - also seemed unconcerned with what foreign visitors considered matters of substance. A Persian writer concluded that "the whole meaningless kingdom is based on words and nothing more."[20] Even the rewards given by the king were words; that is, he rewarded his loyal subjects merely by "pronouncing out loud" their titles or names.[21]

The impact of these titles in everyday life seems to have been no less significant than in the Malay world. In late nineteenth-century Burma "almost every article of use, as well as ornament, particularly in their dress, indicated the rank of the owner."[22] The "shape of the beetle-box", the "horse furniture, even the metal of which (a man's) spitting-pot and drinking cup are made ... all are indications of the gradations of society."[23] Just as in Malay society, rank was not just displayed and defined by the court but was grounded in kingship.

"In the Burman government," explained the Englishman, Michael Symes, "there are no hereditary dignitaries or employments; all honours and offices, on the demise of the possessor, revert to the crown."[24] The Buddhist ruler, therefore, like his Muslim counterpart to the south, was the lynch-pin of a ceremonial structure in which the lives of his subjects both within and beyond the court appear to have been enmeshed.

Again, this structure had spiritual connotations. A Dutch visitor to Thailand in the seventeenth century was told that the people attributed not only their laws but also their religion to the first ruler of that country.[25] It was believed, also, that the Burmese monarchs were members of the "sacred race" from which the Buddha sprang,[26] and there is abundant evidence that the Burmese ruler was thought to be able to influence the spiritual fortunes of his subjects. An inscription of twelfth-century Pagan announces that the Burmese ruler will "drag" his "drowning" subjects across the "river of Samsara", will deliver them from the cycle of birth and rebirth: "I myself would cross and drag the drowning over".[27] In the way that the Malays came to view their ruler as "governing on earth in place of (the Muslim) God", the Burmese ruler was sometimes described as a <u>bodhisattva</u>, or "future Buddha",[28] who was not preoccupied with achieving <u>nirvāna</u> for himself but generously stood upon its threshold assisting the spiritual progress of his followers.

It is true that monarchs making such claims are known to have aroused the ire of the clergy. King Bodawpaya of Burma found only one monastic sect which would support his claim to be the <u>boddhisattva</u>, Metteya;[29] equally, Sultan Mahmud of fifteenth century Melaka was much criticised by the Muslim "priests" at his port when he declared the <u>haj</u> pilgrimage was unnecessary and proclaimed that Melaka was to be "made into Mecca".[30] But the point to emphasise is that, whatever the doctrines of Buddhism or Islam may dictate, the evidence suggests that the rulers claimed, and often achieved in the minds of their subjects, a spiritual pre-eminence which matched the pivotal role they played in the status and ceremonial system of their states. The Southeast Asian ruler was not subject to a priestly class of the Indian type, nor was he required to submit to the egalitarian demands which many modern Muslims claim are implicit in the religion of Islam. In this sense - as a comment by Louis Dumont suggests - the Southeast Asian monarch "fixed a limit" to both Indian and Islamic influence in the region.[31] Whether or not kingship should be considered an indigenous phenomenon its resilience was demonstrated not only in pre-colonial times but also, as we shall see, when challenged by European imperialism.

In Malaya, although the apparently ceremonial monarchs achieved an accommodation with imperialism, historians have tended to dismiss their importance in the colonial period. Burmese kingship, by contrast, was abolished with colonial conquest and we shall see that the consequences of abolition in Burma highlight the need for a re-examination of the significance of monarchy in modern Malaya.

From 1874 the rulers of the different states of Malaya began to submit to the British demand that they maintain at their courts British advisers called 'Residents'. Numerous modern historians have argued that, despite the "fiction" that the "independence and sovereignty of the Sultan" continued into the colonial period, it was the British who held power in, and administered, Malaya.[32] "In theory," to quote Emily Sadka, these British officials were to advise the 'native authority', but the reality was that the "Residents were in fact ruling".[33] The Sultans became ceremonial heads of state who "retired from any active part in government, and were recompensed after a fashion by increases in their wealth, ceremonial and formal honours."[34] The Malay states, argues Dr. Thio, became only "theoretically sovereign entities". In "practice the substance of power gradually passed into British hands."[35] But if the Sultans became so impotent in the colonial period, it must be asked, is the legal continuation of the Malay state to be considered merely as a "fiction"? Is the survival of Malay monarchy during the colonial period therefore of no more than antiquarian interest?

This line of reasoning is undermined, of course, by our discussion of the pre-colonial polity. Can we be confident in contrasting the "substance of power" with "ceremonial and formal" matters when referring to a polity which was always preoccupied with what many foreign visitors regarded as ceremony? When a British-protected Sultan of Selangor, for instance, declared that he did not trouble himself with administration, Sadka assumes that this indicates the decline of the Sultan's position after the commencement of British protection.[36]

Would it not be equally convincing to view the Sultan merely as describing his traditional role? He would not expect to be involved in the mundane matters of state. As the seventeenth century Malay Annals explain, rulers were not customarily concerned with the problems of administration but only with the "good results" which were obtained.[37]

The need for a reconsideration of the significance of Malay monarchy is particularly compelling, however, if British Malaya is compared with British Burma. Of all the countries of Southeast Asia it was Burma where the fate of monarchy was most catastrophic. In this respect the contrast with Malaya could not be more distinct. By 1852 the British had annexed lower Burma; in 1886 the institution of Burmese kingship was abolished, the ruler himself (who had been unwilling to compromise with European imperialism in the manner of his Malay counterparts) was sent into exile, and the whole country brought under British rule. Unlike the Malay states, Burma was acquired by officials whose background was in India. Having entered Burma from India, the conquerors had no appreciation of the importance of monarchy in this Southeast Asian polity: "In all India there was never any nation," explained one sensitive official. The "strongest power we met was the Sikh Kalsa. But that was not a nation, it was a religious organism."[38] On the basis of Indian experience, therefore, the British believed that once the last king, Thibaw, had been overthrown, the fighting would end.

Annexation, on the contrary, was followed not only by years of anarchy, but also by "ideological crisis".[39] Hearing of the departure of their ruler, reported one observer in 1886, "the women, and even the men, in the villages, wept and broke out in lamentations."[40] There was "no disguise to the fact that the removal of the King, who was the representative of the nation and the head of the religion, was resented even by those (in lower Burma) who had been for years the subjects of the British Government."[41] A later writer, Maurice Collis - a scholar official who possessed poetic skills - tried to explain the trauma of annexation by likening kingship to "the pivot of an art integration", a "bit of iconography": when the King was exiled, "a thousand years of dream were splintered, as a magic mirror is splintered by realities."[42]

The impact of annexation on the Burmese has never been examined in depth. What did the ideological crisis entail? In what sense could it be said that "a thousand years of dream were splintered"? Collis remarks that without the King "Burmese art ceased to breathe."[43] It is known also that Burmese drama collapsed after annexation. In what ways was the response to annexation reflected in literature? How representative, for instance, are the lines of Zibani Sayadaw?

> No more the Royal Umbrella
> No more the Royal Palace
> And the Royal Library, no more
> This is indeed the Age of Nothingness
> 'Twere better we were dead.[44]

The characteristics of an Age of Nothingness are difficult to determine on the basis of European records. It seems significant, however, that Fielding Hall observed that with the departure of King and court "has gone all style and fashion".[45] "Manners" also deteriorated.[46] The Burmese, he argues, had "to a great extent lost his pride in being a Burmese."[47] While an Englishman in time of social change could sing "God save the King" and "remember that Our Country still remains to us," for the Burmese "there is no nation."[48] Nationhood, Fielding Hall is reminding us, was in Burma grounded in kingship, so that annexation must inevitably have caused profound dislocation. That the Burmese should have turned so early in the colonial period, and with such energy, to the creation of a modern nationalism was only to be expected.

The degree to which the loss of monarchy brought dislocation to Burmese religious life would require detailed analysis of Burmese as well as English sources. The decline of the "unity, discipline, and dedication to religion" of the Buddhist monks in the British period has often been remarked upon.[49] Even in 1921, a leading Sayadaw of Burma could pronounce that both the laity and monkhood of the country were in a condition of "confusion and disorder."[50] Many writers have emphasized the importance of the removal of the king in bringing the monastic orders into disarray.[51] Was this a consequence merely of administrative change or was it also an aspect of the "ideological crisis"? One observer of the pacification period conjectures, for instance, that, without the spiritual presence of his <u>boddhisattva</u>-like ruler, the Burmese peasant had "to fight his own fight..." When he "lay dying, with a bullet in his throat, he had no one to open to him the gates of heaven ..."[52]

Burmese preoccupation with the monarchy question did not, of course, cease with the consolidation of British rule at the end of the pacification. Their allegiance to the monarchical idea is demonstrated time and again in the colonial period. Not only did rebel leaders fighting British rule claim royal status and adopt a royal style[53] but also modern nationalist leaders, such as U Chit Hlaing and Ba Maw, presented their authority in the language of traditional kingship. U Chit Hlaing, for instance, travelled like a Burmese king with two golden umbrellas. His entrance into a nationalist conference in 1921 was heralded by royal drums playing the royal entry music and the formal opening of the event began with Brahmins reciting Hindu mantras in the manner of a court ceremony.[54] In a period, therefore, when Burmese society was dramatically out of kilter, a people who had wept decades earlier at the loss of kingship appear to have continued to long for monarchy.

To what extent are these developments in Burma an indication of what might have occurred in Malaya? Had the British annexed the Malay states would the results have ben similar to those in Burma? Malays, as has been suggested, were not less wedded to monarchy than were the Burmese and it is possible to assess the likely consequences of annexation from several perspectives.

In the first place, explicit warnings regarding the dislocation which must occur in a raja-less state are found in traditional Malay literature. A text from Patani, for instance, describes a period in which that state "no longer had a raja": everything falls into utter confusion (sangatlah huru-haranya), all the people suffer illness, and customs and orders of procedure cease to exist.[55] The kidnapping of a Raja from a Sumatran state is treated in another text in a less precise but more evocative manner. Seeing their ruler carried off, the people in the palace are

> stiff with fear, there is a din of cries and frightened shouting, a sound of wailing and weeping, all proclaiming that the Raja has been captured. The din is heard as far as the marketplace. Then all is in disturbance.[56]

The utter confusion which reigned in the absence of a ruler is reminiscent of the Age of Nothingness which followed the removal of the "Royal Umbrella" of Burma. In modern terms "Nothingness" or "utter confusion" suggests an ideological and social anarchy which must have provoked a fear of being "rajaless". The possibility that this fear was a critical element in Malay political motivation during the colonial period is given further weight by an examination of three political outbursts in the late nineteenth and twentieth centuries. The two earliest outbursts, the Perak and Pahang uprisings, also helped to set the tone of British protection in Malaya.

Perak was the earliest state to accept a British adviser and the "war" which commenced with his assassination, a minor skirmish by the standards of the Burmese "pacification," can be attributed largely to Malay fear that the British were intending annexation. On 20 January 1874 Sultan Abdullah and certain of the Perak chiefs, in an agreement called the Pangkor Engagement, promised to "receive" a British officer "to be called a Resident" and whose "advice must be asked and acted upon on all questions other than those touching Malay Religion and Custom".[57] The first Resident, J.W.W. Birch, who was appointed at the end of that year, survived less than twelve months. In November 1875 Birch was slaughtered in his bath house and during the next few months Malay forces struggled vainly against the overwhelming might of imperial Britain. The historical sources, and historians themselves, tell more of British than Malay motivations in Perak,[58] but even the English writings of the period provide glimpses of the Malay perception of the way events developed in Perak. From the outset the British Resident must have appeared determined to go beyond the Pangkor Engagement and establish British rule in Perak. Soon after his arrival Birch began to establish an administrative system which, he admitted, paid little heed to the "old customs" of the country.[59] He decided also to appoint chiefs of his own choosing to administer the districts of Perak and believed these chiefs should be "carefully watched".[60] Finally, as regards the lowest level of administration, Birch told the Sultan that the whole system had to be remodelled and that he, the Resident, intended to give all headmen, or <u>pengulus</u>, "fresh acts of appointment."[61]

Faced with such plans Sultan Abdullah was frightened. Diaries written by British officials in that period record, for instance, Abdullah's declaration that he hoped to prevent the British from obtaining the royal regalia because "in that day of truth, this country of Perak will be given over to the English."[62] Abdullah knew that the trend towards direct rule was not sanctioned by the Pangkor agreement and he actually wrote to the Governor in Singapore to ask that the Resident - who was, after all, supposed to advise the Sultan - be made subordinate to the Sultan.[63] Senior Malay officials in Perak shared Abdullah's anxieties. One believed the British "will surely drive us out of the country,"[64] and another enquired as to whether the Resident was "to be under" the Sultan and also whether the Resident would be able to give Perak "laws of his own making."[65] In answering such questions British officials sometimes made reassuring statements regarding their intention to follow the Pangkor agreement but, in fact, the British were rapidly becoming convinced of the need for "English rule" in the Malay states. The Governor himself believed that Perak "should be taken charge of by officers of the British government, assisted by a Malay council,"[66] and by October 1875 it was widely rumoured that Perak was to be annexed.[67]

The suspicions of the Sultan and his people regarding the future of the Sultanate could only have been confirmed by two proclamations issued by the Resident about this time. The proclamations announced that British officers were to become the judges of the country, punishing all crimes, and that these officials would also collect revenue and administer all the affairs of the country. The British government, it was explained, would "administer the government of Perak."[68] To understand completely the impact of these proclamations it would be necessary to see the Malay translations but even in English they are distinctly against the spirit of the Pangkor Treaty. In the context of rumours of annexation they must have been viewed as an intolerable provocation by the Malays. It is significant that it was precisely at the time he was posting the proclamations announcing that Britain would "administer the Government of Perak" that Birch was assassinated. It had been possible, therefore, to persuade the Perak leaders to agree to a treaty in which the Sultan would be advised by a British official in matters other than religion and custom, but the prospect of "English rule" was unacceptable. In one respect there was a connection between the much greater upheaval associated with Burmese pacification and the relatively insignificant hiccup in British expansion which occurred in Perak. The Burmese fighting followed annexation, the Perak war occurred at a time when annexation was anticipated.

In Perak the Malays suffered a decisive military defeat and yet the opponents of British rule did in fact achieve something. The war had a substantial influence upon British official attitudes toward the Malay states in later years. The policies of the Governor and his dead Resident were overruled by the home Government: "neither annexation nor government of (Perak) by British officials in name of Sultan can be allowed," announced a telegram from London.[69] From this point onwards, at least until 1945, the historical record suggests that Malay royal sovereignty was secure. Malays themselves, however, may not have been so confident. Even though annexation was no longer an option, eager Residents tended nonetheless to "govern in name of Sultan." In the words of a Singapore Governor, they forgot "never to hurry Malays."[70] In forcing unpalatable changes on reluctant Sultans and chiefs they aroused the type of suspicions which fuelled the Perak war.

Even more than in the Perak war, the importance of rajaship and the problems of annexation were evident in the events which occurred in Pahang in the 1890's. Although the Pahang uprising - which was the largest anti-British movement of the early colonial period - did not arise out of an explicit threat of annexation, rajaship was used as a rallying cry by the rebels and they were defeated only after the Sultan openly shifted his support to the British cause.

The Pahang uprising[71] commenced at the end of 1891, three years after the first British Resident had been appointed to the state. A small British-led party was ambushed in the interior of the state and, in the next few weeks, attacks were made on many settlements in the region. The leader of the uprising, Dato Bahman, was said to have about one hundred supporters at first but, after his early successes, the number rose to some five or six hundred.[72] These were only the active rebels. "You cannot speak to a Malay in the country," commented a European, "who does not sympathize with (the rebellion)."[73]

A variety of grievances appear to have promoted rebellion, but what is particularly significant for the present purpose is that the Sultan of Pahang, Ahmad, was himself dissatisfied with the Residential system and that his subjects were much influenced by their ruler's view. Although the Sultan did not openly support the rebels, it was known that a "solidarity pact" had been formed between him and his chiefs, including Bahman, before the rebellion.[74] Sultan Ahmad certainly gave little support to British attempts at suppression and, more importantly, his name was employed to give authority to the rebel cause. The extent to which rebel leaders organised in his name is suggested by the fact that the Sultan felt it necessary to reassure the British. An insurgent, he explained, might "make use of (my) name ... so that people believe what he says and obey his authority".[75]

The event which marks the turning point of the uprising is revealing. The rebel leaders began to lose support about April 1892, at which time the Sultan began to be much less closely linked with the movement. In April there were rumours that the most influential chief in Pahang, To Raja, was to lead an important attack in the interior. The Sultan, however, perhaps because the British had convinced him that he would be held responsible for any expansion of the uprising, prohibited the attack. The Malay account of the war relates that the Sultan sent a messenger to the To Raja to restrain him. If he joined the rebels, To Raja was told, "he would be committing Treason" (or derhaka).[76] Derhaka is well known to be a potent word in Malay[77] and the rebels were only referred to as derhaka in the text after the To Raja episode in April.[78] At this time, also, the Sultan gave the resident a war chief's set of clothes and told him that anyone joining Bahman in the act of treason should be destroyed.[79]

Although the rebellion subsided after April 1892, many of the rebel chiefs having fled to neighbouring states, a revealing sequel occurred in 1894. The Pahang rebels based in the state of Trengganu, now bereft of royal support in their own country, acquired the patronage of a new leader, the Islamic holy man, Engku Sayid of Paloh. The holy man gave the rebellion a different, more explicitly Islamic tone. He bestowed on the rebels swords inscribed with texts from the Koran and preached war against the infidel. A fresh invasion of Pahang was soon underway, but this second phase of the Pahang uprising was shorter lived than the first. The rebels received little support in Pahang and, within a few weeks, had fled back to Trengganu.

In this second phase of the rebellion the Sultan's role involved no ambiguity. He presented the British Resident, who was to lead an expedition against the insurgents, with a bracelet which he himself had worn as an invulnerability charm in his own fighting days.[80] Furthermore, the Malay account of events does not hesitate to label the second rebel movement, fighting under the banner of Islam, as treason, or derhaka. Although it is well known that in the twentieth century Islam has become increasingly effective as an inspiration to political action among the Malays, in late nineteenth-century Pahang, at least, only the involvement of the Raja gave potency to the rebellion against the British in Pahang.

In Pahang, unlike Perak, rajaship was not in fact in danger. Yet those Malays who gathered around the banner of the Sultanate had good reason to believe their kerajaan system was threatened. The British officials in Pahang, like their predecessors in Perak, had moved quickly to institute what they considered reforms[81] and, as a consequence, the Sultan and his people must have been apprehensive. Faced with widespread rebellion, the British quickly assured the people that the Sultanate would be respected. They worked through the Sultan to pacify the state and when the rebellion was revived under the patronage of an Islamic rather than royal leader, the people chose to support their ruler. In both the promotion and suppression of the rebellion, therefore, the vitality of the kerajaan ideal is demonstrated. What is more, the decisive importance of the Sultanate both in this Pahang uprising and the earlier Perak fighting illuminates the third and far larger expression of Malay political feeling which will be considered, the protest against the Malayan Union of 1946-8.

For the Malay community, the years between the Pahang uprising and the Japanese occupation which preceded the Malayan Union, particularly when compared with British Burma over this period, were a time of tranquillity and gradual change. In Burma the turmoil of the pacification never really ceased. Crime was so common that "jailing, whipping, collective fines on villages, and the disciplining of errant headmen had little effect."[82] Cultural decline was evident in art, literature and even speech;[83] and the replacement of monastic education by government schools led to a lack of instruction in moral matters.[84] The monkhood itself is often said to have become undisciplined following the removal of royal control[85] and, finally, the alienation of land ownership which followed the substitution of free trade principles for traditional controls meant that the "Burman" was "being squeezed off the land."[86]

Malaya, even more than Burma, underwent dramatic economic change. But the exploitation of the country's tin and rubber, and the development of the administrative and communications infrastructure which accompanied it, had remarkably little impact on the Malay community. It is true that the Malay minorities in the British-governed settlements of Singapore, Penang and Melaka, and in the larger cities on the Peninsula, experienced some social and cultural change,[87] but they formed only a small segment of the Malay population. In general the Malays were affected by only the most gentle Western influence. The hierarchical structure of society remained, and much of Malay custom, or adat, continued to be adhered to after British intervention. Islam was not merely maintaind but has been described as having "had the benefit of far-reaching development as a result of British rule".[88] Finally, as regards occupations, the majority of Malays followed such traditional pursuits as rice-growing. In the pejorative terms of a later critic of British policy, a dual society emerged on the Peninsula. On the one hand, there was a "bustling commercial outfit", on the other there existed what he summed up as a "Malay museum".[89]

The "museum" was only in part a product of British rule. It is true that having seized power in Malaya the British adopted a sympathetic, gradualist and inexpensive policy toward the Malay community. Education policy, for instance, aimed not at radical change but to "make the son of a fisherman a better fisherman and the son of a farmer a better farmer"[90] and in agriculture the British discouraged the peasantry from commercial planting and attempted to keep them in padi and other subsistence farming.[91] The authority of the rulers in Islamic matters was, of course, supported and, even where Malay custom or adat was considered intolerable in terms of British morality, reforms were undertaken with considerable caution.[92] The dominant element in British policy toward the Malays, however, was "pro-Sultanism" and it was the continued presence of the Malay rulers in colonial Malaya which contributed most to the maintenance of the "Malay museum".

"Pro-Sultanism" was not just the result of the moral obligations entailed in the formal treaties of protection but was also a consequence of the fighting in Perak and Pahang. The founding fathers of "British Malaya" saw these Malay uprisings, first, as a warning of the need to placate the Malays while exploiting the resources of their country, and, secondly, as an indication that the restoration of monarchy was the essential element in a conciliatory Malay policy. When Frank Swettenham, for instance, considered the future organization of Malaya in 1893, he concluded that "annexation is impossible" not only because it would mean "breaking faith with the Malays" but also because it was "a serious mistake to overlook the fact that the Malays and their interests are still our first consideration." There were, he reminded his superiors, "100,000 Malays in Perak alone" and it should be remembered "what a trouble a mere handful of discontented people recently gave in Pahang".[93]

In an important sense, therefore, the survival of monarchy cannot be understood merely as a British decision. Not only in the Treaty negotiations, but also in the byzantine political manoeuvrings during the Perak and Pahang fighting, the Malay rulers succeeded in establishing "pro-Sultanism" as the first plank in British policy toward the Malays. What the rulers achieved may be seen as an Anglo-Malay alliance which not only placed constraints upon them but also provided them with protection and opportunities in the period of European domination in Southeast Asia. This alliance, based squarely on the maintenance of the monarchical system, distinguished British Malaya from British Burma. It is the key to understand the tranquillity of the former.

The pro-Sultan policy permitted individual sultans to influence British policy in many respects: they are known to have discouraged, for instance, any attempt to democratize the educational system.[94] But the most important impact on the Malay community of the continuation of the sultanates was ideological. The lives of the vast majority of Malays continued to be oriented around their rulers. The Malay community did not experience the "ideological crisis" which followed the abolition of monarchy in Burma. The ruler remained central to the organization and doctrinal presentation of Islam in his state, headmen in villages were still commissioned on the authority of the ruler,[95] celebrations and ceremonies associated with the court continued and even thrived, and, in strong contrast to Burma, no violent deterioration occurred in Malay manners and cultural life.[96] Although an observer of Burma under British rule could comment that the Burmese believed they possessed "no nation" it was remarked of Malaya that the "great majority" of Malays continued to possess a "strong attachment" to the Sultan.[97] It will be seen that the kerajaan ideology was not immune to threats during the colonial period but there is, nonetheless, a vast difference between the Burmese "Age of Nothingness" and the persistance of Sultanism in the "Malay Museum" of British Malaya.

Perceptive British officials were well aware of the Sultan's importance in Malay society and of the advantages to be gained from placating and supporting him. When Ormsby-Gore visited Malaya in 1928 he concluded that the rajas were "a real and to my mind essential asset". He could have been thinking of the contrast between Malaya and Burma when he added that "but for (the rulers) the Malays would become a mob".[98] In more sympathetic language J.S. Furnivall, in a magisterial study published in 1947, threw light not only on Burma but also on Malaya by a comparison with India. Unlike India, he explained, the Burmese were not "protected against the solvent influence of economic forces by the shield of caste".[99] In both Burma and Malaya, I would suggest, monarchy once had the potential to provide such a "safeguard against social disintegration" but in Burma it was eliminated.

To see Malay sovereignty in British Malay as a "fiction" is thus to misconstrue completely the relationship between the British and Malaya. It must be admitted that the ruler's rôle, to the modern eye, appears to have been largely concerned with religion and ceremony, but this had always been the character of Malay rajaship. The Malay Sultan continued to be a dominant figure in precisely the same ideological and ceremonial spheres which he had occupied in pre-colonial times. As the Sultan of Selangor put it, the rulers of the colonial period did not trouble themselves with administration but left those matters to their British and Malay advisers. The concern of the rulers was to defend and promote, often in the language of ceremony and ritual, the kerajaan ideal. That they had considerable success is suggested by the events of the Malayan Union. When, after the initial shock of the Japanese occupation, the British attempted to unite Malaya under a new system of government, the Malays were presented with a challenge similar to that which confronted the Burmese sixty years earlier. The Malay response to that challenge forms the third and most important Malay political movement of the colonial period.

On returning to Malaya the British government attempted to turn on its head the old pro-Malay policy. The British aimed to implement a Malayan Union in which all the Malay states under British protection, together with Penang and Melaka, would be incorporated into a unified administration under British rule. Although the scheme was designed to prepare Malaya for independence, it was, in the first instance, a consolidation of imperial control. It annulled the treaties on which British protection had originally been founded and which acknowledged and protected the sovereignty of the Malay rulers. Sovereignty was now to be transferred to the British crown, the autonomy of the various Sultans would end, and members of all races would become citizens in the new state.

To the surprise of many foreign observers who had assumed Malays were invariably lethargic as regards political matters, the Malay response to the Union scheme was dramatic. Travelling into the Peninsula from Singapore, a British Member of Parliament found "demonstrations running to thousands of people" at every town and concluded that the country had "become acutely politically conscious overnight."[100] This Malay outcry was, in part, an expression of disappointment that the Sultans had succumbed to British pressure and authorised the constitutional change.[101] Such criticism, however, was levelled at the rulers as individuals. What is striking about the protests is the determination with which they opposed the destruction of the Sultanates as an institution. When the crowds were passionately urging their rulers to abandon the Union agreement the persistent chant was "Daulat Taunku." "Daulat Tuanku"[102] might best be translated as "Power (or Good Fortune) to the Rulers". So strong was this sentiment that even the few left-wing Malay radicals of the time - who might have been expected to seek the downfall of royalty - found themselves in the anomalous position of seeking popular appeal by demanding the restoration of full royal sovereignty.[103]

For some European observers the Malay protest was bewildering. In particular, those who had believed that the sovereignty of the rulers had for decades been a "fiction" found Malay opposition to the Union difficult to explain. Others who felt that the rulers had for long been preoccupied with peripheral matters such as ceremony, rather than the important issues of administration, could see little reason for the Malays to express such loyalty.[104] Those few surviving officials, however, who had been responsible for the shaping of British Malaya - men such as Sir Frank Swettenham - were in no such confusion and vigorously supported the Malays.[105]

The Union scheme, whatever its justification in terms of the future development of Malaya, was, as regards the Malay community, a reversal of seventy years of British policy. In the words of a Malay correspondent in the London Times, the Malay "rightly regards himself as the subject of his Sultan, his loyalty almost amounting to a religious fervour." Although the "more intelligent Malay" was troubled by political division in Malaya, he would not want a union if that meant becoming a British subject and "the transference of his allegiance away from his Sultan."[106]

Other considerations, of course, contributed to Malay anxiety about the Union. Not least of these was the prospect of opening up citizenship rights to vast numbers of non-Malays. Such fears appear to have crystallized, however, around the question of the sovereignty of the rulers. For centuries the Malays had understood political life in the idiom of the Raja. It was not that they approved of every individual ruler but what modern writers might normally define as their political system, the kerajaan, had as its focus the figure of the raja. What is clear is that by 1946 a large majority of Malays continued to view the world through the lens of the kerajaan and that it was therefore to be expected that they would subsume a variety of suspicions regarding Malayan Union beneath a determination to retain the sovereignty of their rulers.

The character of the Malay response to Malayan Union underlines the need to reconsider the British presence in Malaya. The vigour with which the Malays opposed the British scheme in 1946 is a reminder that the survival of Malay monarchy, despite the imposition of British protection, had the most important implications for Malaya. Because of the historian's tendency to be preoccupied with the practical aspects of administration, with "the substance of power", there has been a failure to appreciate that for many Malays the Union was the real beginning of colonial rule. It would end a form of independence which was as significant to Malay people as it has been misunderstood by modern observers. In Malay eyes, at least, the sovereignty of their monarchs in the so-called "British Malaya" was no mere fiction. The ferocity of Malay protest against Union suggests that Malays, even in 1946, continued to believe that the removal of their ceremonial rajas would bring an era of utter confusion, or what was described in colonial Burma as an Age of Nothingness.

Malay pressure led, in 1948, to the replacing of the Union by a Federation in which royal sovereignty was assured. The Malay Sultanates have survived in independent Malaysia and the resilience of the kerajaan ideal was exhibited as recently as 1983-4 when the Malaysian Prime Minister, Dr Mahathir, acting in the name of egalitarian nationalism, attempted to trim the royal powers. Mahathir's failure to achieve his aims underlines the point that Malay nationalism, unlike Burmese nationalism, must compete with royalty as a focus of allegiance and a manner of conceptualizing political and social life. The confrontation between King and Parliament has not only provoked new analyses of the colonial period which denigrate the Sultans[107] but has also revived the taunt that independence or merdeka was not a nationalist achievement. Except for the Union period, it is argued, the subjects of Malay sultans were always independent.[108]

In tracing monarchy from pre-colonial to modern times it is possible to see the colonial period in a different light. The way in which kingship cushioned the impact of the West on the Malay community is brought out particularly by the contrast with British Burma. In Malaysia, and perhaps elsewhere in Southwest Asia, kingship continued to inspire political action even in modern times.

NOTES

1. A useful introduction to Indian political thought is D. Mackenzie Brown, The White Umbrella, Indian Political Thought from Manu to Gandhi, Berkeley, 1968, ch. 2. See also, I.W. Mabbett, Truth, Myth and Politics in Ancient India, New Delhi, 1972, 71-2. For an illuminating comparison between India and Southeast Asia, see L. Dumont, Homo Hierarchicus. The Caste System and its Implications, London, 1970, p. 262.

2. I have discussed Malay kingship in my Kerajaan. Malay Political Culture on the Eve of Colonial Rule, Tucson, 1982.

3. Kassim Ahmad (ed.), Kisah Pelayaran Abdullah, Kuala Lumpur, 1964, 40.

4. Liaw Yock Kang (ed.), Udang Udang Melaka, The Hague, 1976, pp. 62-4, 176.

5. The Hikayat Deli; see my Kerajaan, p. 97.

6. Ibid., esp. ch. 6.

7. Kassim Ahmad, op.cit., pp. 46-7, 125; R.A. Datoek Besar and R.R. Roolvink, eds., Hikajat Abdullah, Djakarta, 1953, vol. 2.

8. F. Swettenham, British Malaya, London, 1908, p. 141.

9. Mahathir bin Mohamed, 'Interaction and Integration', INTISARI, 1, 3 (n.d.), p. 44.

10. I discuss this topic in 'Islam and Malay Kingship', Journal of the Royal Asiatic Society of Great Britain and Ireland, 1, 1981, pp. 51-59.

11. R.O. Winstedt (ed.) 'The Malay Annals; or, Sejarah Melayu. The earliest recension from MS No. 18 of the Raffles Collection in the library of the Royal Asiatic Society, London', JMBRAS, 16, 1938, p. 84. For further references regarding the ruler's prominence in Islamization, see my 'Islam', no. 59.

12. M. Dion (ed.), 'Sumatra through Portuguese eyes: excerpts from Joao de Barros, Decadas da Asia', Indonesia, 9, 1970, p. 140.

13. Milner, 'Islam', op.cit., p. 52.

14. Ibid.

15. Milner, Kerajaan, p. 109.

16. Ibid., p. 107.

17. G.E. Harvey, History of Burma, London, 1967, p. 359.

18. Ibid.

19. N. Gervaise, writing in the seventeenth century, quoted in J. Kemp, Aspects of Siamese Kingship in the Seventeenth Century, Bangkok, 1969, p. 30.

20. J. O'Kane (ed.) The Ship of Sulaiman, London, 1972, p. 143.

21. Ibid., p. 144.

22. M. Symes, An Account of an Embassy to the Kingdom of Ava, London, 1800, p. 310.

23. Ibid. See also F.N. Trager & W.J. Koening (eds.), Burmese Sit-tans 1764-1826, Tucson, 1979, pp. 341, 359, 365, 369, 362.

24. Ibid. See also, Shway Yoe, The Burman, New York, 1963, p. 490; Yule notes that 'the name of every Burman disappears when he gets a title of rank or office, and is heard no more'; H. Yule, Narrative of the Mission to the Court of Ava in 1855, Kuala Lumpur, 1968, p. 194.

25. J. van Vliet, 'Description of the Kingdom of Siam', Journal of the Siam Society, 7 (1910), pp. 8-9.

26. Yule, op.cit., p. 30. See also: Shway Yoe, op.cit., p. 446.

27. Quoted in E. Sarkisyanz, Buddhist Backgrounds of the Burmese Revolution, The Hague, 1965, p. 62.

28. Thaung, 'Burmese Kingship in Theory and in Practice during the reign of Mindon', Journal of the Burma Research Society, 42, 2 (1959), p. 179.

29. E.M. Mendelson, Sangha and State in Burma, Ithaca and London, 1965, pp. 75-6, 88.

30. Milner, 'Islam', op.cit., p. 58.

31. See n.1 above.

32. M. Yegar, Islam and Islamic Institutions in British Malaya. Policies and Implementation, Jerusalem, 1979, p. 39.

33. E. Sadka, The Protected Malay States 1874-1895, Kuala Lumpur, 1968, p. 120. See also pp. 379, 283, 176.

34. Ibid., p. 156. See also p. 175.

35. E. Thio, British Policy in the Malay Peninsula 1880-1910, Singapore, 1969, p. xvii.

36. Sadka, op.cit., p. 171.

37. Winstedt, op.cit., p. 95.

38. H. Fielding Hall, A People at School, London, 1913, p. 51.

39. Sarkisyanz, op.cit., ch. xvi.

40. Ibid., p. 100.

41. Ma Mya Sein, The Administration of Burma, Kuala Lumpur, 1973, p. 122.

42. M. Collis, The Journey Outward, London, 1952, p. 159.

43. Ibid.

44. Quoted in Ni Ni Myint, Burma's Struggle Against British Imperialism 1885-1895, Rangoon, 1983, p. 42. For the decline of Burmese drama, see Maung Htin Aung, Burmese Drama, London, 1956, p. 135.

45. H. Fielding Hall, A People at School, London, 1913, p. 48.
46. Ibid., p. 155.
47. Ibid., p. 158.
48. Ibid., p. 175.
49. D.E. Smith, Religion and Politics in Burma, Princeton, 1965, p. 52.
50. Statement at a meeting in July, 1921, by U Kaw-tha-la. I am grateful to Patricia Herbert for this reference.
51. See, for instance, Smith, op.cit., ch. 2.
52. Fielding Hall, op.cit., p. 59.
53. Ni Ni Myint, op.cit., ch. 2; Toshikatsu Ito, 'Pre-Saya San Peasant Uprisings in Colonial Burma', 31st International Congress of Human Sciences in Asia and North Africa, 1983.
54. U Maung Maung, From Sangha to Laity, Canberra, 1980, pp. 247-8.
55. Milner, Kerajaan, op.cit., p. 109.
56. Ibid., p. 94.
57. C. Northcote Parkinson, British Intervention in Malaya, Kuala Lumpur, 1964, pp. 323-4.
58. See, in particular, ibid. and C.D. Cowan, Nineteenth-Century Malaya. The Origins of British Control, London, 1961.
59. P.L. Burns (ed.), The Journals of J.W.W. Birch. First British Resident to Perak 1874-1875, Kuala Lumpur, 1976, p. 378.
60. Ibid., p. 388.
61. Ibid.
62. P.L. Burns & C.D. Cowan (eds.), Swettenham's Malayan Journals 1874-1876, Kuala Lumpur, 1975, p. xxix.
63. Ibid., p. xxx.
64. Cowan, op.cit., p. 221.
65. Burns and Cowan, op.cit., p. 191.
66. Ibid., p. 337.
67. Parkinson, op.cit., p. 217.
68. Ibid., p. 232; see also Cowan, op.cit., p. 229.
69. Parkinson, op.cit., p. 269.
70. Sir F. Weld, instructions to H. Clifford, in Weld to Secretary of State, confidential, 28 April 1887, Colonial Office 273/144.
71. For a detailed account of the uprising see W. Linehan, 'A History of Pahang', JMBRAS, 14, 2 (1936), ch. 12.
72. Annual Report, Pahang, 1891.
73. Straits Times, 9 April 1892.
74. Smith to Fairfield, private, 6 July 1892, in Smith to Secretary of State, 29 June 1892, C.O. 273/181.

75. Sultan Ahmad to Governor Smith, probably 2 May 1892, in Smith to Secretary of State, 10 May 1892, C.O.273/180. See also Straits Times, 16 April 1892.

76. Hikayat Pahang, rumi text: p. 151; Jawi: p. 57. For a discussion of the different recensions of this Hikayat, see Milner, Kerajaan, p. 135.

77. Ibid., p. 104.

78. I am referring to the Jawi recension. The Rumi one, which would have been considered more accessible to European readers, uses the word 'dehaka' to describe Bahman before this event.

79. Rumi text, p. 188, Jawi text, p. 60.

80. Straits Times, 13 July 1894.

81. See the criticism of the Pahang Resident by T. Shelford, 12 November 1892, in Smith to Secretary of State, 29 November 1892, C.O.273/183.

82. J. Cady, A History of Modern Burma, Ithaca, 1958, p. 175.

83. Ibid., p. 168.

84. Ibid., p. 171.

85. Ibid., p. 169.

86. Ibid., p. 167.

87. L. Richmond Wheeler, The Modern Malay, London, 1928, pp. 206, 234, 240. See also W.R. Roff, The Origins of Malay Nationalism, Singapore, 1967, passim.

88. Yegar, op.cit., p. 264.

89. G. Harrison, M.C.S., quoted in A.J. Stockwell British Policy and Malay Politics during the Malayan Union Experiment, Kuala Lumpur, 1979, p. 31.

90. Philip Loh Fook Seng, Seeds of Separatism: educational policy in Malaya 1874–1940, Kuala Lumpur, 1975, p. 122.

91. Lim Teck Ghee, Peasants and their Agricultural Economy in Colonial Malaya 1874–1941, Kuala Lumpur, 1977, pp. 110–111, 226.

92. Roff, op.cit., p. 70.

93. F. Swettenham, 'A proposal for the better administration of the Malay States now under British Protection', Swettenham Collection, 2/14, in Arkib Negara, Kuala Lumpur.

94. K.K. Ghosh, Twentieth-century Malaysia Calcutta, 1977, pp. 142–3, 303.

95. Sadka, op.cit., pp. 406–7.

96. Apart from Wheeler, op.cit., see, for instance, Alwi bin Sheikh Alhady, Malay Customs and Traditions, Singapore, 1962.

97. Wheeler, op.cit., p. 233.

98. Ghosh, op.cit., p. 304.

99. J.S. Furnivall, Colonial Policy and Practice, New York, 1956, p. 538.

100. Captain L.D. Gammans, quoted in Stockwell, op.cit., p. 89, n. 12.

101. Ibid., pp. 65-6.

102. Ibid., p. 71. See also Tan Sri Syed Ja'afar Albar, 'Sa - Layang Pandang Sejarah Perjuangan UMNO 20 TAHUN', UMNO 20 TAHUN, Kuala Lumpur, about 1966.

103. Stockwell, op.cit., p. 76.

104. Ibid., p. 75, n. 10.

105. Ibid., p. 60.

106. Ismail M. Ali, The Times, 5 July 1945.

107. New Straits Times, 11 November 1983.

108. I spent January and February 1984 in Singapore and Malaysia, and make these observations on the basis of conversations held there at that time.

ABBREVIATIONS

C.O.	Colonial Office
J.M.B.R.A.S.	Journal of the Malay Branch of the Royal Asiatic Society

SELECT BIBLIOGRAPHY

COEDES, G., The Indianized States of Southeast Asia, trans. Susan Cowing, Canberra, 1968.

DARKE, H., The book of government or rules for kings, London, 1960.

ENGNELL, Ivan, Studies in Divine Kingship in the Ancient Near East, 1st Edn, Uppsala, 1943, 2nd Edn, Oxford, 1967.

FRANKFORT, Henri, Kingship and the Gods: A Study of Ancient Near Eastern Kingship as the Integration of Society and Nature, Chicago, 1948.

GADD, C.J., Ideas of Divine Rule in the Ancient Near East, Schweich Lectures 1945, London, 1948.

GARDINER, K.H.J., "Beyond the Archer and His Son : Koguryo and Han China", in Papers in Far Eastern History, (Canberra), XX, September, 1979.

GARDINER, K.H.J., The Early History of Korea, Canberra, 1969.

GIBB, H.A.R., An interpretation of Islamic history, Lahore, 1957.

GONDA, J., Ancient Indian Kingship from the Religious Point of View, Leiden, 1969.

GULLICK, J.M., Indigenous Political Systems of Western Malaya, London, 1965.

HALL, K.R. and WHITMORE, J.K., eds., Explorations in Southeast Asian History: The Origins of Southeast Asian Statecraft, Ann Arbor, Michigan, 1976.

HENTHORN, W.E., A History of Korea, London, 1971.

HOLT, P.M., LAMBTON, A.K.S., LEWIS, Bernard, eds., Cambridge history of Islam, Cambridge, 1970.

HOOKE, S.J., ed., Myth, Ritual, and Kingship: Essays on the Theory and Practice of Kingship in the Ancient Near East and in Israel, Oxford, 1958.

JAYASWAL, K.P., Hindu Polity, 3rd Edn., Bangalore, 1955.

KULKE, H., The Devaraja Cult, trans. I.W. Mabbett, New York, 1978.

LEWIS, Bernard, Islam, New York, 1974.

LEWIS, Bernard, The World of Islam, London, 1975.

MENDENHALL, George E., The Tenth Generation: The Origins of the Biblical Tradition, Baltimore, 1973.

PICKTHALL, M.M., The meaning of the glorious koran, Mentor Book, 14th printing.

POSENER, Georges, De la divinité du Pharaon, Cahiers de la Société Asiatique, XV, Paris, 1960.

RAYCHAUDHURI, H.C., Political History of Ancient India, 6th Edn., Calcutta, 1953.

RIZVI, S.A.A., Shāh Walī-Allāh and his Times, Canberra, 1980.
RIZVI, S.A.A., Shāh 'Ahd al-'Aziz, Canberra, 1982.
ROSENTHAL, F., The Muqaddimah, New York, 1958.
THE SACRAL KINGSHIP: Contributions to the Central Theme of the VIIth International Congress for the History of Religions, Rome, April 1955, Leiden, 1959.
SHARĪF, M.M. (ed.), A history of Muslim philosophy, Wiesbaden, 1966.
SHARMA, J.P., Republics in Ancient India, c.1500 B.C. - 500 B.C., Leiden, 1968.
SHEMESH, A. Ben, Taxation in Islam, Leiden and London, 1958.
SINGH, Sarva Daman, Ancient Indian Warfare with Special Reference to the Vedic Period, Leiden, 1965.
WATT, W.M., Islamic political thought, Edinburgh, 1968.
WHITTING, C.E.J., Al-Fakhrī, London, 1947.

GLOSSARY

The following abbreviations are used:

A	Arabic, Perso-Arabic
C	Chinese
K	Korean
S	Sanskrit
S-J	Sino-Japanese

Ahl al-ra'y (A)	Competent to give an opinion
Ansar (A)	Helpers, applied particularly to the citizens of Medina, who assisted the Prophet Muḥammad when he was obliged to fly from Mecca
Arthaśāstra (S)	Ancient Indian text on politics, traditionally though implausibly attributed to Kauṭalya (late 4th cent. B.C.)
Baray (Khmer)	Reservoir
Cakravartin (S)	Universal Emperor
commandery	Chinese, _chün_. The most important administrative unit used in the Chinese empire from the third century B.C. to the sixth century A.D. At the beginning of the first century A.D. the empire comprised 83 commanderies and 20 kingdoms
Daṇḍa (S)	King's rod of punishment; the power of the state to punish, coerce or sanction
Dawla (A)	Kingship
Devarāja (S)	Name of a royal legitimising cult in ancient Cambodia
Dharma (S)	Law, duty, obligation; moral burden of religion
Dharmavijaya (S)	Righteous conquest
Dhimmī (A)	Non-Muslim protected subject in an Islamic state paying _jizya_
Dīn (A)	Religion
Dīwān (A)	Lit. 'Register'; department of finance and revenue
Fai (A)	Revenue rights

Fiqh (A)	Islamic jurisprudence
Ghanīma (A)	Booty
Han-shu (C)	A history of the former Han Dynasty (202 B.C.-A.D. 9) written by the historian Pan Ku (32-92)
Ijmā' (A)	Consent of the people competent to express opinion
Jizya (A)	Poll tax
Kāfir (A)	Infidel
Kharāj (A)	Land revenue
Kojiki (S-J)	The earliest extant Japanese history, completed in 712
Kṣatra (S)	Protective power; warrior-aristocratic element
Kṣatriya (S)	Warrior-aristocratic order in society
Liṅga (S)	Phallic emblem of Hindu god Śiva
Mahāsammata (Pāli)	Great Chosen One
Mātsyanyāya (S)	The law of the big fish devouring the small ones
Mawla (A)	Patron
Muhājirūn (A)	Those who abandon their country, particularly applied to Prophet Muhammad's companions who moved from Mecca to Medina
Mulk (A)	Sovereignty
Nihongi (S-J)	The second major history of Japan, coming down to 697 and completed in 720
prefecture	Chinese hsien; a subdivision of a commandery
Purohita (S)	Royal chaplain
Rājan (S)	King
Rāṣṭra (S)	Territory
Ratnin (S)	Lit. 'Jewel-bearer'; high official or representative of people
Sadaqa (A)	Alms
San-kuo-chi (C)	'The Record of the Three Kingdoms', covers the period of civil war and upheaval following the fall of the Later Han Dynasty at the end of the second century A.D., terminating with the unification of most of China by the Western Chin Dynasty which came to the

	throne in 265. The author, Ch'en Shou (233-297), served successively under the kingdoms of Shu and Western Chin
Sharī'a (A)	Islamic law
Shih-chi (C)	A general history of the Chinese world written by Ssu-ma Ch'ien c. 100 B.C.
Sonno-bu, Chollo-bu, Sunno-bu, Kwanno-bu, Kyeru-bu (S-J)	The five tribes which made up the old confederacy of Koguryo
Umma (A)	Muslim community
Viś (S)	People
Wei-lüeh (C)	A lost history of the third-century kingdom of Wei in northern China, written by the otherwise unknown Yü Huan. The book survives only in the notes compiled by the fourth-century scholar P'ei Sung-chih to Ch'en Shou's San-kuo-chi

THE CONTRIBUTORS

HAROLD BOLITHO (Ph.D., Yale), Associate Professor, Department of Japanese, Monash University. Specializes in the history of Tokugawa Japan, and has published Treasures Among Men (Yale University Press, 1974) as well as several articles. Currently working on the Meiji Restoration.

BRIAN E. COLLESS (Ph.D., Melbourne; Th.D., Australian College of Theology), Senior Lecturer in Religious Studies, Massey University. Has produced numerous publications on early cultural links between Western Asia and Eastern Asia.

K.H.J. GARDINER (B.A., Ph.D., Lond.), Senior Lecturer, Asian History Centre, Australian National University. Lectures on the early and mediaeval history of China, also on early Korea. Publications include The Early History of Korea (Canberra, 1969) and numerous articles dealing with early Korea and the history of the Chinese frontier in the Han and Three Kingdoms periods. He has also published on the early history of Vietnam and on the historiography of Western Europe in the Dark Ages. Currently working on an annotated translation of the Koguryo section of the Samguk-sagi and, together with Dr I. de Rachewiltz, on a translation of Paul the Deacon's History of the Langobards.

I.W. MABBETT (M.A., D. Phil., Oxon), Reader in History, Monash University. Lectures on early Asian history. Publications include A Short History of India (Cassell Australia, 1968; Second Edition, Methuen, 1983), Truth, Myth and Politics in Ancient India (Thompson Press, New Delhi, 1972); various books and articles, chiefly on ancient South-East Asia. At present working on the Mūlamādhyamikakārikās of Nāgārjuna.

A.C. MILNER (M.A., Malaya; Ph.D., Cornell), Lecturer, Department of History, Australian National University. Has published Kerajaan. Malay Political Culture on the Eve of Colonial Rule (Tucson: Association for Asian Studies Monograph, 1982), and, with Virginia Matheson, Perceptions of the Haj (Singapore: Institute of Southeast Asian Studies, 1984).

S.A.A. RIZVI (M.A., Ph.D., D.Litt, Agra, India), Reader, Centre of Asian History, Australian National University. Lectures on Muslims in South Asia and Islamic West Asia; has published A History of Sufism in India, Vol. 1 (New Delhi, 1978); Vol. II (New Delhi, 1982); Shāh Walī Allāh and his Times (Canberra, 1980); Shāh 'Abd al-'Azīz, Puritanism, Sectarianism, Polemics and Jihad (Canberra, 1982); Iran, Royalty, Religion and Revolution (Canberra, 1980).

PAUL RULE (Ph.D., Australian National University), Senior Lecturer in History and Religious Studies, La Trobe University. Teaches courses in Chinese History and Religious Studies. Has published several articles on Chinese history and religion. Forthcoming works include Mao Zedong (University of Queensland Press, 1984), and K'ung-tzu or Confucius? The Jesuit Interpretation of Confucianism.

SARVA DAMAN SINGH (M.A., Ph.D., Lond., Ph.D., Queensland, F.R.A.S.), Associate Professor, Department of History, University of Queensland. Lectures on South and Southeast Asian Civilizations and Religion and Art in Asia; and has published Ancient Indian Warfare with Special Reference to the Vedic Period (Lucknow, 1972); and Polyandry in Ancient India (Delhi, 1978), besides many papers. At present working on the Art of Mathura; Eroticism in Indian Art.

INDEX

Ashikaga, Japanese ruling house, 36, 37
Ashurbanipal, King of Assyria, 145, 154n.
Aśoka, Indian emperor, 14, 15, 101
Assyria, 18, 138, 139, 142, 145, 146, 147, 148, 150
Atharva Veda, Sanskrit text, 88, 89
Aurangzeb, Aurangzebe, Mughal emperor, 7

Ba Maw, 167
Ba'al, 137
Babur, Mughal ruler of India, 16, 21
Babylon, 133, 137, 138, 140, 146, 150
Baghdad, 127
Bahman, Dato, leader of Pahang uprising, 170, 171, 182n.
Bakufu, Japanese government, 42n.
Bāṇa, Sanskrit author, 97
baray, reservoir, 10
Basham, A.L., 22
Baṣra, 115, 118
bay'a, pledge of allegiance, 116, 117, 118, 121
Bernier, F., 7
Bihar, 10
Birch, J.W.W., 168, 169
Bodawpaya, Burmese ruler, 163
Bodde, D., 23n.
bodhisattva, Buddhist saviour, 163, 166
brahmanas: class in Indian society, 6, 90, 91, 93, 94, 98, 99, 101, 104n.; Sanskrit texts, 90, 92
Bṛhadāraṇyaka Upaniṣad, Sanskrit text, 89, 93
Bṛhaspati, Indian god, supposed author of Sanskrit text, 99

British: in Burma, 164, 165; 174, 175 in Malaya, 168-178
Brundage, B.C., 23n.
Buddha, 30, 95, 163
Buddhism, Buddhists, 11, 18, 19, 29, 32, 67, 70, 72, 73, 76, 88, 94, 105n., 158, 163, 165, 172
bureaucracy, 9, 30, 53, 68n., 76, 79, 141, 142
Burma, Burmese, 77, 158, 162, 163-169, 172, 174, 175, 178
Burrow, T., 100

cakravartin, Indian concept of universal ruler, 92, 100
Caliphs, caliphate, 5, 111-119, 121-127, 161
Cambodia, 79. See also Chenla, Angkor
Canaan, 137, 146, 156n.
Candragupta Maurya, Indian emperor, 21
Ceylon (Sri Lanka), 11, 94
Champa, 72, 75
Chandogya Upaniṣad, Sanskrit text, 93
'Chenla', Chinese name for Cambodian kingdoms, 76
Chi Ch'ao-ting, 13
Ch'ien-lung, Chinese emperor, 54
Ch'in, Chinese dynasty, 15, 50
Chin-shu, Chinese historical text, 65
Ch'ing, Chinese dynasty, 51, 52, 54
Chou, Chinese dynasty, 5, 14, 16, 17, 49
Christianity, 110, 111
chu-pu, Chinese official position, 62
Coedès, G., 73, 76